VICTORIAN VALUES

PROCEEDINGS OF THE BRITISH ACADEMY · 78

VICTORIAN VALUES

A Joint Symposium of
the Royal Society of Edinburgh and the British Academy
December 1990

Edited by
T. C. SMOUT
Fellow of the British Academy
Fellow of the Royal Society of Edinburgh

Published for THE BRITISH ACADEMY
by OXFORD UNIVERSITY PRESS

Oxford University Press, Walton Street, Oxford OX2 6DP
Oxford New York Toronto
Delhi Bombay Calcutta Madras Karachi
Petaling Jaya Singapore Hong Kong Tokyo
Nairobi Dar es Salaam Cape Town
Melbourne Auckland
and associated companies in
Berlin Ibadan

Oxford is a trade mark of Oxford University Press

Published in the United States
by Oxford University Press, New York

British Library Cataloguing in Publication Data
Victorian Values: Joint Symposium of the
Royal Society of Edinburgh and the
British Academy, December 1990. —
(Proceedings of the British Academy; v. 78)
I. Smout, T. C.   II. Series
941. 081
ISBN 0-19-726119-1
ISSN 0068-1202

Typeset by Falcon Typographic Art Ltd,
Fife, Scotland
Printed in Great Britain by
Bookcraft (Bath) Limited,
Midsomer Norton, Avon

Contents

Proceedings of the British Academy, **78**, 1–7

Introduction

T.C. SMOUT
University of St. Andrews
Fellow of the British Academy
Fellow of the Royal Society of Edinburgh

THE papers in this collection arose from the first joint symposium between the British Academy and the Royal Society of Edinburgh, which took place in the Society's rooms in Edinburgh, December 12–14, 1990. The theme for this historic meeting had been proposed to the councils of each organisation as peculiarly apt, bearing in mind the great contemporary interest in 'Victorian values' as an exemplar to modern Britain, and Scotland's own distinctive contribution to nineteenth-century moral systems. The details were then worked out by a joint organising committee, consisting of the editor of the present volume as chairman, Lord Briggs of Lewes, Professor J.W. Burrow and Professor F.M.L. Thompson, FBA, and Professor R.S. Downie, Professor F.W. Robertson and Dr. W.D.I. Rolfe, FRSE.

Almost all the texts printed here are substantially the same as delivered at the symposium, apart from minor corrections and adjustments in the light of discussion at the meeting. The main exception is Raphael Samuel's paper on Margaret Thatcher's use of the concept of 'Victorian values', which is the development of a strand in his original contribution on 'Victorian values and the working classes', and a theme much enlarged upon throughout the symposium: we gathered in Edinburgh, after all, within a month of the Prime Minister's dramatic fall from office. Because of its different character, it comes first in this collection.

The final contribution, also, has a special character. Dr. A.J.P. Kenny, as President of the British Academy, provided a reflective tail-piece which was not, he insisted, an academic research paper but the reflections of a philosopher on a field not his own. We prevailed upon him to allow its publication providing this proper distinction was made.

The symposium was structured to allow the Victorian system of values to be examined from many angles, in the belief that light from only one approach would inevitably fail to illuminate its vast complexity. On the first afternoon, R.J. Morris led us off with a fine-tuned exploration into the Scottish contribution to Victorian values which he described as a 'mixture of the practical and the moral'. In a country that had a sharp awareness of its distinctiveness yet no central machinery of government, where aristocracy was often despised but the dominant religious tradition stressed each soul's egalitarian responsibility to answer to God, the 'value of the individual operating in the moral framework of small communities' was well developed. Mark Girouard, by contrast, speaking of the upper classes in a British perspective, distinguished three types – the earnest Victorian, responsible, respectable and puritan; the Victorian swell, as profligate and stylish as any eighteenth-century progenitor; and the Victorian gentleman, a conflation inspired by ideas of chivalry and natural leadership. Each of them, in their common easy assumption of the importance of the high-born as an example to society at large, were miles removed in their value systems from the tortured, boot-strap approach to life of Samuel Smiles of Haddington and his middle-class readership. Raphael Samuel speaking on Victorian values and the working class again stressed variety. The independent artisans of the East Midlands, proud to stand on their own two feet, were distant from the swells and the gentlemen: but working-class mutuality and ability to make the most fun out of life was also far removed from the strait-laced and atomistic Victorian world of popular conception.

The following morning we explored religion and literature. S.J. Brown introduced us to Thomas Chalmers' subtle attempt to marry 'concern for individual morality and personal salvation' with 'the desire to organise society into closely-knit communities independent of upper-class patronage and State paternalism': he showed us how traditional this was in Scottish life, and how, therefore, Chalmers' territorial ideals of church organisation had a powerful grip in Scotland long after his death. Perhaps an even greater service that Professor Brown provided for the symposium, however, was to throw into sharp relief how Chalmers epitomised one peculiarly enduring strand of the popular notion of Victorian values, as standing for the dignity of an individual's independence from state help. Clyde Binfield next explored the interplay between community and the networks of related or mutually admiring individuals in English non-conformity, and beautifully drew for us the mind-set of those to whom Mr. Gladstone was practically a deity. This essay as printed is substantially longer than as delivered. Valentine Cunningham brought out the anti-materialist values of Victorian literature, the critique of money-grubbing and compassion for the poor illustrated in Dickens, Arnold, Elliott, Brontë and Kingsley; but the writers themselves lived in fear and distaste of slum and its denizens, and coped in a materialist world of unbalanced accounts and opportunistic publishers.

Saturday afternoon began with science and medicine. In a most illuminating and wide-ranging introduction to nineteenth-century evolutionary ideas from the pre-Darwinian Scottish evolutionists, through Darwin and Huxley to the non-Darwinian early twentieth-century theorists, Peter Bowler again reminded us of the perils when historical myths are used to support modern values; 'the familiar images begin to blur when the past is studied in more detail'. The true originality of Darwin was obscured when Huxley used his own interpretation of *The Origin of Species* as a weapon to take control of the scientific community, and Herbert Spencer allied with Huxley in promoting notions of liberal social evolutionism, 'a naturalistic interpretation of the Protestant work ethic'. Non-Darwinian ideas, Lamarkian theories of cycles of evolution and decline, had wide currency among anthropologists and palaeontologists at the start of this century, and were used to support racialist theories that had no basis in Darwin's thought at all. So while it is true that most Victorians and Edwardians came to accept the general concept of evolutionism, the authentic originality of Darwin's discoveries was overlaid and perverted, and had to be rediscovered in much more recent times.

The medical profession was the subject of William Bynum's paper focusing on the response to competition in the market place. 'The most striking features of this adaptation were the growth of an occupational diversity and increasing reliance on the state as an important patron'. The 1911 National Health Act thus came as a culmination of processes which had been in train since 1834. He reminds us that for Sir John Simon the essence of his age was not simply the growing wealth and power of the community but 'the constantly increasing care of the community at large for the welfare of its individual parts'.

This perspective interlocked neatly with that of José Harris on the founders of the welfare state. She contrasted Mrs. Thatcher's view of Victorian values as individualistic with those of Corelli Barnett, whose *Audit of War* portrays the contemporary welfare state as the major inheritance of soft-centred Victorian Christianity and sentimentalism. The fathers and mothers of the welfare state in fact drew their ideas from admiration of the culture and institutions of the late Victorian and

Edwardian organised working class and found in its unions and friendly societies what appeared to them to be a model for an escape route from the poor law. The framers of the welfare state, notably Beveridge, went to great lengths to imitate the self-help rules of the big trades unions, with their Draconian penalties for misbehaviour, though they found almost insuperable problems in imposing them. Correlli Barnett thus looks quite wrong, Mrs. Thatcher closer to the truth, but authentic Victorian values had always flourished in a less commercial and consumerist world than ours.

On Sunday we heard three very different papers. Anne Crowther followed the previous theme in examining the workhouse. The Victorians neither invented this institution nor found themselves able to get rid of it. Some supported its principles against what Chadwick's assistant called 'anti-poor-law, pseudo-philanthropic agitators': others became enmeshed in controversies about the relationship between the poor house and charity. But no-one even in our century has been able to deny for long the need for some sort of less eligibility principle. Anne Digby took us into the realm of women's relationship with Victorian values, examining the ideological divide between the public sphere, viewed as a masculine domain of work and politics, and the private sphere, viewed as a female domain of home and family. The important territory here was the shifting border between public and private spheres, and the ability of the women's movement to turn it into a moving frontier of expanding opportunity. Little protest was heard from men while women pushed the frontier forward through work in philanthropy, social work or even local government: the threshold was crossed in the campaign for parliamentary suffrage and in other manifestations of 'unladylike' behaviour.

The last paper, unfortunately not available for publication in this collection, was Clive Dewey's examination of the export of Victorian values to India. The conquerors were anxious that the empire should be administered by Victorian gentlemen – definitely upper class, but preferably not by the earnest and certainly not by the swells of Mark Girouard's three-fold classification. While the rules did not totally exclude natives, or whites of relatively humble origin, the demand that admission to higher administrative grades should include proof of ability to ride and jump meant that many literally fell at the last fence.

So our symposium was a very rich mélange – too fruit-filled a mixture, some might say, to stick together or to be easily digested. Yet the emphasis on diversity, even a certain incoherence, does better justice to Victorian values than the simplicities of political slogans. As José Harris put it in her paper:

'Victorian Britain was a large, ramshackle, complex, diverse society that lasted a very long time and embraced a multiplicity of cultural traditions – and is therefore open to a wide variety of often mutually-conflicting stereotyped interpretations'.

We were only able to begin to indicate just how large, ramshackle and complex the value system was.

The editor may perhaps allow himself a final tailpiece and speculation of his own. If one considers Mrs. Thatcher's own version of Victorian values (which is the starting point of the chapters that follow) it is clear that it was very selective: but we can now see that the immense complexity of that value system made selectivity inevitable. More to the point, it was selected from a range of attitudes in many respects (not in all) close to those expressed by Thomas Chalmers. There will be scholars who will want to emphasise, as S.J. Brown would, that Chalmers was fundamentally more of a communitarian than Mrs. Thatcher, and that the drive of his evangelical message was the need to redeem capitalism, which he saw as basically selfish though capable of conferring great benefits, by an infusion of traditional Christian community values, the very cement of which was unstinted generosity of time and money by the rich and attention to work, subordination and familial responsibility by the poor. It was to be a true Godly Commonwealth, and a true community. Chalmers, however, was vulgarised and misunderstood by contemporaries, few of whom could respond to the sternness of his call for unstinted sacrifice of wealth and time on the part of the middle and upper classes, and preferred to emphasise another, equally real part of his message: that the poor could not evade a personal responsibility for their own plight, and that automatic entitlement to poor relief did more harm than good by undermining the motivation, thrift and work ethic of recipients and their families. This deep suspicion of welfare, and the belief that virtue was equated with thrift, sobriety and family responsibility, undoubtedly bit deep into Victorian attitudes, especially in Scotland.

As the twentieth century progressed, the sun at last set on the great reputation of Thomas Chalmers. The ethic of the welfare state, however hedged about with thrifty Victorian qualifications insisted upon by Beveridge and others, replaced the ethic both of Thomas Chalmers and of the English poor law. In public speeches in the twentieth century, politicians took the line that if there was a genuine social need, a way should somehow be explored to relieve it, rather than the Victorian line that if there absolutely had to be relief, a way must be found to ensure that it did not destroy the motivation and character of the recipient. The post-war world that had listened to Keynes and Beveridge considered *laissez-faire* a dirty word, and generally regarded those who still emphasised those values in economics and social philosophy, balefully or indifferently.

One such leopard who would not change his spots was the eccentric Professor of Political Economy at Thomas Chalmers' own University of St. Andrews, J. Wilkie Nisbet, who was wont even in the 1950s and 1960s to deliver public diatribes against the welfare state and who continued to regard Chalmers as an inspiration. In his small corpus of published work is a paper in the *Scottish Journal of Political Economy* for 1964 on the neglected thought of Chalmers, whom he described as an 'intellectual giant . . . and a remarkable exponent of Political Economy'. He praised in particular his views on 'Voluntary Action' in welfare as opposed to public intervention. Nisbet, though something of a figure of fun to Keynesian colleagues elsewhere, was a memorable teacher, with a reputation for looking after his students. Several moved into positions of influence in the financial establishment: a few became extremely able luminaries of the New Right, notably Lord Harris of High Cross, and Sir Alan Peacock who also began his academic career in the Political Economy department in St. Andrews. Sir Alan's aphorism, 'the true purpose of the welfare state is to teach people how to do without it' was deeply rooted in the tradition of which Chalmers was such an a major proponent, and his scepticism about the appropriate role of the state in economic life was also entirely in tune with that tradition.

It is not suggested that Mrs. Thatcher and the economists of the New Right retired with a copy of Chalmer's *Political Economy in connexion with the Moral State and Moral Prospects of Society* on their bedside tables, but it is easy to see that some of the foremost economists with whom she was associated came from a stable where certain basic ideas of Thomas Chalmers were still thought relevant. Her own internalised version of the meaning of Victorian values arises, Raphael Samuel suggests, from the values of her Methodist shopkeeper, preacher father, and an East Midland radical root. Certain key intellectual mentors, however, drew their understanding of Victorian values from a Chalmerian Scottish professor. When they came together in the world of inflation and growing doubt about Britain's economic, social and political performance – not to say moral fibre – in the 1970s, their union conflated two parts of the nineteenth-century mental legacy into Thatcherism – out of Grantham, by St. Andrews, as it were.

Mrs. Thatcher is often justly compared to Mr. Gladstone, alike in their hegemony over the British political scene for so long, setting the political agenda even for their opponents, and successfully claiming the high moral ground. It is tempting to say they also shared the legacy of the chapel (Grantham) and the kirk (St. Andrews), but the inheritance even from those institutions is deeply ambiguous. Whereas the north and the west had adored Mr. Gladstone in his day, the same areas gave only scant support to Mrs. Thatcher a hundred years later. The voters of Scotland, Wales and the North of England also inherited Victorian values from Mr. Gladstone's admirers, but in their own selectivity from the past they apparently gave that old-fashioned Liberal belief in mutuality some priority over belief in the individual. As is clear from many papers in the book, both were left to posterity in the Victorian will.

On an occasion like this, so many debts of gratitude are incurred by the organising committee and the participants that it is odious to single out particular names. It would be most ungracious, however, not to take this opportunity to thank Mr. Peter Brown of the British Academy, and Dr. William Duncan and Sandra Macdougall of the Royal Society of Edinburgh for the enormous effort that they put in to making the symposium a success.

Proceedings of the British Academy, **78**, 9–29

Mrs. Thatcher's Return
to Victorian Values

RAPHAEL SAMUEL

University of Oxford

I

'VICTORIAN' was still being used as a routine term of opprobrium when, in the run-up to the 1983 election, Mrs. Thatcher annexed 'Victorian values' to her Party's platform and turned them into a talisman for lost stabilities. It is still commonly used today as a byword for the repressive just as (a strange neologism of the 1940s) 'Dickensian' is used as a short-hand expression to describe conditions of squalor and want. In Mrs. Thatcher's lexicon, 'Victorian' seems to have been an interchangeable term for the traditional and the old-fashioned, though when the occasion demanded she was not averse to using it in a perjorative sense. Marxism, she liked to say, was a Victorian, (or mid-Victorian) ideology;[1] and she criticised ninetenth-century paternalism as propounded by Disraeli as anachronistic.[2]

Read 12 December 1990. © The British Academy 1992.

Thanks are due to Jonathan Clark and Christopher Smout for a critical reading of the first draft of this piece; to Fran Bennett of Child Poverty Action for advice on the 'Scroungermania' scare of 1975–6; and to the historians taking part in the 'History Workshop' symposium on 'Victorian Values' in 1983: Gareth Stedman Jones; Michael Ignatieff; Leonore Davidoff and Catherine Hall.

[1] Margaret Thatcher, Address to the Bow Group, 6 May 1978, reprinted in Bow Group, *The Right Angle*, London, 1979.

[2] 'The Healthy State', address to a Social Services Conference at Liverpool, 3 December 1976, in Margaret Thatcher, *Let Our Children Grow Tall*, London, 1977, p. 81.

Celebrating, at one moment, the achievements of Victorian philanthropy and quoting the example of Dr. Barnardo, she was ready, at the next, to strike at one of its taproots, and to proclaim her freedom from what she derisorily termed, in an early address as Party leader, 'bourgeois guilt'.[3]

Mrs. Thatcher's traditionalism was perhaps more a matter of style than of substance. If in one voice she regretted lost stability, in another she seized on what was new and developing. Monetarism was the 'modern view' of the role of government rather than (or as well as) a revival of 'old-fashioned laissez-faire'. Privatisation was hard-nosed realism. For all her denunciation of permissiveness and 'TV violence', Mrs. Thatcher felt no compunction about licensing Cable TV (in the name of free consumer choice), or conveying a knighthood on that pioneer of 'bubbly' journalism, the editor of the *Sun*. Her well-advertised attachment to the work ethic did not exclude an enthusiasm for hi-tech industry or a willingness, indeed eagerness, to contemplate the robotisation of the motor-car factories, or the substitution of nuclear power for coal. 'Enterprise culture', the flagship of Mrs. Thatcher's second term of office, probably owed more to the inspiration of contemporary America (or Japan) than to the railway mania of the 1840s. BUPA, Mrs. Thatcher's preferred alternative to the National Health Service, was modelled on Medicare, the corporation-funded medicine of the United States; the great working-class friendly societies of the nineteenth century, the Buffaloes, the Oddfellows or the Foresters, though monuments to the spirit of self-help, might have existed on another planet for all the attention they received.

In her modernising moments, Mrs. Thatcher had a radical contempt for the antiquated and the out-of-date. Restrictive practices were a relic of nineteenth century industrial relations. Government subsidies or 'hand-outs', were a throw-back to the past 'protecting yesterday's jobs and fighting off tomorrow's.[4] Manning agreements, though supported by unions and management, were a recipe for industrial decline, ossifying labour where it should be mobile, strangling innovation at birth.[5] Mrs. Thatcher believed that 'traditional' British industries unless they adopted advanced technology, would vanish, and that without a radical restructuring of the labour market, enterprise would wither.[6] Whatever the pain associated with redundancy and the return of mass unemployment, she feared entropy more, a Britain (as she warned the Institute of Directors in 1976) 'living in the nostalgic glories of a previous industrial revolution', a 'Museum

---

[3] Address to the Institute of Socio-economic Studies, New York, reprinted in ibid., p. 4. As she acknowledges, she owed the phrase to Helmut–Schoeck, *Envy*, London, 1969.
[4] Margaret Thatcher, *The Revival of Britain*, London, 1989, p. 98.
[5] Speech to the Conservative Party Conference, *The Times*, 17 October 1981.
[6] The *Guardian*, 9 October 1982.

Economy' dedicated to obsolete practices and wedded to the production of uncompetitive goods.[7]

Mrs. Thatcher's attitude to traditional institutions, so far from being reverent, was iconclastic. She deregulated the City of London and destabilised (or abolished) the County halls. She attacked by turns those erstwhile pillars of the Establishment, the Higher Civil Service, the Church of England, the House of Lords, the Universities and the Bar. She was even impatient, it seems, with monarchy. Nor did she demonstrate any particular regard for things Victorian. As one who made a fetish of never using public transport, her attitude towards that 'typical illustration and symbol of the nineteenth century, the railway train',[8] was the reverse of nostalgic, and she was equally unsentimental about such relics of Victorian achievement as free libraries and the penny post. Above all, identifying it with jobbery and bureaucracy, extravagance and sloth, she attempted to put an axe to what is arguably the most substantial twentieth-century legacy of the Victorian era, the public service ethic.

Yet it was as a traditionalist that Mrs. Thatcher set out her stall as Party leader, and made a pitch for the minds and hearts of her followers. She presented herself as a conviction politician, standing up for old-fashioned values where others were apologetic or shamefaced. In a climate of permissiveness – or what many Conservatives thought of as moral anarchy – she called for a restoration of the authority principle in society. She denounced those who were 'soft' on crime. She defended the family as the bedrock of national life. She advocated 'parent power' in the schools. Economically, she declared her faith in the principles of laissez-faire, quoting John Stuart Mill on the perils of over-government, Adam Smith on the need for the unfettered pursuit of wealth.[9] She appeared concerned to vindicate nineteenth-century capitalism and rescue it from the opprobrium of posterity. She argued that 'the heyday of free enterprise in Britain' was also 'the era of selflessness and benefaction'. She complained (in 1976) that 'the Victorian Age' had been very badly treated in socialist propaganda. 'It was an age of constant and constructive endeavour in which the desire to improve the lot of the ordinary person was a powerful factor'. She quoted with approval Samuel Smiles, a joke figure to generations of progressives, enlisting him to support the proposition that 'the sense of being selfreliant, of playing a role within the family, of owning one's own property, of paying one's way, are all part of the spiritual ballast which maintains responsible citizenship, and provides

[7] Address to the Institute of Directors, 11 November 1976, in *Let Our Children Grow Tall*, p. 70.
[8] Havelock Ellis, *The Nineteenth Century. A Dialogue in Utopia*, London, 1900, p. 144.
[9] For Adam Smith, *Let Our Children Grow Tall*, pp. 15, 98, 212; for J.S. Mill, *Sunday Times*, 6 February 1975.

the solid foundation which people look around to see what they might do for others and themselves'.[10]

Mrs. Thatcher aimed in the modernising programme to restore business to a place of honour in national life, and reverse a century of denigration by those, in her Party's own ranks as well as among its opponents, who affected to despise money-making and who wanted to keep commerce and trade at arm's length. She adopted business maxims as her watchwords – e.g. 'Value for Money' – drafted in businessmen as her advisers, watchdogs and trouble-shooters; advocated business patronage for the arts and the appointment of businessmen as the governors of schools and colleges. 'The discipline of market forces' was government's sovereign remedy for social ills; the revival of enterprise the object of its policy. Historically, Mrs. Thatcher was concerned to identify business with the creative forces in national life, the risk-takers and the innovators, the doers and the makers. She gave it a heroic pedigree, offering an alternative version of the national epic, in which there was a merchant-adventurer in every counting-house, a village Hampden in every store. In place of constitutional development – the traditional basis of Whig narrative – or its Tory counterpart, statesmanship and the rise of government, she offered, as the national epic, the romance of trade, conjuring up an age of primitive virtue where nothing was easy and everything had to be earned.

Mrs. Thatcher seems to have stumbled on the phrase 'Victorian Values' as a rallying cry, by accident, conjuring the phrase out of nowhere, and launching it on its public career in the course of an interview with 'Weekend World' (January 16, 1983).[11] Only those who are privy to the secrets of the television studio will know whether it was an inspiration of the moment, or a premeditated plant. However that may be, it was a rhetorical trope which seemed both to thematise her causes and to give them a retrospective dignity. In the following weeks she elaborated it, invoking on the one hand 'the Puritan work ethic'[12] on the other a leitmotif of the election campaign – 'family values'. Her followers added inflections of their own. Thus Mrs. Winterton, the candidate for Congleton, who 'agreed wholeheartedly' with Mrs. Thatcher's Victorian Values, interpreted them benignly as 'thrift, kindness and family values'[13] On the other hand, Dr. Rhodes Boyson, Minister of State for Education, and himself an ex-headmaster (and an ex-historian), argued that they meant a return to strictness.[14]

---

[10] *Let Our Children Grow Tall*, p. 101.
[11] Interview with Brian Walden, Weekend World, 11 January 1983. Typescript in the writer's possession.
[12] *Daily Telegraph*, 29 January 1983; *Guardian*, 29 January 1983.
[13] *Daily Telegraph*, 25 April 1983.
[14] *Daily Telegraph*, 23 April 1983.

He said parents did not want their children to be taught 'deviant practices by proselytising homosexuals'. What parents want is for their children to learn discipline, self-discipline, respect, order, punctuality and precision . . . Parents expect their children to be punished when they step out of line . . . No discipline, no learning. Good old-fashioned order, even Victorian order, is far superior to illiterate disorder and innumerate chaos in the classroom.

It seems possible that, as so often when speaking her simple truths and advertising her hostility to the post-war social settlement, Mrs. Thatcher was deliberately courting outrage. If so, she was duly rewarded by the chorus of indignation which greeted her remarks. For Labour, already convinced that the Tories were planning to destroy the National Health Service and dismantle the welfare state, it was proof positive that they wanted to turn the clock back. It showed yet again that the Tories were 'uncaring' and was of a piece with their 'callous indifference' in other spheres. Just as, in the sphere of family policy, the Tories supposedly wanted to return women to the kitchen sink, and were even toying (it was believed) with eugenics, so in welfare they wanted to go back to the Poor Law. 'Victorian Values', we were told by the opposition, meant each man for himself and the devil take the hindmost. Some invoked the spectre of the workhouse, some of child labour, some of the Dickensian slum. 'Victorian Britain was a place where a few got rich and most got hell', Mr. Kinnock, then shadow minister of education, told the Labour Club at Workington. 'The "Victorian Values" that ruled were cruelty, misery, drudgery, squalor and ignorance'.[15]

Victorian Values, though a latecomer to Mrs. Thatcher's political platform, had been anticipated in a whole series of prior tropes. She had come to the leadership of the Conservative Party, in 1975, on a gospel of 'self-reliance and thrift'.[16] In government she liked to say that her monetarist policies were inspired by 'an old-fashioned horror of debt'. The 'work ethic' was her favoured idiom when arguing for fiscal reform. 'Privatisation' was her tonic for energising the economy and 'rolling back the frontiers of the state'. 'Personal responsibility' was the mantra of her addresses on moral questions, 'parent power' her grand specific for schoolroom disorder and youth unrest.[17] It was not hard to slot 'Victorian Values' into this continuum.

'Victorian Values' were also of a piece with Mrs. Thatcher's personal mythologies. She presented herself to the public not as a scholarship girl

[15] *Daily Telegraph*, 23 April 1983.
[16] Russell Lewis, *Margaret Thatcher*, London 1975, p. 113; *Let Our Children Grow Tall*, p. 34.
[17] *The Times*, 8 May 1977.

who had found her vocation in the city of dreaming spires, nor yet as a successful tax lawyer and denizen of Chelsea, but as a grocer's daughter from Grantham who was still living, metaphorically speaking, above the shop. Her father, as she portrayed him in countless interviews, was a very personification of the Victorian worthy, a self-made (and self-educated) man who had left school at thirteen and who had pulled himself up by the bootstraps, ending up as an alderman on the town council and a lay preacher at the chapel. In Mrs. Thatcher's account of Victorian Values, as also when she spoke of 'traditional' Christianity, there was a conflation between the precepts of her Grantham childhood there and those of an earlier past. 'I was brought up by a Victorian grandmother' she told an *Evening Standard* reporter:

> 'we were taught to work jolly hard. We were taught to prove yourself; we were taught self-reliance; we were taught to live within our income. You were taught that cleanliness is next to godliness. You were taught self-respect. You were taught always to give a hand to your neighbour. You were taught tremendous pride in your country. All of these things are Victorian values. They are also perennial values'.[18]

In another and earlier interview, she describes these values as follows. 'You didn't live up to the hilt of your income; you respect other people's property, you save; you believe in right and wrong; you support the police'.[19]

If the call for a return to Victorian Values struck a chord in 1983, it was perhaps because it corresponded to widespread disenchantment with the modernisations of the 1960s, together with a post-1960s awareness of the limits of economic growth, and also to transformations in the perception of past-present relations. Perhaps, too, it drew subliminal strength from the revival of period styles and the rage for the restoration of 'period' interiors. A concurrence of different influences could be hypothesised here. In the property market, the conversion of run-down Victorian terraces and the elevation of Victorian mansions to the status of 'period' residences: in marketing the mushroom growth of what came to be known, in the 1980s, as the 'Laura Ashley' look, and in heritage, the proliferation of open-air and industrial museums. All of them had the effect, so far as popular taste was concerned, of rehabilitating the notion of the Victorian and associating it not with squalor and grime, but on the contrary with goodness and beauty, purity and truth.

Victorian Values also created a metaphorical space for the expression of moral anxiety. As a rhetoric, it spoke to those who felt bewildered or alarmed by the shape of cultural change. It ministered to the belief, widely

---

[18] 'The Good Old Days', *Evening Standard*, 15 April 1983.
[19] Reference temporarily mislaid.

canvassed in the public press, that Britain was becoming ungovernable, in Mrs. Thatcher's words, 'a decadent, undisciplined society'. It played on fears that the family was in crisis and marriage falling apart. In one aspect, the invocation of Victorian Values was a counterpart to Conservative demands for a 'crack-down' on crime; in another it was perhaps an alarmed response to the coming out of previously stigmatised (and criminalised) sexual minorities. It could be seen as a late echo of the purity campaigns of the 1970s and the mass mobilisations of the Festival of Light.[20] Affirming the need for clearly-defined standards of right and wrong, it questioned the wisdom of past reforming House Secretaries. Against the pleasure principle, it counterposed the worth of self-control and self-restraint.

One aspect of moral anxiety was fear of 'welfare scroungers', seen as early as 1975–6, when a whispering campaign against welfare state 'spongers' swelled into a chorus of newspaper complaint (even, it has been argued, an orchestrated campaign) against those who were allegedly living it up on the dole.[21] With the acknowledgement of unmarried mothers and single parent families as categories in need, numbers dependent on social security payments had risen to new heights. At the same time the extension of 'supplementary benefit' to take account of previously unrecognised contingencies (e.g. rent, mortgage payments, clothes and more generally 'child poverty') narrowed the gap between waged and unwaged almost to vanishing point at the bottom of the social scale. Those caught in the 'poverty trap' (it was then argued) had little or no inducement to get out. Welfare was producing the very condition it was supposed to alleviate, reducing its recipients to a state of dependence and calling new classes of idlers into being.

Mrs. Thatcher appealed directly to this sentiment, indeed anticipated its public expression by some months, when, campaigning for the leadership of the Conservative Party in January 1975, and addressing the annual conference of the Young Conservatives, she appealed to the Party to 'back the workers and not the shirkers'; she coupled this, in a five minutes *credo*, with a ringing declaration of faith in the individual as earner. 'The person who is prepared to work hardest should get the greatest rewards and keep them after tax. It was not only permissible but praiseworthy to want to benefit your own family by your own efforts'.[22] In the years of

---

[20] For the Festival of Light, Dallas Cliff, 'Religion, morality and the middle class', in ed. Roger King and Neill Nugent, *Respectable Rebels, Middle Class Campaigns in the 1970s*, London, 1979.

[21] For an excellent account of this 'moral panic' and the very effective political campaign which followed in its wake, Peter Golding and Sue Middleton, *Images of Welfare: Press and Public Attitudes to Poverty*, Oxford, 1982.

[22] Lewis, op.cit., p. 129.

opposition these were her constant themes. People wanted to be left to get on with their own lives 'and have more of their own pay packets to spend'.[23] Welfare hand-outs sapped initiative.[24] Food subsidies 'had gone to people who did not need them',[25] housing benefits unfairly advantaged the Council tenant:

> 'The Britain I want is a land where a man can know that if he works hard and earns money for his family, he will be allowed to hold on to most of what his efforts have brought him rather than have it seized to build Ministerial empires . . . The Britain I want is a land where people are not ground down in the name of false equality to the point where a man is better off on the dole than at work'.[26]

In the leadership election, Mrs. Thatcher opined (presciently as it turned out) that these sentiments would have as much resonance on the working-class council estates as in the dormitory towns and suburbs. In the following years she was to deploy them with singular effect, discovering, or creating, a new constituency of Tory voters, many of them working class. They were quite undeferential to the rich but had a considerably developed hostility to those further down the social scale. Here is a letter in 1983 from one of them, a real-life original, it may be, of that 'Essex-man' who by the end of Mrs. Thatcher's term in office, was to be recognised as her most faithful supporter.[27]

> Returning to Britain after a five-year absence, I have noticed a wonderful transformation. People are tired of featherbedding for those too lazy or inadequate to fend for themselves. They want an end to our sick, inefficient welfare state. They realise the nation is not a charitable institution and has no business running free hospitals and soup-kitchen benefits, or interfering with private enterprise. They applaud the curbing of the union and want to see our nation great once more. Who has brought about this change? Mrs. Thatcher, of course. Her resolution in rebuilding our country after decades of mismanagement is awesome. A new spirit walks abroad – and this is only the beginning. Well done, Maggie. It's great to be back.
> ALEX THIRLE
> Colchester, Essex.

II

When, in the early days of her Party leadership, Mrs. Thatcher called for a 'restoration' of parental authority, as later when she took up the

---

[23] *Sunday Express*, 8 February 1976.
[24] *Let Our Children Grow Tall*, p. 108.
[25] *Financial Times*, 18 July 1976.
[26] The *Sun*, 2 May 1979.
[27] The *Mail on Sunday*, 24 April 1983.

call for a return to Victorian Values, what mattered was less the words themselves than the character she projected of one who was not afraid of sounding reactionary, but on the contrary gloried in old-fashioned ways. As a piece of symbolic reassurance it was magnificent, convincing her Party followers that Conservatism was returning to the paths of faith. It enabled her to magnify differences with her predecessor – always, it seems, a consideration with Tory leaders – and further to distinguish herself not only from Mr. Heath but also from Mr. Wilson and Mr. Macmillan. Where they made a fetish of tacking to the winds of change, she was by contrast sternly inflexible.

One of Mrs. Thatcher's strengths, and not the least of the reasons why she was able so frequently to wrong-foot her opponents, was that of translating policy issues into questions of what has been called, in another context, 'moral economy'. Even the Poll Tax, the wildly unpopular reform which helped to bring her down, was conceived of as an act of justice, applying nineteenth-century principles of fair play and fair shares to local government taxation, and bringing home a sense of personal responsibility to the local electorate. Private enterprise, Mrs. Thatcher argued, was not only economically efficient, it was also ethically beautiful, harnessing the self-regarding virtues to the higher good. Protectionism, whether in the field of trade unionism, state intervention or local government, bred monopoly; welfare was enervating; bureaucracy was an invitation to extravagance and sloth. Competition on the other hand was bracing, putting workers and employers on their mettle. The market generated an equitable distribution of the available goods, making producers directly accountable to consumers. Job-shedding was a way of losing weight and producing a leaner, fitter labour force. Monetarism was an exercise in frugality, applying the principles of household budgeting ('living within your means') to the management of the national economy. 'Some say I preach merely the homilies of housekeeping or the parables of the parlour', she told the Lord Mayor's banquet in November 1982, when anger about monetarism was at a peak, 'But I do not repent. Those parables would have saved many a financier from failure and many a country from crisis'.[28]

Mrs. Thatcher used 'Victorian Values' as a way of conjuring up lost innocence. Against a background of inner-city disturbances, such as those which swept the streets of Toxteth and Brixton in 1981, she pictured an older Britain where parents were strict, children good-mannered, hooliganism (she erroneously believed) unknown. At a time when both the struggling and the prosperous were mortgaged up to the hilt, she recalled the virtues of penny saving. In a contracting economy, where,

[28] Speech at Lord Mayor's Banquet, November 1982, reported in Hugo Young, *One of Us*, London, 1989, p. 5.

under the shadow of microchip technology every occupation was under actual or potential threat, she looked back to a time when labour was a means of self-fulfilment, when occupations were regarded as callings, and when jobs – or businesses – were for life. In the face of multi-culturalism, she resurrected the mythology of a unified national self.

In all these instances, Victorian Britain was constituted as a kind of reverse image of the present, exemplifying by its stability and strength everything that we are not. The past here occupies an allegorical rather than temporal space. It is a testimony to the decline in manners and morals, a mirror to our failings, a measure of absence. It also answers to one of the most universal myths, which has both its left-wing and right-wing variants, the notion that once upon a time things were simpler and the people were at one with themselves. Like the small town America of Mr. Reagan's rhetoric – God-fearing, paternalistic, patriotic – Mrs. Thatcher's Victorian Britain is inhabited by a people living in a state of innocent simplicity. Instead of nationalised industries there are small businesses and family firms. Work is accorded dignity, achievement rewarded rather than taxed. Families hold together and put their savings by against a rainy day. People know right from wrong. By a process of selective amnesia the past becomes a historical equivalent of the dream of primal bliss, or to the enchanted space which memory accords to childhood. By metaphorical extension, Victorian Values thus passed from the real past of recorded history to timeless 'tradition'. They were, Mrs. Thatcher assured us, like those of Christianity, 'perennial', the values which had made Britain great.[29]

Other people of Mrs. Thatcher's generation and earlier, it is worth noticing, recall things with a different emphasis. In working-class accounts of the 'good old days', as recorded in oral history and written memoirs, it is the images of sociability that prevail – the sing-songs in the pubs, the funeral processions, the 'knees-up' street parties, the summer outings. The canvas is crowded with characters; street performers will sometimes get a page or two to themselves and there may be a whole chapter for Whitsun or Bank Holiday. Shopping is remembered for its cheapness – 'packet of fags and a pint of beer and you could still get change from two bob'. People are forever in and out of each other's houses: 'everyone was in the same boat together' 'everyone was the same'. Children make their own toys, stage their own theatre, invent their own games. The street is their playground, waste lots their battlefields, bunkers their lairs. Pleasures, though simple, are treasured. As Lionel Bart put it, both

---

[29] *Evening Standard*, 15 April 1983.

sentimentally and sardonically, in his musical *Fings Aint What They Used to Be*:

> It used to be fun
> Dad and ole Mum
> Paddling dahn Southend
> But now it ain't done
> Never mind chum
> Paris is where we spend our outings.

Mrs. Thatcher's version of the 'good old days' is altogether more severe. Her lost Eden is one where resources were scarce and careful husbandry was needed to ensure survival. She remembers her childhood not for its pleasures but for its lessons in application and self-control. Reading is not a form of escape but a means of improvement; library visits are compulsory.[30] There are no outings or beanos, though she goes to chapel three times a day on Sunday, no remembered holidays (though at Guides she learnt the lifelong motto 'be prepared'),[31] no secret gardens or ways of playing truant. 'Was she happy?' a journalist asked in an interview. 'We didn't take happiness as an objective. We did a lot. Our parents worked. Our house was always spotless. Cleanliness and hard work were next to Godlines'.[32]

Mrs. Thatcher's values, as many commentators have pointed out, were Puritan values. A literal belief in the devil[33] may help to account for her readiness to discover 'enemies within', while a Puritan alertness to backsliders might be seen in the vigour with which she attacked fainthearts and waverers in the ranks or, worse, in her immediate Cabinet entourage. As a political leader, Mrs. Thatcher was happiest in the role of an evangelist confronting the country with uncomfortable truths. She despised 'soft' options:[34] she used the word 'easy' in a consistently pejorative sense 'a generation of easy liberal education has accustomed many to suppose that Utopia was soon to be achieved';[35] 'freedom is not synonymous with an easy life';[36] 'the world has never offered us an easy living'.[37] She made a fetish of plain speaking, 'calling things by their proper names'. She prided herself on never flinching from making 'painful' decisions, following unpopular

---

[30] Young, op.cit., Margaret Thatcher, *The Revival of Britain*, London, 1989, p. 63.
[31] *Sunday Mirror*, 31 July 1972.
[32] Interview with Jilly Cooper, *Sunday Times*, 19 September 1976.
[33] Address at St. Lawrence, Jewry, 30 March 1978, reproduced in *The Revival of Britain*, pp. 67–8.
[34] Speech to Conservative Party Conference, *Guardian*, 7 October 1981; *Sunday Express*, 8 February 1976.
[35] *The Right Angle*, p. 4.
[36] *The Revival of Britain*, p. 70.
[37] Ibid., p. 98.

courses, or speaking up for unfashionable truths. She relished the idea of struggle, picturing herself romantically as travelling rugged roads, navigating shoals and rapids, braving stormy weather. Even after eleven years in office she still pictured her life as a succession of uphill fights. 'Work is the ethic', she told an interviewer shortly after her resignation[38]

> . . . Decide what you think is right to do and try to persuade other people to try *your* way. That was instilled in me in childhood . . . That's my life. If you believe something passionately and do something that is really worthwhile you will get opposition from people who believe differently, so my life will always be uphill all the way . . . I have never been worried about being unpopular if I thought I was doing right'.

In nineteenth century terms, Mrs. Thatcher spoke in the accents of chapel rather than the church. Brought up a Methodist and a provincial, with a father who had left school at thirteen and started his own business, she seems to have felt an elective affinity with the culturally under-privileged, and a corresponding suspicion of those who used to be called 'the comfortable classes'. Her version of Victorian Values reflects this, invoking the plebeian virtues of self-reliance and self-help rather than the more patrician ones of chivalry and *noblesse oblige* and in her radical contempt for paternalism, and her suspicion of philanthropically-minded 'do-gooders', whether in the socialist or the Conservative ranks, it is not difficult to find echoes of her Northamptonshire shoemaker forbears – 'the radicallest set of fellows in the radicallest town in England', as one of their number told the *Morning Chronicle* Commissioner when he visited Northampton in 1850.[39] If, as Arthur Marwick has interestingly suggested, the post-war social consensus was sustained by a kind of 'secularised Anglicanism';[40] and if the Attlee welfare state was, as Gareth Stedman Jones has eloquently put it, 'the last and most glorious flowering of late Victorian liberal philanthropy',[41] then Mrs. Thatcher's revolt against it might be seen as nineteenth-century Methodism's revenge.

Mrs. Thatcher's values were also grammar school values, those of a scholarship girl who had come out top of the form. Hence, it may be – the matter is speculative – her insistence that she had been born with 'no privilege at all', and had had 'precious little' of it in her early years[42] – a distinctive note in her leadership campaign of January 1975, as it was to be in that of her successor, John Major, – and her fierce resentment of

[38] Interview in *The House Magazine*, reported in the *Independent*, 15 December 1990.
[39] 'The Manufacturing Districts . . .', *Morning Chronicle*, 1850.
[40] Arthur Marwick, *British Society Since 1945*, Harmondsworth, 1982.
[41] Gareth Stedman Jones, *Languages of Class, Studies in English working class history, 1832–1982*, Cambridge, 1983, p. 246.
[42] Lewis, op.cit., pp. 112, 115.

those who, whether by reason of hereditary title and wealth, or expensive education, or, as in the case of one of her adversaries, Mr. Wedgwood Benn, both[43] – had started life with unfair advantages. Hence, too, one could argue her belief that the failures in life were the lazy. Like that other grammar school star to whom she has some uncanny resemblances, Mr. Wilson, she made a great point of having all the facts and figures at her fingertips, of being prodigiously industrious and well-prepared. Her economics, too, has a distinctively prefectorial tang. Competition kept people up to the mark; 'merit' and 'distinctions' spurred them onwards. Success was a recognition of ability: progress was achieved by diligence, application and efforts. The virtues ascribed to Mrs. Thatcher's Methodist upbringing – 'order, precision and attention to detail'[44] – were, of course, also grammar school values. It was Mrs. Thatcher's originality to project them out to the national stage.

All this has some political relevance if, rather than seeing the cultural revolution of the 1960s as an outcome of the campus revolt (which followed rather than preceded it), one were to seek its roots instead – as I have tried to argue elsewhere[45] – in a prior sixth-form dissidence. It may be that at the heart of the 1970s call for a return to 'standards' was outraged grammar school sentiment, the bewilderment and anger of those who found that the very qualities which had served them so well in life were, under the impact of the counter-culture, deliberately transgressed. It is strikingly the case that, from the publication of *The Black Papers on Education* (1969) down to current calls for a return to the 3Rs, the crusade for the defence of 'standards' has been voiced most urgently by right-wing scholarship boys, Professor Cox, the editor of *The Black Papers*, Mr. Boyson, an erstwhile Lancashire lad, Paul Johnson, a Merseyside Catholic and by his own account a youthful swot being striking cases in point. Mrs. Thatcher, from the moment she was elected Party leader, weighed in on their side. 'Our schools used to serve us well' she told Party Conference in 1975. 'A child from an ordinary family, as I was, could use it as a ladder, as an advancement. The socialists, better at demolition than reconstruction, are destroying many good grammar schools. Now this is nothing to do with private education. It is opportunity and excellence in the state schools that are being diminished'.[46]

Mrs. Thatcher's Victorian Britain, like that of Asa Briggs – one of the 'new wave' social historians who, by their scholarly work, prepared the

[43] Patricia Murray, *Margaret Thatcher*, London, 1980, p. 178.
[44] Young, op.cit., p. 6.
[45] Raphael Samuel, 'Born-again Socialism' in ed. Robin Archer *et al.*, *Out of Apathy, Voices of the New Left Thirty Years On*, London, 1989.
[46] Speech at Conservative Party Conference, *Guardian*, 11 October 1975.

way for the rehabilitation of Victorian Values – is an 'age of improvement'.
There is space for the Mechanics Institute, but hardly for the free-and-easy
nor yet for that class who are so inescapable a presence in the novels of the
period, the shabby genteel. While not exactly filled by Grammar school
types, it is peopled by humble, striving, God-fearing folk who might be
thought of as their spiritual ancestors. They are artisans and tradesmen
rather than carriage folk, the industrious sorts of people rather than those
who were called, in the literature of the time, the Upper Ten Thousand.
People rise, but they do so in a modest way, advancing socially by degrees,
rather than meteorically, by flying upward leaps. Tradesmen prosper not
by speculation (or the adulteration of goods) but by punctilious attention
to their ledger books. School leavers learn to educate themselves, in the
manner of Mrs. Thatcher's own father. The self-made men whom she
celebrates are not the commercial adventurers, like Mr. Merdle, nor
the fraudulent projectors, like those presiding over the Anglo-Bengalee
company in *Martin Chuzzlewit*, nor the stock jobbers attempting to corner
the market in cotton on Manchester or Liverpool 'Change. They are rather
the patient who better themselves, moving up in the world without losing
their family roots.

III

Mrs Thatcher's rhetoric of Victorian Values was, on the face of it, a
remarkable example of 'a political attitude' struck for purely symbolic
rewards. Except for the restoration of hanging – something which she
voted consistently whenever the issue of Capital Punishment came before
the House of Commons – Mrs. Thatcher showed no signs of wanting
to translate it into legislative enactment or administrative practice. No
attempt was made to impose any modern equivalent of the workhouse test
on welfare claimants (during Mrs. Thatcher's period of office the number
of those depending on supplementary benefits rose by leaps and bounds,
from 3.4 million in 1979 to 5.6 million in 1988). For all her well-advertised
horror of debt, Mrs. Thatcher made no attempt to curb consumer credit;
indeed if her precepts had been taken seriously, the economy would have
been in ruins. In the consumerled boom of the 1980s, when credit facilities
multiplied, outstanding debt (excluding home loans) grew in real terms by
3% a quarter between the end of 1981 and the first quarter of 1988, rising
from 8% of annual household disposable income in 1981 to 14% in 1987.
In the same period personal savings (excluding life assurance premiums)
fell from 16.3% in 1980 to a mere 1.3% in late 1988. Frugality and thrift,

in short, so far from staging a come-back during Mrs. Thatcher's period in office, all but disappeared.[47]

If one turns, however, from the real to the imaginary, and from literal to figurative meanings, then it can be seen that, if short on legislative pay-offs, the metaphor of Victorian Values was a rich political source of psychic satisfactions. It confirmed misanthropists in the belief that the country was going to the dogs, while rallying traditionalists to the defence of 'standards'. In a more egalitarian register, it peopled the past with familiars, picturing Britain as a nation given over to honest toil. As an allegory of the bourgeois virtues, it celebrated ordinariness, treating humble origins as a mark of distinction and family fortune as the sign of grace. It gave serious money a pedigree and offered class exiles – among them, one might suggest, Mrs. Thatcher – an ideal home, a little commonwealth where birth and breeding counted for nothing, and character was all.

Victorian Values also helped the Conservatives to turn the tables on their opponents by presenting Labour as ossified and sclerotic and the Conservatives as the true radicals, destabilising the Establishment. Where its opponents kept whole armies of wage-earners in thrall, Conservatism was emancipatory: Victorian Values also released the more Utopian strains on Conservative thought, and in its more exalted moments, seizing on privatisation as a token of the shape of things to come, the party could even appropriate the old Marxist dream of the 'withering away' of the state. They pictured the new Britain which 'enterprise culture' made possible as a capitalism without classes and a society without the state. Equipped with the precepts of self-help, claiming the protective mantle of tradition for a born-again radical individualism, and evoking that archetypal figure of national myth, the Free-born Englishman, Conservatives could thus present themselves *both* as the party of the future, championing what was new and developing where their opponents were stuck in a time-warp *and* as the party of precedent, restoring a spirit of republican independence to national life and character.

Within the Conservative Party, Victorian Values gave a voice to the Tory unconscious, licensing the public expression of sentiments which would have been forbidden in the liberal hour of the 1960s. It also provided an idiom or code within which intra-party differences could be fought out. For Conservative loyalists, adopting laissez-faire economics as though it was a long-lost Tory creed, monetarism was a test of stamina; state intervention,

[47] Ivor Crewe, 'Ten Years on', *Daily Telegraph*, 4 May 1989; Sarah Hogg, 'How did we do under Thatcher?', *Sunday Telegraph*, 25 November 1990; Vivien Goldsmith, 'Thatcher's Legacy to Homeowners', *Independent on Sunday*, 25 November 1990; Christopher Huhne, 'From the horn of plenty to the poisoned chalice', *Independent on Sunday*, 25 November 1990.

however benevolently intended, a confession of weakness; Conservative
dissidents, the high Tories or 'Wets', plucking up courage to speak for the
unemployed, or, during the strike of 1984–5, for the miners, but fearful
of being tarred with the brush of post-war 'consensus' politics, invoked
the counter-tradition of nineteenth-century paternalism and philanthropy.
In the coded meanings that, in the 1980s, seemed *de rigeur* at Party
conferences, they invoked a Disraelian notion of 'one Nation' against
the laissez-faire 'dogma' of the government. The rhetoric of Victorian
Values could be seen as an example of what the post-modernists call
'double-coding' and sociologists 'cognitive dissonance' – i.e. of words which
say one thing, while meaning another and camouflaging, or concealing,
a third.

Mrs. Thatcher's traditionalism allowed her to act as an innovator –
arguably the most ruthless of our twentieth-century Prime Ministers –
while yet sounding as though she were a voice from the past. By turns
radical and reactionary, modernising and atavistic, she moved from one
register to another with the dexterity of a quick-change artist. Her political
career exhibits the same paradoxes. At one moment she was the Little
Englander, proclaiming the virtues of splendid isolation, or speaking up for
old-fashioned sovereignty; she was a globetrotter at the next, making the
world her oyster, and trying out the part of statesman on an international
stage. In one role, sniping at the mandarins of Whitehall and Westminster
from her Downing Street redoubt, she was the insider playing the system
against itself; in another speaking up for 'ordinary people', she was the
great outsider, rallying the country against the court. Victorian Values
were similarly double-coded, a programme for the future disguised as a
narrative about the past. The watchwords may have been conservative, but
they were used for subversive ends, to destabilise established authority; to
mobilise resentment against the *status quo*; to give historical precedent to
what was essentially a new turn. She could thus appear simultaneously as
a fierce iconoclast and a dedicated restorationist, an avatar of the future,
pointing the way forward, and a voice from the past, calling on the British
people to return to its traditional ways.

In each of the different phases of her career, Mrs. Thatcher, taking up
the age-old radical cry of corruption in high places, pictured herself as
at war with an *ancien regime*. In a remarkable inversion of the Marxist
theodicy not capital but labour appeared as the fetter on the forces of
production, the feudal integument which had to be broken if capitalism was
to resume its forward march. There were in the first place the trade unions,
with their privileged immunities, and oligarchic government, strangling
innovation by restrictive practices and over-manning. Their leaders were
accused of being overmighty 'barons', holding the country to ransom, as

in the 'winter of discontent' which did so much to bring Mrs. Thatcher to power. Shop stewards, too, were overmighty subjects, with their flying pickets intimidating the public and defying the forces of the law. Then there was the Labour Party, with its vested interest in the extension of public sector employment, its 'client' vote, its state monopolies, its town hall 'czars' and regional fiefs. It was, Mrs. Thatcher argued, a paternalism turned sour, a benevolent despotism whose day was done, protecting dying occupations, shoring up declining industries, multiplying benefits to hold on to a contracting electorate. It fed on the weakness of its constituency, levelling down rather than up in the schoolrooms, maintaining claimants in a state of dependence, lording it over council house tenantry and preventing individuality and excellence from leaving their mark:[48]

> It is now our turn to take a major step towards extending home ownership to many who have until now been deliberately excluded. Councils, particularly socialist councils, have clung to the role of landlord – they love it because it gives them so much power – so that more than 2 million families have seen themselves paying rent for ever. Petty rules and restrictions, enforced dependence. There are the marks of this last vestige of feudalism in Britain.

The Welfare State, under this optic, appeared as Old Corruption writ large, a gigantic system of state patronage which kept its clients in a state of abject dependence, while guaranteeing a sheltered existence for its officials and employees. A hundred years of collectivism (one of Mrs. Thatcher's new circle of intellectual advisers argued) had produced powerful interest groups and influential lobbies whose privileges were bound up with the extension of the public service. 'Every reform ends up by increasing the number of jobs for the boys'. The Whitehall world of 'big government' was a Dracula devouring an ever-increasing quantity of both human and financial resources, and insatiable in its appetite for more (public expenditure consumed 40% of the national product in Mr. MacMillan's premiership; under Mr. Callaghan the proportion had risen to 55%). In office, Mrs. Thatcher translated these precepts into practice, abolishing at least a token number of Quangos, the advisory bodies of the great and the good which had grown up to serve the machineries of state intervention, deprivileging the higher civil service: attempting to restrict supplementary benefits, and to disqualify whole classes of claimants; imposing cash limits on health and hospital authorities, slashing education budgets, ratecapping local councils, cutting off the life support for ailing industries, selling off state assets. But the 'nanny state' turned out to be a many-headed hydra, with Establishments in every reach of public life, and sympathisers in the highest circles in the land. Professional bodies, such as the British Medical

---

[48] Speech to Conservative Party conference, *Guardian*, 7 October 1981.

Association and the Royal College of Nurses, sprang to its aid; the House of Lords and the Church of England came to its defence; the universities and the polytechnics, notwithstanding the attempt to introduce business patronage, remained wedded to the idea of public service, the schools to the principles of universalism, the town halls to the provision of welfare. One adversary was no sooner slain than others rose in their stead.

Victorian Values formed part of a wider discourse in which Mrs. Thatcher sought, with remarkable success, to replace the antique divisions between capital and labour, or class and class – 'pernicious relics' of the nineteenth century as she called them – with a whole set of new 'Us' and 'Them' antitheses which pitted private sector against public sector employment, business against the professions, 'enterprise culture' against 'the dependency' state. Consciously or otherwise, she brought into requisition the age-old radical opposition between the 'productive' and the 'unproductive' classes, the 'industrious sorts of people' and the idle rich. 'Business', a term which by metaphorical extension included both workers and employers – was cast in the role of the wealth-producing sector of the community. The professions, by contrast, with the privileged exception of the army and the police, were treated as social parasites, feeding off the country's 'trading base', running up inflationary costs. The 'caring' professions, with their heartland in the Welfare State, and their outriders in the churches and the charities, were particularly suspect, protecting their privileges and comforts while pretending only to be concerned with others. In another frequent opposition the free market economy was contrasted to the dependency state, the one a democracy of strivers, the other a protectionist racket. In either case business, like the agricultural interest of the nineteenth century was 'the backbone of the country', the doers rather than the talkers, the hardheaded rather than the soft-hearted, the active rather than the passive. As in other matters where 'tradition' was at stake, Mrs. Thatcher was able to relate these antinomies to her own family history. She told a TV interviewer:[49]

> . . . My father (was) a grocer . . . he employed some people in the shop and in another small shop at the other end of town. So he having left school at thirteen provided employment for other people. There was a great fashion in that time that (the) next generation should go into the professions because quite honestly in our town the people who had the greatest security were in the professions. So I took a science degree and I was employed in a scientific job and then I came into law and politics. I with much higher education have not actually created jobs. And I often think of my father when I hear some academics pontificating about how to solve the unemployment problem . . .

[49] TV interview with Gill Neville, reproduced in Sheila Harding, *Orderly Freedom: The Common-sense of Margaret Thatcher*, Sheffield, 1985, pp. 7–8.

I'm tempted to say to them well if you find it so easy to solve why don't you go out and start a business by your own effort and employ – five, ten, fifteen, twenty, a hundred, two hundred. Why don't you? I will tell you why – because you can't. It's easier to tell other people what to do about it than it is to sort it out for yourself. But in the end we have to provide the kind of society where people who can do this who can build up a business are prepared to start . . . Of course . . . you've got to have the good administration in government . . . you've got to have good education – you've got to have good health – don't think you can do without the professions . . . But in the end we rely on those who say . . . 'I've always wanted to build up a business' . . . because they are the people who spot what you and I will want . . . – and they are the people who create the jobs.

Politically, Victorian Values may have made some contribution to the degentrification of the Tory Party, a process which Mrs. Thatcher's successor, with his declared attachment to 'classlessness', shows no sign of wanting to reverse. It offered an alternative tradition to that of the Altar and the Throne, or for that matter of Empire 'Kith and kin'. It had no place for the great public schools (though many of them were Victorian foundations), no room for stately homes, not even those such as Hatfield which had been the country seats of Tory leaders. The parson and the squire were not there, nor were the Upper Ten Thousand, i.e. the world of rank and fashion, the metropolitan rich, or those whom Mrs. Merdle called 'Society'. The most interesting absentee of all was the nineteenth-century Tory Party itself. Perhaps because of its nineteenth-century association with protection and paternalism, Mrs. Thatcher was happier to invoke the liberal-radical John Stuart Mill and the ex-Chartist Samuel Smiles. She has a good word for the nineteenth-century trade unions, quoting them as an example of public-spiritedness, none at all for the Marquess of Salisbury.

After her own fashion, Mrs. Thatcher was offering her Party 'a history from below', one which gave pride of place to those whom she called 'ordinary people'. Mrs. Thatcher had no feel for the traditions of the British governing class, or perhaps, despite the Falklands War, for the imperial dimension of British history. She did not, like her rival, Mr. Heseltine, set herself up as a country gent: and a lifetime spent in politics seems to have insulated her from, rather than drawn her towards, the mystique of Westminster and Whitehall. She reached out instead to the provincial England of her childhood and constructed out of it a family saga. In the process she domesticated the idea of tradition and feminised it. Her narrative concentrated on the small details of everyday life. It was exclusively concerned with the private sphere, omitting such traditional ingredients as wars and diplomacy, monarchy and government, the nation and the state. As she put it in perhaps her best-known aphorism, 'There is no such thing as society, only individuals and their families'.

Victorian Values, if the argument of the foregoing is accepted, was modernisation in mufti. It marked a historic check to the collectivist idea which had been gathering strength, almost unopposed, ever since the discovery (or rediscovery) of the social question in the 1880s. It signalled a sea-change in attitudes to poverty and welfare. It dramatised public disenchantment with the cult of planning. It registered the exhaustion of the programme of state-led modernisation, an idea which has been on the agenda of British politics ever since the Safeguarding of Industries Act (1922) and the formation of the National Grid; which had been vigorously canvassed by 'middle opinion' in the 1930s; and which the 'comprehensive redevelopment' and state-engineered amalgamations of the 1960s had seemed to carry to new heights.

In economics, the call for a return to the market cloaked a rationalisation of British industry more ruthless than ever before. It put trade unionism on the defensive and heralded a remarkable erosion of those craft practices which had survived and indeed flourished in the interstices of modern industry; it heralded the emergence of 'flexible' work-forces and the spread of part-time employment. Most interestingly of all – for the term 'Victorian Values' was coined in the pit of a recession – it seized on what were to be some of the leading strengths of 'born-again' capitalism, in particular the new vitality of small-scale enterprise, and the emergence of the market as a universal panacea for political and social skills, a phenomenon not less marked, at time of writing, In Russia and Eastern Europe than it is in Britain. 'Back to the future', in a word, has proved a more convincing paradigm for change than 1960s gigantism or 'going-for-growth'.

In education, the call for a return to the traditional standards, though framed, by the *Black Papers* of 1960s, as an anguished plea by traditionalists in the humanities has now broadened out into a covert, concerted assault on its predecessor – the idea of a 'liberal education', campaigned for in Matthew Arnold's *Culture and Anarchy*. When the Minister of State attempts to resurrect 'Payment by Results' it is not Matthew Arnold who is the presiding spirit, but if one were to look for Victorian Values in the current revival of the idea of 'useful' knowledge, and the talismanic importance currently being attached to 'performance indicators', it is Mr Gradgrind who is the presiding spirit.

As one who traced a line of descent from the Northamptonshire shoemakers, whose father was a lay preacher and who had herself a strict chapel childhood, Mrs Thatcher has better credentials than most for speaking about Victorian Values. Historians, however much they might want to qualify or question her version of the nineteenth century, ought to acknowledge their indebtedness; as those who assembled last December for the British Academy conference on the subject acknowledged, we would be envious of one of our colleagues who, ten years on, was still able to kindle the fires of scholarly controversy. But it is a sad irony of our time that Mrs Thatcher, though espousing the work ethic, presided over a decade which saw more job losses than at any other time in twentieth-century British history, and which witnessed (or confirmed) a decisive shift from a manufacturing to a service economy. There is no reason to doubt the sincerity of Mrs Thatcher's professions of faith, but if one were to look for those who, during her period of office, most obstinately stood out for Victorian Values generally, whether one interpreted them in terms of family solidarity, the dignity of work, the security of the home, or simply the right of the Free-born Englishman to stay put, it would be not the Prime Minister, but the miners defeated in the strike of 1984–5 – her 'enemy within' – who would have the stronger claim.

Proceedings of the British Academy, **78**, 31–47

Victorian Values
in Scotland and England

R.J. MORRIS
University of Edinburgh

A DISCUSSION of Victorian values taking place in Edinburgh invites and demands a comparison of England and Scotland with an insistence that would be unlikely in a London context.[1] Responding to this demand presents many problems. Victorian values is a sharply contested concept as the initial 1983 debate showed all to clearly.[2] In addition we have the hidden guest at the feast, namely Britain, once centre of an Empire. Scotland, itself, remains part of a contested relationship, Scotland-Britain, in other words the Union of 1707. It is a contest which has filled the political, cultural and indeed daily life of Scotland for nearly 300 years. Thus in his 'Auld Licht Idylls' J.M. Barrie described Snecky Hobart, the bellman of the weaving settlement of Thrums; 'Though Scots in his unofficial conversation, he was believed to deliver himself on public occasions in the finest English.'[3] It was a careful and instinctive balancing of English power and Scottish community. From an English perspective, the relationship England-Britain is unproblematic. In discourse as varied as Raphael Samuel's splendid essay

Read 12 December 1990. © The British Academy 1992.
[1] I am grateful to David McCrone, Graeme Morton, Lindsay Patterson, Nick Phillipson and Jim Smyth for help, advice, information and ideas which have contributed to this paper in a very substantial way. In an area of debate which can be contentious, I hasten to add that I take full responsibility for the views and arguments in the final product.
[2] *New Statesman*, 27 May 1983; James Walvin, *Victorian Values*. A companion to the Granada Television series (London, 1987); Eric M. Sigsworth (ed.), *In search of Victorian Values. Aspects of 19th century thought and society* (Manchester, 1988).
[3] J. M. Barrie, *Auld Licht Idylls* (London, 1892), p. 210.

on patriotism to the campaign speeches of Michael Hesletine in the 1990 Conservative leadership contest, the two words are interchangeable.[4]

Central to the relationship has been the major contribution which Scotland made to the creation of Victorian values themselves. That contribution we call the Scottish enlightenment is well known. Less acknowledged are a series of innovations in social and cultural practice which were developed in early 19th-century Scotland and then exported south to become a successful part of the dominant values of the 19th century. Mechanics Institutions began in Glasgow and were exported to London in 1824. In the following three decades their diffusion was widespread.[5] Savings Banks came from rural Ayrshire. They were enshrined in an act of parliament in 1817 and experienced an even more rapid diffusion across the major urban centres of England.[6] Temperance was brought down from the Belfast-Glasgow axis to the industrial areas of England. The Scottish cultural produce was widely adopted. The original movement was interested in banning spirits drinking, the cause of much distress in Scotland. It took the English a few years to find that this was of little value in the beer drinking counties. On the initiative of a small group of men in Preston, the formula was changed to teetotalism.[7] It is an interesting and rare example of a policy developed for Scotland being foisted on the English. We should notice that these cultural products all came from an area of social action in which middle and working class people sought to act without reference to the state. Central to the contested nature of Scotland is the lack of clearly identifiable state institutions. There is no head of state, no parliament, no cabinet but that did not mean no Scotland.

At a personal level the sons of northern manufacturers and whig aristocrats came north to keep a term or so in Scotland's universities. The graduates of Scotland went south. They took with them a much broader philosophical base from which to contribute to the values of British society. They brought the Scotch philosophers' sense of history

---

[4] Raphael Samuel, 'Introduction: exciting to be English', in Raphael Samuel (ed.), *Patriotism. The Making and unmaking of British National Identity, Vol one, History and Politics* (London, 1987).

[5] Mabel Tylecote, *The Mechanics Institutions of Lancashire and Yorkshire before 1851* (Manchester, 1957); James Hole, *An Essay on the History and Management of Literary, Scientific and Mechanics Institutions* . . . (London, 1853), pp. 4–12; Henry Brougham, 'Practical Observations upon the Education of the People, 1825' from *The Speeches of Lord Henry Brougham*, vol. 3, (Edinburgh, 1837), pp. 110–13.

[6] John Tidd Pratt, *The History of Savings Banks* (London, 1830); H. Oliver Horne, *A History of Savings Banks* (Oxford, 1947).

[7] Brian Harrison, *Drink and the Victorians. The Temperance Question in England, 1815–1872* (London, 1971); Daniel C. Paton, 'Drink and the temperance movement in nineteenth century Scotland' (Edinburgh PhD, 1977).

and progress over time. They brought a tradition of organized knowledge and teaching. They were more adept in the use of abstract or, as the English would have it, 'metaphysical' concepts. By way of the Holland House whigs Edinburgh graduates were in at the start of Victorian values, demanding limits on the power of the Crown and representation for property as part of parliamentary reform.[8] Thomas Chalmers in *The Christian and Civic Economy of Large Towns* united his evangelical concerns with political economy, and an acute sense of the importance of community which is not just rural but also particularly Scottish.[9] Scotland had a weak eviscerated state but a strong sense of community. When James Kay, Edinburgh graduate, went south he took with him not just a medical qualification but the values gained sitting at the feet of Thomas Chalmers to whom he dedicated his first book.

> You, who minister in the sacred office, must have more frequent opportunities than I, of observing with regret, that many who recognize the constant presence of a presiding Providence, fail in practically acknowledging the perpetual influence of a mighty source of moral causation . . .

The mixture of practical and moral is the key element here. Kay attacked the Poor Law, '. . . depriving the virtuous poor of the incentives to industry and glutting the market with labour'. His views of education were still partially formed; '. . . There is no sufficient provision for the education and the religious and moral instruction of the poor; and their ignorance and misery often tempt them to desperate deeds.'[10]

Kay took the traditions of the statistical movement from Scotland to his enquiries in English towns like his fellow Scottish graduate G.C.Holland in Sheffield.[11] Others were active in the formation and spread of the Mechanics Institutions. Kay joined Southwood Smith and Leonard Horner amongst the inspectorate of the new civil service of the 1830s.[12] Those who grew up in Scotland learnt to act at the level of community and to

---

[8] Anand C. Chitnis, *The Scottish Enlightenment and early Victorian English Society* (London, 1986), esp. pp. 160–62; George Davie, *The Democratic Intellect. Scotland and her Universities in the 19th century* (Edinburgh, 1961).

[9] Thomas Chalmers, *The Christian and Civic Economy of Large Towns*, 3 vols (Edinburgh, 1821); Stewart Mechie, *The Church and Scottish social development, 1780–1870* (London, 1960), pp. 47–63; see also the contribution of Professor Stewart Brown to this symposium.

[10] James Kay, *Moral and Physical Condition of the Working Classes* (Manchester, 1832; reprint Didsbury, 1969) pp. 4 and 16.

[11] M.J. Cullen, *The Statistical Movement in Early Victorian Britain. The Foundations of Empirical Research* (Brighton, 1975); G Calvert Holland, *The Vital Statistics of Sheffield* (London, 1843).

[12] Richard Johnson, 'Educational Policy and Social Control in Early Victorian England', *Past and Present*, **49** (1970).

combine moral and civil imperatives. The two states within which they
lived were weak or distant. The ruling class to which they might relate was
increasingly bound into the larger dominant element of those two states
and their attendant cultures.

The English in return found something cold and chilling about the
organized practical logic which the Scots brought with them. 'Scotch
feelosopher' was a term of abuse for Cobbett. Dickens, when he wanted
to sum up all that was wrong with working class education, choose a
Scottish stereotype, Mr. McChoakcumchild.[13] Another form in which
Scottish influence came south was the classroom teaching which David
Stow developed in Glasgow in the 1830s.[14] The Scots had a clear notion
of themselves not just as better educated at certain levels but able to
argue in a more thorough and abstract manner. When Hugh Miller,
the stonemason, geologist, newspaper editor for the evangelical wing
of the Kirk travelled through England, he sat in the public room of his
inn in Newcastle eavesdropping on an argument about the atonement
involving two Sheffield mechanics. He was scathing: 'the methodists
were wild nondescripts in their theology'. The remark would scarcely
have arrested a theologic controversy on the same nice point in Scotland,'
he commented after one silence, 'certainly not among the class of peasant
controversialist so unwisely satirized by Burns'. 'You Scotch are strange
people,' one of the commercial travellers told him. 'The development of
the popular mind in Scotland is a result of its theology', was Miller's
reply.[15]

Scottish cultural exports south were more than this. When Samuel Smiles
left Haddington in 1829, he carried with him a letter from his father. It was
a chilling mixture of affection, discipline and family identity. There was a
powerful sense of an all seeing, all powerful God and a distrust of anything
beyond the boundaries Haddington, East Lothian, Scotland. Duty and guilt
were writ large between the lines.

> Haddington 17th October 1829
> Dear Son,
> You are now about to leive us, permit us to give you an advice, the place in
> which dwelling for a time wher much depravety and wickedness is prevelant
> now when you are away from our parential eye, think on Hagar's prayer,

---

[13] Chitnis, p. 183.

[14] David Stow, *The Training System adopted in the Model School of the Glasgow Educational
Society* (Glasgow, 1836), pp. 67–75 and 235–7; David Hamilton, *Towards a Theory
of Schooling* (London, 1989), pp. 75–115 traces the emergence of the classroom or
'simultaneous' teaching in the context of early 19th century Glasgow and looks back to
the ideological influence of the thought of Adam Smith.

[15] Hugh Miller, *First Impressions of England and its People* (Edinburgh, 1877), pp. 8–10.

my God Seith me, be ernest at a thron of Grace . . . Your conduct from
this time forward will either be a joy or sorrow to your affectionate father
and mother and be assured if you do as becometh a Son who venerates
their parents, nothing shall be wanting on our part for your good, you will
be provided with the meins of making you respectable in the worald, you
will also have our prayers and Affectionally esteimed by us; but, if you act
contrary, to your own disgrace, and our Shame, your now fair prospects will
be forever blasted, we will withold our support, and give it to another if more
deserving, but we cherish the hope that your conduct will be as becometh
a Christian and be deserving of our approbation . . .[16]

So Smiles went to the big bad city of Edinburgh with this tucked in his
pocket. He took it with him when he went south. It is the only document
which survives from this period. The end product was 'Self-Help' and
its associated lectures and books. As all close readers of this literature
know this was not a heartless product. It was the product of a man who
advocated self reliance, struggle and self creation as the only sound way to
respect and independence.[17] It was a lesson that had begun in the chilling
but affectionate eye of God Almighty in Haddington. As his intellectual
and political interests expanded in the south, the lesson was extended in
the face of the aristocrat led state and the threatening mass politics of
Chartism. The experience of middle status Scotland was an experience of a
state managed by an increasingly remote aristocratic elite. From Highlands
to borders, the middle ranks of Scotland learnt to distrust the aristocratic
families which ran the state. That distrust was more complete and without
recourse to mitigation than the English experience. The message of 'Self
Help' appealed to many English middle and working class people. By
the 1850s it was a British message despite its Scottish origin. These rags
to riches tales were not of course new in the 1850s. What Smiles had
contributed in his great secular sermons was a keen sense of morality and
moral self creation. In much the same way Thomas Carlyle had taken the
radical hero Cromwell and turned him into a moralized example of self
creation and leadership.[18] Again compare *Chamber's Edinburgh Journal*,
product of two Edinburgh brothers, with the *Penny Magazine*. One is
warm, moralizing and human in its content. The other is as cold as an
encyclopedia. The Edinburgh product was written for the respectable
middle and working class by some of their own number. The London
product was written for the same group by their social and intellectual

[16] Leeds City Archives, SS/A III/1.
[17] R.J. Morris, 'Samuel Smiles and the Genesis of Self Help; the retreat to a Petit Bourgeois
Utopia', *The Historical Journal*, **24** (1981), 89–109; Ken Fielden, 'Samuel Smiles and Self
Help', *Victorian Studies*, **12** (1968), 155–76.
[18] Ian Campbell, *Thomas Carlyle* (London, 1974).

superiors and it shows.[19] Much has been written about the anglicization of Scotland; more thought needs to be given to the Scottish input to this process in the first half of the 19th century. Already three features which lay behind Scotland's contribution to Victorian values begin to show. The lack of a central state capable of integration with Scottish society, a direct and bitter confrontation with aristocracy beyond anything experienced in England and an individualistic relationship with a chilling but affectionate God.

This enormous and fruitful exchange was possible because Scotland and England were a part of the same urbanizing industrial society, the same market economy.[20] This means that any attempt at comparison is dangerous ground, a world of carefully shaded meaning. The most secure ground comes from the Act of Union itself. Surely, the church and the law are different, and as a result the education system and the physical and legal structure of property is different. Scotland claims a better educated and worse housed population than England. Yet on closer examination how real are these differences. In 1851, some 58% of English and 61% of Scots were in church on census Sunday. There was one difference. Scottish attendance tended to be better in the urban areas whilst the English were better attenders in the rural parts.[21] Careful calculation suggests that the Scots spent much the same proportion of their resources on education as the English, although outcomes in terms of third quarter of the 19th century literacy seem to favour Scotland.[22] The cities full of tenements can be related to the transfer costs of the Scottish property system but equally they were a product of the lower incomes of the Scottish working class, some 5% lower in the 1880s.[23] The Scottish economy was the low income, export orientated margin of the British 19th-century economy.[24] This fact was as important as Kirk and Court of Session in interpreting shades of

[19] William Chambers, *Memoir of Robert Chambers with the Autobiographical Reminiscences of William Chambers* (Edinburgh, 1876); Richard D. Altick, *The English Common Reader. A social history of the mass reading public, 1800–1900* (Chicago, 1957) pp. 332–8.

[20] R.J. Morris, 'Introduction,' and 'Urbanization and Scotland,' in W. Hamish Fraser and R.J. Morris (eds), *People and Society in Scotland*, vol. 2, 1830–1914 (Edinburgh, 1990).

[21] Callum G. Brown, 'Religion, class and church growth', in Fraser and Morris, op.cit.; Callum G. Brown, *The Social History of Religion in Scotland since 1730* (London, 1987).

[22] E.G. West, 'Resource Allocation and growth in early nineteenth century British Education', *Economic History Review*, 2nd series, vol. 23 (April 1970) 73–7; R.A. Houston, *Scottish Literacy and the Scottish Identity: illiteracy and society in Scotland and northern England, 1600–1800* (Cambridge, 1985) 1–19.

[23] R.G. Rodger, 'The Law and Urban Change', *Urban History Yearbook* (1979) 77–91; R.G. Rodger, 'The Invisible Hand, Market Forces, Housing and the Urban Form in Victorian Cities', in Derek Fraser and Anthony Sutcliffe (eds), *The Pursuit of Urban History* (London, 1983).

[24] R.H. Campbell, *The Rise and Fall of Scottish Industry, 1707–1939* (Edinburgh, 1980).

difference in values. The Poor Law was different. There was a greater use of outdoor relief, a less authoritarian regime in the poorhouse (which was not a workhouse), but then the poor, especially the able bodied poor, had no rights. In some respects the two systems converged. In the 1830s, the rate of pauperism in England and Wales was a massive 7%, whilst Scotland recorded 3.25%. By the 1860s the gap had narrowed and was gone by the end of the century when both countries were just over the 2% mark.[25] The Scots imported many values and practices from the south, but retained a greater faith in outdoor relief and profited from a much weaker form of central supervision.

One consequence of the greater poverty and community base of Scottish society is a suspicion that 'family' meant something different in Scotland. The English image of family was very household centred. The Scottish concept of family was a more chaotic set of relationships. It had to be. In the cities the dominance of single and double ends made the disciplined family ideal of sexual discipline and gender and age hierarchies difficult to locate in the household. In the countryside, tied housing made the concept of a secure home difficult to conceive. For middle and working class people alike, long distance migration changed the meaning of family ties. In the 19th century Scotland lost huge portions of its population to migration. Family was not home sweet home but the ballads of parting and the attempts to maintain contact by letter.[26] The need to see family as a set of relationships may have been one influence on Poor Law policy. Scotland was far more prepared to use outdoor relief for the aged poor and was much earlier in the use of fostering for pauper children, practices which were not only cheaper but embedded the poor in networks of relationships rather than institutional categories. In terms of modern culture I ponder on the cosy turmoil of the family networks of the Broons and compare this with a cultural product of northern England, the Andy Capp cartoon with its sexist and household violence.[27]

It was in the nature of Scottish national identity that the divergences were most apparent. Let me consider a number of images. The first is the suffragette march along Princes Street in 1909 (Figure 1). The Women's Social and Political Movement came late and cautiously to Scotland and was imported from England, yet the several banners are in Scots and the march was led by a women piper. Now by the end of the 19th century

[25] Ian Levitt, *Poverty and Welfare in Scotland, 1890–1948* (Edinburgh, 1988); Ian Levitt, 'Poor Law and Pauperism', in John Langton and R.J. Morris (eds), *Atlas of Industrializing Britain* (London, 1986) pp. 160–3.

[26] M.A. Anderson and D.J. Morse, 'The People', in Fraser and Morris (op.cit.).

[27] This owes much to a conversation with Ian Levitt and other 'Sunday Post' readers; see *The Broons, selected from the Sunday Post* (Dundee [Christmas], 1977).

the bagpipes had become firmly male and military in their identity, so that the challenge involved in this could only be fully understood in a Scottish context.[28] Next, Empire Day in Aberdour with the Scottish Lion rampant central to the celebration of the British Empire (Figure 2). Central to Scotland's Victorian values was a particular sort of patriotism which recreated Scotland as a nation within a nation. Scotland gathered together a wide variety of cultural symbols during the 19th century.[29] There was Burns, and by mid century Burns suppers, and then Walter Scott and his monument which dominated Edinburgh's Princess Street. Tartan was transformed from its highland origins to a universal symbol of Scottish identity. With tartan came Bonnie Prince Charlie and Mary Queen of Scots, two Catholics who became the romantic heroes of a Protestant nation.[30] The crown jewels were taken out of a box in 1818 for the Prince Regent. Mons Meg was returned to Edinburgh castle at the request of Walter Scott in 1829.[31] In the second half of the century the gateway and esplanade of the 'medieval' Edinburgh castle were laid out. These provided a great stage set upon which the nation could display its regiments and set out the memorials to its dead. The new middle class suburbs filled with villas and superior tenements which were decorated with stone thistles, saltires and baronial turrets. The meaning of this national identity was different from the aggressive expansionist meaning of British/English. The work of Mr. Graeme Morton on the Edinburgh middle classes shows quite clearly that the dominant form of nationalism was a unionist nationalism. The Society for the Vindication of Scottish Rights was firmly against anglicization but equally pro Union. This perception of nationalism was expressed in Noel Paton's proposal for a national monument in 1859. It was to feature Wallace and Bruce (two more symbols)

> Intelligent Englishmen know full well the source of Britain's strength and greatness, and that to the independence achieved under Wallace and Bruce, the UNION of Scotland with her sister kingdom, on terms satisfying to both, owes not only all its practicality, but the greater portion of its success.
>
>   In my design . . . the recognition of the peaceful triumphs of a later and

[28] Elspeth King, *The Scottish Women's Suffrage Movement* (Glasgow, The People's Palace, 1978).

[29] David McCrone, 'Representing Scotland: Culture and Nationalism', in David McCrone, Stephen McKendrick and Pat Straw (eds), *The Making of Scotland: nation, culture and social change* (Edinburgh, 1989).

[30] Alexander Smith, *A Summer in Skye* (London, 1865) shows how these elements were brought together in the mind of a Paisley pattern designer cum Edinburgh poet in the 1850s.

[31] *McDowall's New Guide in Edinburgh, being a description of all the localities, antiquities and buildings of any interest in the city and vicinity* . . ., (Edinburgh, c. 1850) reference from Mr. G. Morton; H.J. Hanham, *Scottish Nationalism* (London, 1969).

Figure 1. Suffragette demonstration, Edinburgh 1909. *People's Palace (Glasgow Museums and Art Galleries).*

Figure 2. Empire Day, Aberdour 1902. *National Museums of Scotland.*

happier day, when the sword of intestine war had been for ever sheathed in these lands, and the Scotch and the 'auld enemies', the English, had become, under the providence of God, one great, free and united people.[32]

By 1900, Scottish people had created clear choices for themselves, Scottish or British. To be Scottish might overlap with being British as in the celebration of the Empire. It could be antagonistic as in the formation of the Scottish football league. It could be complementary as in the formation of the Scottish TUC and Scottish elements of the labour movement.[33] Note that these expressions of Scottish identity often involved plundering cultural resources from England. Thus football, a major form of nationalist expression for all classes in Scotland was lifted from the English public schools. The constitutional theory was implicit, at the union in 1707, foreign affairs, trade and military policy together with representative legal powers had been handed to the Westminister parliament and that was all. The most fundamental assertion of Scottish national identity in the 19th century had been the Disruption of the Church of Scotland in 1843, when nearly half the ministers and members walked out of the Assembly in a dignified procession. The issue was the interference of lay patrons in the conduct of the church and the support of that interference by the courts and parliament of Westminister. The leaders and supporters of the Disruption believed that the Westminster government had a duty under the Union to sustain the institutions of Scottish society, law, church and education, but had no right to interfere in the nature of those institutions.[34]

The legal and religious existence of Scotland combined with the weak Scottish government bequeathed by the Union produced another aspect of Scottish values and practice. Scotland had a higher regard for community and locality as a basis for action than the English. It is this that lies behind the paradox of the Scottish Poor Paw which was at once meaner but less authoritarian than the English version. The poor had fewer rights but were subjected to a weaker discipline. After the Union, Scotland happily ignored Poor Law legislation with the connivance of the Court of Session which decreed that any law which was ignored for a few years no longer applied. Even when the law caught up with Scotland in 1844, the parish remained the unit of administration.[35] At first this ensured the authority of property

[32] 'Proposal' in Edinburgh Room, George IV Bridge, qYNA 9355W, Acc 42194, again reference from Mr. G. Morton.

[33] Ian MacDougall, *Labour in Scotland*, (Edinburgh, 1978).

[34] Revd Thomas Brown, *Annals of the Disruption* (Edinburgh, 1893); Callum Brown, *The Social History of Religion in Scotland since 1730* (London, 1987) pp. 38–40.

[35] Audrey Patterson, 'The Poor Law in nineteenth century Scotland', in Derek Fraser (ed.), *The New Poor Law in the nineteenth century* (London, 1976); Ian Levitt and Christopher Smout, *The State of the Scottish Working Class in 1843* (Edinburgh, 1979).

owners but by 1920s allowed considerable influence to local democracy in the application of poor law directives from a weak Board of Supervision. When the parish basis of welfare administration was abolished in 1929, it was admitted that this 'would disturb one of the foundation stones of Scottish society.'[36]

This same sense of locality and community was evident in Scottish town government. Low incomes, the instability of the economy, cramped housing and the surplus population of a well ordered countryside all put intense pressure on Scottish urban conditions. At the same time central direction was weaker than anything experienced in England. At times this failure of central direction was almost comical as with the 1866 Sanitary Act which proved unworkable in Scotland because the final appeal was in the English Court of Queen's Bench. Attempts to provide general legal powers for urban authorities lagged well behind England. The first public health act only appeared in 1867. However Scottish towns carried with them the authoritarian traditions of the Royal Burghs. Building regulations were stricter than anything in England. Crowded working class housing was ticketed, giving the police power to raid homes at any time of day or night to check overcrowding.[37] At their best the Scottish towns became centres of innovation and initiative. The early days displayed a rather charming faith in community as at Stirling which attempted draining and paving by voluntary subscription.[38] This rapidly gave way to a spectacular series of local initiatives in the large cities. Glasgow carried out the Loch Katrine water supply scheme as early as 1859. The 1866 Glasgow Improvement Act remodelled 88 acres of the city centre.[39] By the 1880s the Trust acting for the Corporation had been drawn into building and in 1902 the Corporation owned 2,488 houses. In Edinburgh improvements carried out under the patronage of Lord Provost William Chambers paid attention to housing, sanitation and communication. At the other end of the scale were places like Coatbridge which had hardly begun to think about water supply. Although transatlantic observers saw Glasgow as the leading innovator in

[36] Ian Levitt, *Poverty and Welfare in Scotland, 1890–1948*. p. 160, quoting Walter Elliott. Elliott moved poor law responsibilities to the country and burgh, doubtless hoping that this would dilute the influence of labour and communist councillors in the more socially homogeneous parishes.

[37] R.J. Morris, 'Urbanization', in W.H. Fraser and R.J. Morris (eds), *People and Society in Scotland*, vol. ll, 1830–1914 (Edinburgh, 1990) p. 83–7.

[38] Finlay McKichan, 'A burgh's response to the problem's of urban growth: Stirling, 1780–1880', *Scottish Historical Review*, vol. 57 (1978) pp. 68–86.

[39] Tom Hart, 'Urban growth and Municipal Government: Glasgow in Comparative context, 1846–1914', in A. Slaven and Derek H Aldcroft (eds), *Business, Banking and Urban History* (Edinburgh, 1982) pp. 193–216; Bernard Aspinwall, *Portable Utopia. Glasgow and the United States. 1820–1920* (Aberdeen, 1984).

the 1900s, England can produce the same range of the active and the squalid, but there is not the same respect for local initiative and power that Scotland provided. An extreme version of this respect was embodied in the Lindsay or Burgh Police (Scotland) Act of 1862, which allowed extensive powers for the self creation of burghs. Seven ratepayers in any community with more than 700 people could, with the help of the Sheriff declare themselves a burgh. One result was a rash of police burghs around Glasgow which provided a variety of havens from the taxes and from the building regulations of the big city.[40]

But Victorian values is as much a debate about the 1980s and the relationship of perceptions of the past to power, policy and morality in the 1980s as it is a debate about the nature of the past itself. The 1980s was a decade in which visions of the future died. Socialism and Marxism had both sunk in a welter of bureaucracy and self interest. Keynesian control had died in a bout of inflation and growth economics was threatened by ecological perceptions. The invisible hand of the market economy was turning out to be neither invisible nor universally benevolent. Hence that mixture of economic freedom and social authoritarianism which we call Thatcherism turned to history for justification; 'I was brought up to work jolly hard, . . . to live within our income.' Family, patriotism, self reliance, self respect, personal responsibility, in short, traditional values, '. . . were the values when our country became great.' It all seems to have started with a television interview in 1982 and the debate and its rhetoric spread rapidly around the 1983 election campaign.[41] It was a powerful reuse of history to legitimate a far reaching bundle of policies designed amongst other things to weaken the welfare capacity and responsibilities of the state. The response both positive and critical was immediate, but it was almost all an English and a British response.[42] The conclusion was clear, Victorian values was a partial, partisan and trivialized version of the values and practices of the Victorians but an excellent and effective justification for changes taking place in the 1980s. That is, except in Scotland. In Scotland, there was no debate. Local authority housing was purchased with caution and the change of ownership brought no political dividend. The political response reduced the number of Tory MPs in Scotland to only ten in 1987. In 1988, it was Scotland's turn. After the general election of the previous year the Tories were clearly convinced that Scotland had got it wrong and that with a little persuasion, voters would change their minds. Margaret Thatcher

[40] R.J. Morris, op.cit., p. 88.

[41] Margaret Thatcher, *The Revival of Britain. Speeches on Home and European Affairs, 1975–1988* (London, 1989).

[42] *New Statesman*, 27 May 1983; *The Listener*, 2 June 1983; these were followed by the Granada television series in 1986, see Walvin, op.cit.

made a number of key speeches in that year in Scotland. Central to this was the 'Sermon on the Mound', delivered to the General Assembly of that year. [43] The sense of quiet outrage this provoked is difficult to reconstruct. It was believed to have been an attack on Scottish values and identity. Yet a re-reading of the speech shows very little which most members of the Kirk could take exception to. It was about faith, family, personal responsibility and patriotism. Yet this speech probably brought hopes of a Tory revival in Scotland to a premature end for two reasons both related to the use of history. The first was a matter of place. For that very English Prime Minister to lecture the premier assembly of the national church was an intrusion which caused deep unease. The Presbyterian Church of Scotland has always reserved the right to comment on the lay sphere of politics but has been equally jealous of interference from government. In addition, this was a period in which the Thatcher establishment made a ferocious and counterproductive attack on the Scottish identity. Speeches by Lawson and Tebbit accusing the Scots of being junkies for state handouts were followed by a headline in *The Sun*, 'stop yer snivelling Jock.' A week before Mrs. Thatcher had addressed the Tory women's conference at Perth claiming, '. . . the Scots invented Thatcherism' with frequent references to Adam Smith. The British Empire, the ladies were told, could not have flourished if the Scots had not been there to build the roads and cure the sick. Edinburgh was praised for its scenery, '. . . not to mention a handy golf course and a distillery or two.' These were powerful historical references, but the Scots engineer of Kipling's poems had long gone and the image of Scotland as a tourist resort led easily from the golf course to the grouse moor. The correspondence and editorial columns of *The Scotsman* rocked with gentile anger and hostility. The chair of the Scottish Council on Disability defended Adam Smith, his was 'a socially responsible and moral system of economics.' It was 'effrontery' 'to use his name for ideological purposes.' Adam Smith, said another correspondent '. . . showed a deep moral concern for the long term outcome of commercialism'. [44] This disastrous period for the Scottish Tory party was completed when '. . . the English Prime Minister presented the Scottish Cup at Hampden Park . . .' to the enthusiastic booing of the crowd, who had been thoughtfully provided with red cards to 'send off' Thatcher. Malcolm Rifkind, the Secretary of State for Scotland, in his kindly and patient way explained that the Tories were the oldest party in Scotland and that the Union was one of the finest achievements of the Scottish people and should be defended as

[43] The General Assembly of the Church of Scotland takes place annually in the Assembly Hall which lies behind New College on The Mound which links the Old and New Towns of Edinburgh, hence the ironic title given this speech by the Scots.
[44] *The Scotsman*, 17 May 1988.

such.[45] As we have seen his was a correct reading of a powerful historical tradition in Scotland, but meanwhile Thatcher and her Victorian values were send homeward, although whether it was 'to think again' must be a matter of some speculation.

So where does all this leave the status of Victorian values in the relationship between the identities of Scotland and England.

First, there was a flow of ideas south. These ideas were conceived in the context of a weak central government in Scotland. They were also influenced by the much poorer integration of aristocratic power into the hierarchies of Scottish society. The anti landlordism of the late-19th-century Liberal Party really had meaning in Scotland. The Scottish input to Victorian values were based upon a confident juxtaposition of evangelical and materialist systems of meaning; God and geology in Hugh Miller, faith and political economy in Thomas Chalmers. There was the confidence in self creation exemplified in the writing of Samuel Smiles. In all of them there was a sense of the value of the individual operating in the moral framework of small communities.

How was all this transformed in England? These ideas had to come to terms with the deep seated aristocratic paternalism located in the state as well as in a powerful urban Tory presence. It had to come to terms with a stronger state; the state of inspectors and boards. Hence, in that context the Scottish ideas of individuality, self creation, the interpenetration of moral and material concerns, the faith in community and locality came to acquire a much firmer anti state meaning. In England these ideas had to come to terms with a more fragmented religious practice and system of meaning.

Secondly we can identify a variety of contrasts and convergences in the social and ideological nature of two closely related societies operating in the same urban industrial market economy. The most important divergence was in the manner in which the Scots provided themselves with a choice of identities by living within a recreated Scottish identity which sustained an equivocal independence within a unionist imperialist British identity, and was very different from the English/British imperial amalgam generated further south.

But the real contrast was in the response to the Victorian values of the 1980s. The attempts to incorporate Scotland into this system of legitimation were at best failures and usually counterproductive. Indeed the response to such attempts at incorporation may well have meant that 'Victorian values' became in themselves a stimulus to cultural innovation within Scotland. The Scottish cultural revival of the last 20 years has always had a strong historical content, from the 7:84 Theatre Company's, *Cheviot, the Stag and the Black*

---

[45] *The Scotsman*, 12 May 1988.

Black Oil to the 'Dance called America' from the music group Run Rig.[46]
The Scottish Constitutional Convention, which recently issued its report,
placed itself firmly 'in the mainstream of Scotland's constitutional history.'
(Canon Kenyon Wright, chair of the Convention's Executive) The opening
document was a 'Claim of Right' which referred back to a document of the
same name which had justified the 1843 Disruption of the Kirk – just one
of the ghosts which had been raised by the 'Sermon on the Mound'.[47] After
long discussion, this Convention opted for 'Home Rule' a constitutional
arrangement which the late 20th century refers to as devolution. This
looks very like a late 20th century version of independence within the
Union. The document has a confidence and sense of innovation which is
rarely reflected in English perceptions of Scotland. The Convention clearly
saw itself as a source of innovation which will benefit the constitutional
structure of Britain as a whole. In the products of the Convention as in
the responses to the 'Sermon on the Mound' there was a notable absentee,
namely Protestant Scotland. As late as 1923, the General Assembly had
approved documents which referred to the Catholic Irish as a threat to
Protestant Scotland.[48] In the Convention, this exclusive nationalism had been
replaced by an inclusive nationalism which referred to the economy, society
and culture located on the territory of Scotland. The title 'Claim of Right'
has historical references with very deep Protestant significance, yet it was
used with scarcely a comment by a body dominated by the Scottish Labour
Party, an organization which in the 20th century had done more than any
other to bring the Catholic Irish into Scottish political life.

Does Scotland's lack of response to Victorian values display a much
greater assurance in national identity in the 1980s than England has
achieved? There were other signs that this was so. Football violence
was identified with England. Ranger's Football Club proudly evicted a
fan for racist comments about once a year.[49] In Scotland anti poll tax
demonstrations were dignified, orderly, constitutional and ignored. Quite
different from the violence and hysteria further south. The cult of 'heritage'
has a much less pervasive hold in Scotland. Cultural disputes surrounding
Glasgow's role as European City of Culture in 1990 involved major failures
for two institutions. The much valued People's Palace failed to gain political
support, and a temporary commercial venture called Glasgow's Glasgow
failed to gain the support of the paying public. Ignored in the row was
the real winner, the Burrell Collection, a great magpie's nest up on the

[46] McCrone, op.cit.
[47] Owen Dudley Edwards (ed.), *A Claim of Right for Scotland* (Edinburgh, 1989).
[48] Callum Brown, op.cit. p. 238 quotes the document: the Irish 'by reason of their race . . .
(were) . . . dividing Scotland, racially, socially and ecclesiastically.'
[49] *The Scotsman*, 23 November 1990.

hill where Glasgow and its public revel in European culture. In the 19th century, Scotland learnt to be a nation within a nation. This identity did not mean independent statehood, but it did include the defence of valued institutions like the national church. The availability of this choice of identities may well be one reason why Scotland, despite horrific economic pressures, has handled the problems of Britain's loss of empire and world standing more gracefully than England, and why the prospect of Scotland in Europe seems to hold fewer fears than the prospect of the loss of English/British sovereignty in Europe. After all having formed Scottish Victorian values under the shadow of a London government, who is afraid of forming Scottish post modern values in the shadow of Brussels? Perhaps the English should read more Scottish history.

Proceedings of the British Academy, **78**, 49–60

Victorian Values
and the
Upper Classes

MARK GIROUARD

AN article under this title could adopt two radically different approaches. It could deal with the extent to which the Victorian upper classes accepted or rejected a specific group of 'Victorian Values', so called because they in some way encapsulated the essence of Victorianism. Or it could be a discussion of all the values which informed the upper classes in the Victorian period.

In fact it opts for the second approach. In the welter of sets of values which were to be found at work in different groups and circumstances during the sixty-three years of Victoria's reign, it seems neither possible nor desirable to try to select one group as quintessentially Victorian. Whereas the values to be found among the Victorian upper classes at least provide a real object of enquiry, even if a far from simple one. It is complex because there is so much variety. What common ground is there, for instance, between the 4th Marquis of Hastings, who wasted his fortune, dissipated his health, and died worn out and near bankrupt at the age of 26 in 1868, and his almost exact contemporary the 2nd Viscount Halifax, politician and pillar of the High Church, who died, reverenced by all, at the age of 93 in 1934. And yet both were, in rather extreme forms, representative of different sections of the High Victorian upper classes.

Not only were upper class values varied; they cannot be fitted into a drawer labelled 'upper class only', as distinct from middle or lower class values. A more convincing model is one in which different sets of values are

Read 12 December 1990. © The British Academy 1992.

seen working through different (though sometimes overlapping) sections of all classes. One can see this model at work, more generally, in all the different interests and enthusiasms which informed the Victorians. Almost any Victorian activity can be followed up the social pyramid to a peak made up of aristocrats or upper gentry. Those lower down the pyramid looked for such people, if possible to lead them, but at least to give their group or movement the seal of upper class approval, and, as it were, symbolize and sanctify for them their own enthusiasms. And so the High Church looked to Lord Halifax in England or Lord Glasgow in Scotland, the evangelicals to Lords Shaftesbury, Harrowby, Tollemache and Radstock, the Catholics to the Earl of Shrewsbury and, later, the Duke of Norfolk and the Marquis of Bute; the Temperance movement to Lord Stanhope, Lord and Lady Carlisle, Lady Henry Somerset and Sir Walter Trevelyan; the racing fraternity to the grandees of the Jockey Club; scientists to the 7th Duke of Devonshire, pugilists to Lord Queensberry, astronomers to Lord Lindsay, firemen and fire brigades to the Duke of Sutherland, musicians to Lord Dudley, botanists to Lord De la Warr, widows to Lord Cholmondeley, and so on and so on.[1] In every county the farming community looked up to an inevitable peer, who was chairman of their county agricultural society; and farmers all over Britain could feel that Lord Hartington spoke for them when he said that the proudest moment of his life was when his pig won first prize at Skipton Fair.[2]

It is worth picking out three large, and certainly not mutually exclusive groups from the complex Victorian scene, and looking at them in more detail with particular emphasis on the upper classes. These are earnest Victorians, Victorian swells, and Victorian gentlemen.

'Earnest Victorians' is perhaps too vague a category but it does correspond to something which anyone who has studied the Victorian period will recognize. It entails an attitude to life both serious and moral, characteristic of people who took their religion and their marriage-vows seriously, and believed that they were put in this world to cultivate their talents and assets for the benefit of others, not themselves, and had a duty to do so. The earnest middle-class Victorians have been much written about. The earnest working-class Victorians included all those serious-minded artisans who attended chapel, temperance meetings and evening lectures, and became the backbone of the Co-operative movement and the Trades Unions. It was a commonplace amongst the Victorians themselves that the Victorian upper classes, or at least a significant section of them, had also

---

[1] Much of this list derives from the list of the relevant societies and their chairmen in the 1860s editions of *Whitaker's Almanack*.
[2] Bernard Holland, *Life of Spencer Compton, 8th Duke of Devonshire* (1911), vol. 2 p. 226.

become earnest in this way. As Charles Kingsley put it, in 1862, 'the attitude of the British upper classes has undergone a noble change. There is no aristocracy in the world, and there never has been, as far as I know, which has so honourably repented, and brought forth fruits meet for repentance; which has so cheerfully asked what its duty was, that it might do it.'[3]

Duty is the operative word. In 1844 Lord Shaftesbury condemned Eton and approved of Rugby in these terms: 'It does not make the man required for the coming generation. We must have nobler, deeper, and sterner stuff; less of refinement and more of truth; more of the inward, not so much of the outward gentleman; a rigid sense of duty, but a delicate sense of honour; a just estimate of rank and property, not as matters of personal enjoyment and display but as gifts from God, bringing with them serious responsibilities, and involving a fearful account; a contempt of ridicule, not a dread of it; a desire and a courage to live for the service of God and the best interests of mankind . . .'[4]

Florence Nightingale, who used the clarion call of duty to drive the supremely aristocratic Sidney Herbert to his death, portrayed him as follows: 'Eager and enthusiastic in duty, cared little for the reward, and not at all for the credit. No assertion of self; purity of nature and high principle'.[5] Writing about himself and his home he commented that: 'There is not a spot about Wilton which I do not love as if it were a person. If one had nothing to do but consult one's own taste and one's own ease I should be too glad to live down here a domestic life'.[6]

When the 1st Duke of Westminster died in 1899 one of his obituaries wrote of him that 'he thought of himself not so much as a private millionaire as the head of a great public institution or trust'.[7] The biographer of the 5th Marquess of Lansdowne wrote as follows about that most patrician of late Victorian statesmen: 'A great noble, cultivated and accomplished, the owner of historic titles and of historic houses, he was one of those who, from motives of duty and patriotism, deliberately chose the toil and responsibility of political life in preference to the existence of cultured ease and pleasure which was within his reach'.[8]

At the head of this particular pyramid Queen Victoria and the Prince

---

[3] Charles Kingsley, 'Preface to the Undergraduates of Cambridge' in the 1862 edition of *Alton Locke*.

[4] Edwin Hodder, *The Life and Work of the 7th Earl of Shaftesbury. K.G.* (London, 1886), vol. 2, p. 77.

[5] Cecil Woodham-Smith, *Florence Nightingale 1820–1910* (London, 1950), p. 70.

[6] Ibid.

[7] Gervase Huxley, *Victorian Duke* (London, 1967), p. 145.

[8] Lord Newton, *Lord Lansdowne; a Biography* (London, 1929), p. 491. Lansdowne was at Balliol and Jowett had impressed on him that 'wealth and rank are means and not ends, and may be the greatest evil or the greatest good as they are used'. Ibid., p. 7.

Consort set the supreme example of domesticity, purity, religious serious-ness and devotion to duty – killing devotion, in the case of the Prince Consort as of Sidney Herbert. They are sometimes considered to have been adopting middle class values in doing so.[9] It is surely more meaningful to say that they epitomized and encouraged a trend which could be found in all classes, and had roots running well back into the early decades of the century. There was a sizeable section of the Victorian upper classes who lived very different lives from those lived by Victoria and Albert, who were disapproved of by Victoria and Albert and a powerful section of the middle classes in consequence – and who made fun of Victoria and, especially, Albert in their turn. But there was an equally important section who gave Victoria and Albert their admiration and devotion and were all that they in their turn could have wished for: high-minded, church-going families, to give an example from many, like the Lytteltons of Hagley, so perfectly presented in the diaries of Lucy Lyttelton, later Lady Frederick Cavendish.[10]

No doubt this kind of seriousness was stimulated by members of the middle classes, by Arnold at Rugby, for instance, or Jowett at Balliol. But this is to say no more than that upper class life-styles have always been influenced by idea-preaching and image-creating members of the classes below them – in a very different way, for instance, by Beau Nash and Beau Brummel in Georgian days. There does not seem much point in trying to give class tags to movements of ideas, and to argue about the contribution to the Tractarians of the upper class Pusey, and the middle class Keble and Newman, or to radical thought of the upper class Shelley and the middle class Godwin.

The contrast, in an upper class context, between earnest Victorians and the world of Victorian swells is beautifully made in *Left Hand, Right Hand*, the first volume of Osbert Sitwell's reminiscences. He compares the character of his paternal grandmother Louisa Lady Sitwell with his maternal grandparents, the Earl and Countess of Londesborough.[11] Lady Sitwell (an Irish Earl's daughter) was a good and pious Evangelical, who refused to go to the theatre, moved in a circle of Low Church clergymen, founded a home for fallen women, and poured out her religious meditations into her diary; she was the widow of a baronet who had been as serious-minded

---

[9] For example James Laver, *Victorian Vista* (London, 1954), p. 26. 'Each age seems, on retrospect, to be dominated by one particular class, the features of whose life we regard as characteristic of the whole epoch. In this sense, the Victorian era was essentially middle class. Even royalty cultivated the bourgeois virtues . . .'

[10] *The Diary of Lady Frederick Cavendish*, ed. John Bailey, 2 vols, (London, 1927).

[11] O. Sitwell, *Left Hand, Right Hand* (London, 1945), esp. pp. 128–47 (Londesborough), 147–159 (Sitwell).

as herself – and a friend of Lord Shaftesbury's. Lord Londesborough was one of the richest peers in England. Sitwell quotes a description of him at the Henley Regatta: 'Swell, I love that word, for a person of extreme elegance and splendour. Our permanent local swell, and a big one at that, was Lord Londesborough. The scene . . . of his entertaining Henley parties was a houseboat, named the Ark, from which, however, we could issue if we wished, and take a little tour in punts or canoes or skiffs on the crowded river. But the company it was that so greatly delighted me . . . theatrical stars of both sexes, with the very prettiest of the actresses, together with a select band of our host's innumerable friends, for the most part, like himself, of noble rank . . . Lord Londesborough was a patron of the stage, and was reputed to have lost £30,000 in one production . . . Babel and Bijou, a musical spectacle'. As his grandson put it: 'Yachts, races, coaches, carriages, sport of every kind, especially shooting, speculation and the stage, were the chief channel he had found for ridding himself of his earthly burden'.[12] The quintessential scene of his glory was the intensely fashionable annual cricket week at Scarborough which he inaugurated and presided over from his Scarborough house, Londesborough Lodge. When at Scarborough he would process down to the sea front on three-quarters of a mile of red carpet, laid down for the occasion.[13]

Dash and style were the qualities expected of a swell. He was exquisitely turned out; he shone and glowed all over, whether in Piccadilly or on the hunting field, and the same care informed his grooms, his footmen, his beaters, his gleaming horses and carriages. Lord Londesborough's was one of the four equipages so faultless that it was allowed inside the railings at Buckingham Palace on state occasions (a piece of information we owe, rather unexpectedly, to the diarist Kilvert).[14] The main claim to fame of the 5th Earl of Hardwicke is that he invented a preparation which gave an extra sheen to his top-hat. 'I can see him now', wrote Lady Battersea, 'in faultless attire, with his carefully arranged black satin tie, his beautiful pearl pin, his lustrous hat balanced at a certain angle on his well-brushed hair, his coat-sleeves always showing precisely the same amount of white cuff, his pleased-with-himself-and-the-world expression'.[15]

Swells were not expected to be faithful to their wives; having mistresses or affairs with married women of their own class was acceptable and even admired. Nor were they expected to pay their tradesmen, or bother about money, except about ways of getting rid of it. As Captain Donald Shaw, writing as 'One of the Old Brigade', put it in *London in the*

[12] Ibid., p. 30, quoting W.B. Maxwell, *Time Gathered* (London, 1937).
[13] Ibid., p. 131.
[14] *Kilvert's Diary*, ed. W. Plomer (London, 1938–40), vol. 2, p. 177 (7 April 1872).
[15] Constance, Lady Battersea, *Reminiscences* (London, 1922), p. 153.

Sixties, there were only two unforgiveable sins: buggery and cheating at cards.[16]

There is no question who was at the top of the hierarchy of swells: to Queen Victoria's grief it was the Prince of Wales. She grieved because the world of the swells lacked so entirely the values which her husband had bequeathed to her. As Lady Warwick, who moved in the Prince of Wales's set as a young married woman, wrote in her recollections, 'we considered the heads of historic houses who read serious works, encouraged scientists, and the like, very, very dull, and they had only the scantiest contact with us . . . On rare occasions, if a book made a sufficient stir, we might read it, or, better still, get somebody to tell us about it, and so save us the trouble'. But, as she put it, 'of course the Marlborough House set had glamour; indeed, glamour was its particular asset'.[17]

Glamour was expensive. Racehorses, actresses and lavish entertaining cost money, not least entertaining the Prince of Wales. Among mid-Victorian swells both Lord Londesborough and Lord Chaplin had to sell substantial portions of their estates. Lord Hardwicke went bankrupt in 1881. Christopher Sykes, the Prince of Wales's especial friend, would have gone bankrupt, if the Prince had not baled him out.[18] Lord Hastings ran through almost all his very large fortune in four years, mainly on the race-course. He lost his money in style. In 1867 he was cheered on the race-course at Ascot because he had lost £120,000 in a week's racing, had taken the loss so coolly and paid up so promptly.[19] That was the style of a swell. It was a long way removed from Lord Shaftesbury, presiding over missionary meetings at Exeter Hall.[20]

The line of the swells, whose great days were in the sixties, seventies and eighties, can be traced back to the dandies and bucks of late Georgian and

---

[16] Donald Shaw, *London in the Sixties* (1908), p. 145, quoting George Payne. The first offence is not specifically named, but the quoted example of the 'recent H – affair' involving the brother of a peer and major in a crack regiment seems to refer to Charles Hammond, Lord Arthur Somerset and the Cleveland Street scandal.

[17] Frances, Countess of Warwick, *Afterthoughts* (London, 1931), pp. 40–1.

[18] Sitwell, op.cit., pp. 71, 132–33 (Londesborough); *Dict. National Biography*, supplement II (Chaplin); Frederic Boase, *Modern English Biography* (London, 1892–1912) **5** (Supplement II), entry under Hardwicke; Christopher Sykes, *Four Studies in Loyalty* (London, 1946), pp. 11–39. Other Victorian swells who experienced serious financial troubles included Lord Dupplin, Charles Buller, the 8th Duke of Beaufort, and Sir Frederick Johnstone. No doubt their situation was exacerbated by the agricultural depression in the last decades of the century.

[19] Henry Blyth's readably slapdash *The Pocket Venus: a Victorian Scandal* (London, 1966) appears to be the only reasonably full-length study of Lord Hastings, and contains some good contemporary quotations.

[20] If one tried to relate swells to Matthew Arnold's barbarians one might say that all upper class swells were barbarians, but not all barbarians were swells.

early Victorian days, and forward well into the century to peers like the 'Yellow Earl' of Lonsdale, or the young men of title who waited for their girls at the stage door of the Gaiety – and sometimes married them.[21] But they can also be traced down the social scale through the middle class to the working classes. At every level one can find men who sought for the same qualities of dash and style in dress or behaviour, and were careless about money and ready to throw it about, whether or not they had it.

An obvious image creator is George Leybourne, both in himself and in his music-hall role as Champagne Charlie:

> From coffee and from supper room
> From Poplar and Pall Mall
> The girls on seeing me exclaim:
> 'Oh What a Champagne Swell'

This hit-song, which he first sang on the stage of the Canterbury Music-Hall in 1868, was promoted off the stage by his enterprising manager Bill Holland and by the Moët Champagne company, which put up the necessary money. Leybourne, dressed as a swell and smoking a big cigar, drove round London in a spanking turnout pulled by glistening horses, visiting public houses to distribute free champagne. He was to have numerous imitators on and off the music hall stages, and himself, in faultless turnout, to continue to sing Champagne Charlie and related songs, until he sank out of sight in the 1880s, almost literally beneath a sea of alcohol.[22]

'Champagne Charlie' became a familiar metaphor, sometimes for a swell of any class (Lord Hardwicke, for instance, was nicknamed Champagne Charlie),[23] but more especially for a middle or working class swell. Here, for instance, is G.R. Sims describing life in and around the Haymarket in 1867: 'Devil-may-care dukes, madcap marquises and eccentric earls mingled freely with the Champagne Charlies of the counting house and the counter'.[24]

Who were these Champagne Charlies? Clearly, they did not have chapel values even if they were occasionally chapel by birth. In a Lancashire context John K. Walton has perceptively analysed the division in the middle classes between non-conformist Liberals and Church of England Conservatives;[25] and perhaps middle class swells were more likely to come

---

[21] Eight Gaiety girls married into the peerage between 1884 and 1924. See W. Macqueen-Pope, *Gaiety: Theatre of Enchantment* (London, 1949), *passim*.

[22] *The Illustrated Victorian Songbook*, ed. Aline Waites & Robin Hunter (London, *c.* 1979), pp. 92–4; interview with William Holland, q. *Blackpool Gazette*, 3 January 1896.

[23] Battersea, loc. cit.

[24] G.R. Sims, *Glances Back* (London, 1917), p. 14.

[25] John K. Walton, *Lancashire: a Social History, 1558–1939* (Manchester, 1987), pp. 221–38.

from the latter. One would expect a sizeable number of them to have been connected with the entertainment world, the drink trade, up-market shops, horses, racing or sport of one kind or another. But even outside those directly working in these worlds one does not have to penetrate very deeply into Victorian society to realize that a substantial section of the Victorian middle classes fail to correspond to the puritanical, straight-laced image which has been popularly attached to them. The size and strength of this other world helps explain the fervour with which earnest Victorians attacked it. I can't pretend to have investigated it with any thoroughness, but here are a number of examples – samples, I am sure, from a much larger population.

From the public-house world comes Colonel Baker (1841–99), of Baker Brothers, who started business with his brothers as a licensed victualler in the 1870s, established a string of large London pubs, cafés and hotels around Leicester Square, became a Colonel in the Honourable Artillery Company, and had a family and a substantial house in Cumberland Terrace, Regent's Park – and a mistress and a second family in Gordon Square.[26] His career is reminiscent of that of Alfred Roger Ackerley in the next generation, as so brilliantly portrayed by J.R. Ackerley in *My Father and I*: very much a young swell in the 1880s, going on to become a partner in Fyfe's banana business, earning the nickname 'The Banana King', and fathering two families, both illegitimate and unaware of one another's existence.

The middle classes' answer to the Marquis of Hastings was H.E.S. Benzon, son of an iron-master, and author of that curious little book *How I Lost £250,000 in Two Years* (1889). One of the ways in which he lost it, in addition to betting and wearing a new shirt every day, was in giving a ball at the Royal Hotel, Scarborough, in Cricket Week, for the girls of the Gaiety Theatre, when they were on tour.[27]

John Hollingshead, who became manager of the Gaiety in 1868, was something of a swell, and his successor, George Edwardes, even more of one, to judge from contemporary accounts.[28] So was Frank Matcham, the best and most successful architect of Victorian theatres, and the actor-manager Sir Augustus Harris, with his roulette board in the garden and impulsive outings to Monte Carlo.[29] So was the irrepressible and exquisitely turned out entrepreneur of Champagne Charlie, Bill Holland,

[26] For Baker see M. Girouard, *Victorian Pubs* (2nd edn, London and New Haven, 1984), pp. 95–8, Pl. 60, and accompanying references.
[27] Op. cit. and M.B. Hawke, 2nd Baron, *Recollections and Reminiscences* (London, 1924), p. 317.
[28] Macqueen-Pope, op. cit., especially pp. 215–17.
[29] *Frank Matcham, Theatre Architect*, ed. B. Mercer Walker (Belfast, 1980), pp. 1, 7–8, 17, especially cartoon on p. 55.

who moved on from London to help establish Blackpool as a working class holiday resort.[30] So was the locally-born owner and builder of Blackpool Tower, Mayor of Blackpool, jauntily turned out yachtsman and lover of royalty, John Bickerstaff.[31] And one would like to know more about Edward Barker Cox, steel-bar manufacturer, enthusiastic fox-hunter, and owner and builder, in the 1870s, of the Talbot public house and music hall in Nottingham – 'the flaunting Talbot, a source of immorality and degradation', according to the, one suspects, non-conformist Nottingham town clerk.[32] In general, investigation into the background of the managers, owners, promoters and backers of theatres, music halls and variety theatres all over England, could be one of the most fruitful ways of exploring the world of the middle class swell.

An earnest swell is an impossible concept, and a Christian swell an unconvincing one. But the idea of a Christian gentleman is entirely acceptable, and so is that of an earnest, or at least serious-minded gentleman. The whole concept of the gentleman, as developed in the nineteenth century, and the set of values attached to it, was to be of the greatest importance to the Victorian upper classes. One reason for its importance is that it provided a synthesis of two sets of values. It made serious things glamorous, and glamorous things serious.

One of the main ways it did this was by reviving and adapting the concept of chivalry. It was as modern knights, heirs to a great and glamorous tradition, that Victorian gentlemen could come to the rescue of the oppressed – whether by building model cottages or serving in East End Settlements – woo their wives, be courteous to their inferiors and protective to all women, despise mere money-making or too much cleverness (for character, it was stressed, was more important than intellect), and train their bodies in manly exercise or sporting tournaments with their fellow knights. They dedicated their lives to others; but the seal of knightliness set them apart from and above the rest of mankind.[33]

The ideals of the Victorian gentleman, like other ideals adopted by the upper classes, were worked out, preached or put across by both upper and middle class propagandists – by the upper class Anglo-Irishman Kenelm Digby, by Lord John Manners and the aristocratic youths of Young England, by upper class Christian Socialists like Tom Hughes, Lord Sydney Osborne or Lord Goderich, by upper class novelists like

---

[30] For Holland see M. Girouard, *The English Town* (New Haven and London, 1990), pp. 292–4, 298–303.
[31] Ibid., pp. 293–4.
[32] R.S. Tresidder, *Nottingham Pubs* (Nottingham Civic Society, 1980), p. 20.
[33] This section adds nothing to the much fuller discussion in my *Return to Camelot: Chivalry and the English Gentleman* (New Haven and London, 1981).

Charlotte M. Yonge – but just as much by a powerful company of middle class writers, teachers and artists, by Carlyle, Kingsley, and Tennyson, by the journalists of *Fraser's Magazine*, by Maclise, Watts, William Morris and Burne Jones, by Mrs. Craik of *John Halifax, Gentleman* in London, or Sir Noel Paton in Edinburgh.

Just as with other sets of values, the ideal of the gentleman operated at all social levels. By the second half of the nineteenth century the distinctive question for most better-off Victorians was not whether they belonged to the upper or middle classes, but whether or not they were gentlemen. And if the working classes could not aspire to be as it were fully paid-up gentlemen, a substantial portion of them could and did aspire to gentlemanly values, as the success of the Boy Scout movement among them was to make clear.

Of all the forces and agencies which spread the ideals of gentlemanly behaviour through the upper and middle classes, and provided a common code of behaviour and values for both of them, none was more important than the Public Schools. The reforming movement which undoubtedly started with Dr. Arnold's headmastership of Rugby in the 1820s, spread to other public schools, and led to the remodelling of existing grammar schools in the public school image, and the founding of further public schools all over the country. The two most prestigious and upper-class-oriented public schools, Eton and Harrow, changed along with the schools which catered primarily for the middle classes, so that the similarities between them became more obvious than the differences.

But between the 1820s and 1900 the nature of the public-school movement changed. Of the three types of training with which it was concerned, of the brain, the character, and the body, Arnold had concentrated on the brain and character, but his successors shifted the emphasis to the character and body. Arnold would have been horrified by the change; it is ironic that one of its instruments was the best-selling *Tom Brown's Schooldays*, written by his pupil and passionate admirer Thomas Hughes, with its much-quoted statement 'I know I'd sooner win two school-house matches running than the Balliol scholarship any day'.[34] Implicit in the remark was that devotion to team spirit, which was to become such a feature of later public schools. And behind both team-spirit and stress on bodily training was the inspiring image of the brave and manly knight, who trained his own body in order to serve others, and was loyal to the fellowship to which he belonged. Victorian knights were prepared to fight real battles, in a just cause, as well as moral ones, and believed in the purifying and exalting effects of war, as Dr. Arnold, or for that matter Lord Shaftesbury, surely did not.

The code learned at the public schools could be practised in after life

[34] T. Hughes, *Tom Brown's Schooldays* (small illustrated edn, 1874), p. 282.

by officers in the armed forces, clergymen, members of the professions, colonial officials, and even by manufacturers and businessmen – though not too easily by these, for Victorian gentlemen were taught to look down on trade. This last attitude was as much a feature of middle class as upper class public schools, and perhaps helps to explain Britain's economic decline in the 20th century. Clifton College was opened in 1862 on the edge of commercial Bristol. Bristol businessmen sent their sons there, but as the official school history puts it, in reference to its greatest headmaster, John Percival, 'Trade and business and money-making generally were looked at rather askance by Percival, and by very high minded Cliftonians who accepted his ideals'.[35]

But the landed classes had no problem in following the gentlemanly ideal. A stereotype emerged to which members of the country aristocracy and gentry were expected to conform, both by their equals and their social inferiors. The ideal upper-class gentleman excelled in manly sports. He looked after his tenantry and the poor. He was courteous to members of all classes. He did not boast or brag. He was not expected to be clever or a patron of the arts, although it was not necessarily held against him if he was. He wore the right things at the right times. He was a keen farmer, but more concerned with winning prizes at agricultural shows than making money – money, in fact, in all its aspects, he left to his agent and his lawyer. If they were as gentlemanly as he was, this did not always lead to financial success.

These are the characters who, no doubt slightly edited for public consumption, crowd the pages of the volumes of country notabilities which were published by the dozen towards the end of the 19th century. They are not quite earnest, and not quite swells. They occupy, very solidly, a middle ground. A quick dip into *Norfolk Notabilities*, published in 1893, produces the following. Captain the Hon. A.E. Fellowes is an able officer, a keen sportsman, and a sound but progressive conservative MP. He has little or no sympathy with Socialists and political agitators, but knows how to show reasonable respect for the opinions of his opponents. He has been President of the Norfolk Chamber of Agriculture. He is beloved by his tenants and by all who know him, being held up as a model landlord and a typical English gentleman. Lord Hastings (only a very distant connection of the spendthrift Marquis) has won the Derby and the Leger, is a fine shot and owns very good preserves. He is President of North Norfolk Conservatives Association, and a successful exhibitor of his herd of Norfolk red-polled cattle. His wife is enthusiastic in looking after the welfare of the poor. He himself is exceedingly popular with his tenantry and all classes in

[35] O.F. Christie, *A History of Clifton College, 1860–1934* (1935), pp. 122–3.

the country. 'He is, indeed, the beau-ideal of an English nobleman and country-gentleman'. A similar accolade is given to Nicholas Henry Bacon, of Raveningham Hall: 'Courteous in conduct, kindly in disposition, and modest in manner, he is a splendid specimen of that perfect gentleman which we all admire'.[36]

And didn't they just all admire him. It was stated at the beginning of this article that there is no one value which encapsulates the essence of Victorianism. But there is one which, if not universal, is to be found at all levels and in all classes throughout the Victorian period. This is the belief in social hierarchy, the resulting deference which this led to in those who were not at the top of the hierarchy, and the automatic assumption of the right to lead by those who were. As E.C. Grenville-Murray, writing in no very friendly spirit in 1881, put it in his *Sidelights on English Society*, 'Thackeray's Book of Snobs has not cured a man or woman of the national itch for lord-worship'.[37] This is not, I imagine, one of the Victorian values of which Mrs. Thatcher was thinking, but its importance cannot be ignored.

[36] C.A.M. Press, *Norfolk Notabilities* (Norwich, 1893), pp. 55–6, 79, 97–9.

[37] E.C. Grenville-Murray, *Sidelights on English Society: Sketches from Life Social and Satirical* (2nd edn, London, 1883), p. 271. Murray was the illegitimate son of the 2nd Duke of Buckingham, the most sensationally bankrupt, or near-bankrupt, of Victorian swells.

Proceedings of the British Academy, **78**, 61–80

Thomas Chalmers and the Communal Ideal in Victorian Scotland

STEWART J. BROWN
University of Edinburgh

On 14 April 1915, a public meeting was held in Glasgow's St. Andrews Hall to mark the centenary of Thomas Chalmers's arrival in Glasgow and the beginning of his celebrated experiments in the urban parish ministry. It is significant that amid the carnage of the war that was bringing an end to the Victorian age, Glasgow took this opportunity to commemorate a Scottish clergyman and his parish ideal. Among the speakers were leaders of the two largest presbyterian Churches, the Church of Scotland and the United Free Church, while representatives of eight other denominations appeared on the platform. The Lord Provost of the city presided. The principal speaker of the evening was another Scottish eminent Victorian, Lord Rosebery, the leading figure behind the creation of the Scottish Office in the 1880s, former leader of the Liberal party, and former prime minister. For Rosebery, Chalmers had been 'one of the greatest of our race', a man to be ranked with John Knox in shaping the Scottish identity. Chalmers's whole life had been informed by a grand vision: 'his ideal was to raise the nation by Christianity, by Christian co-operation, Christian education, Christian worship. He thought that by these means he would be able to rear a character and a race which would disdain State aid or State patronage, and be independent of all but faith'. This ideal had, to a large extent, defined the values and aspirations of nineteenth-century Scotland. None the less, Rosebery maintained, the dream was dying. 'The world creeps on in its blind course . . .', he observed with melancholy, 'we know not whither, but it certainly

Read 13 December 1990. © The British Academy 1992.

does not seem to tend towards the aims of Chalmers'. 'He was indeed', Rosebery continued, 'the Moses of his country, pointing to a land of promise into which neither he nor his countrymen entered or were destined to enter'.[1] Amid the horrors of World War, of great powers employing the technologies of mature industrial society for the grim work of mass killing, Chalmers's vision of a Christian commonwealth of small, co-operative communities did indeed seem but a utopian dream of a lost world.

Thomas Chalmers was widely acknowledged as the greatest Scottish Churchman of the nineteenth century. He was a powerful preacher, who stirred congregations with torrents of rich language, and brought many to share his evangelical faith. He was a theologian and natural philosopher, who combined the 'common sense' thought of the later Scottish Enlightenment with a traditional Calvinist orthodoxy, and who sought evidence of a beneficient design in the natural and social realms. He was a political economist, the leading disciple of Thomas Malthus, who accepted the doctrine of free trade, but who also recognized the darker aspects of unrestricted economic competition and economic individualism. Above all, he was a social reformer, the most creative social theorist of the nineteenth-century Scottish Church, who developed a practical programme of comprehensive Christian communal reform, emphasizing benevolence, co-operation and shared sacrifice. It was as a social thinker that Chalmers exercised his most lasting influence on Victorian Scotland. His scholarly contributions in theology, natural philosophy and political economy did not long survive his death in 1847; they were soon overshadowed by advances in Biblical criticism and biological science, and by the waning of Malthusian economics.[2] But his social reform activities and his Christian communal programmes exercised a pervasive influence on Scottish social thought and philanthropic activity throughout the nineteenth century.[3]

In recent years, scholars have devoted considerable attention to Scottish social thought in the nineteenth century – especially to the distinctive Scottish response to the challenges of urbanization and industrialization.

---

[1] *Scotsman*, 15 April 1915.

[2] For early views of waning influence of Chalmers's contributions in theology, philosophy and political economy, see [W.H. Smith], 'Dr. Chalmers as Political Economist', *Blackwood's Magazine*, vol 73 (May 1853), 598–616; [I. Taylor], 'Dr. Chalmers's Works', *North British Review*, vol. 26 (Nov. 1856), 1–71. In a perceptive recent study, Boyd Hilton sees Chalmers as a leading representative of those evangelical social thinkers who viewed the world primarily as a scene of trial and suffering – a world view that was waning amid the relative prosperity of the 1850s and 1860s. See *The Age of Atonement: The Influence of Evangelicalism on Social and Economic Thought, 1785–1865* (Oxford, 1988).

[3] For an eloquent expression of this argument, see A.C. Cheyne, 'Thomas Chalmers: Then and Now', in A.C. Cheyne (ed.), *The Practical and the Pious: Essays on Thomas Chalmers* (Edinburgh, 1984), 9–30.

There has been a new appreciation of the survival of a distinctive Scottish culture amid the expansion of urban-industrial society. The literary historian, William Donaldson, has demonstrated that, contrary to long accepted views, nineteenth-century Scottish fiction was not predominantly escapist and remote from the problems of urban society. On the contrary, there was a rich and diverse Scottish urban fiction which was published, not through the London book trade, but rather through serial editions in the popular newspaper press.[4] Christopher Harvie has noted the enduring importance of religion on Victorian social thought, while Donald Withrington has directed attention to the distinctive Scottish contributions to late nineteenth-century British idealism. Olive Checkland has described the rich diversity of Victorian Scottish urban philanthropy, Bernard Aspinwall has explored the pioneering achievements of late Victorlan municipal collectivism in Glasgow, and Ian Levitt has considered the development of Scottish social policy in the nineteenth century.[5] Such work has demonstrated that Victorian Scotland devoted more attention to organized philanthropy and the problems of the city than was previously recognized, and that Scotland's social attitudes were profoundly influenced by its communal traditions. This essay will explore the influence of Thomas Chalmers and his social vision on Victorian Scotland, directing attention to his role in reviving and preserving Scotland's communal traditions during a period when Scotland's weak central government and rapid industrialization might otherwise have resulted in intolerable strains on the social fabric. It will also consider the social engagement of the mainstream presbyterian Churches during the high tide of evangelicalism, between the 1830s and 1880s, and suggest that the evangelical social ethos was not as individualistic and obsessed with personal salvation as is sometimes supposed.

Thomas Chalmers was born in 1780, into a merchant family of modest means in the small east Fife coastal burgh of Anstruther.[6] He attended St. Andrews University, where he studied for the ministry and nurtured

---

[4] W. Donaldson, 'Popular Literature: The Press, the People and the Vernacular Revival', in D. Gifford (ed.), *The History of Scottish Literature*, vol 3 (Aberdeen, 1988), 203–15.

[5] C. Harvie, 'Industry, Religion and the State of Scotland', in D. Gifford (ed.), *The History of Scottish Literature*, vol 3, op. cit., 23–42; D. Withrington, '"A Ferment of Change": Aspirations, Ideas, and Ideals in Nineteenth Century Scotland', Ibid., 43–63; O. Checkland, *Philanthropy in Victorian Scotland* (Edinburgh, 1980); B. Aspinwall, *Portable Utopia: Glasgow and the United States 1820–1920* (Aberdeen, 1984), 151–84; I. Levitt, 'Welfare, Government and the Working Class: Scotland, 1845–1894', in D. McCrone, S. Kendrick and P. Straw (eds), *The Making of Scotland: Nation, Culture and Social Change* (Edinburgh, 1989), 109–22.

[6] For a fuller discussion of Chalmers's life and work, see S.J. Brown, *Thomas Chalmers and the Godly Commonwealth in Scotland* (Oxford, 1982).

ambitions to cut a figure in the literary world of the later Scottish Enlightenment. In 1802, he was ordained to the Fifeshire parish of Kilmany, a stable agricultural parish with a population of about 800. For nearly a decade, he neglected his parish, while he pursued literary recognition and academic preferment. Then, in 1811–12, following a prolonged illness, he experienced an evangelical conversion. He became a leading figure in the Scottish Evangelical Revival, an intense preacher and forceful advocate of missionary societies. In 1813, he directed his energies to his rural parish, beginning regular house-to-house visiting and embracing his responsibilities for parish poor relief and education with new zeal.

Chalmers's rising fame as a preacher brought him a call to Glasgow's Tron parish, where he began his ministry in July 1815. Profoundly disturbed by what he perceived as the collapse of social responsibility in Glasgow, he fastened on the need to restore the communal values of rural Scotland to the urban environment. During his four years at the Tron, from 1815 to 1819, he developed programmes designed to translate the rural parish ideal to the emerging industrial city. Recognizing that the supervision of a large urban parish with over 12,000 inhabitants was beyond the capacity of a single parish minister, he organized the lay members of his predominantly middle-class congregation for the work of house-to-house visiting on what he termed the principle of 'aggression'. Religion and education were to be pressed upon the people, as they had no natural appetite for these things. He organized a parish Bible society, and encouraged all his parishioners to contribute generously in support of a cause, that of overseas missions, which transcended their material self-interests and bound them together in shared sacrifice. His experiences convinced him that the radical evil of the emerging urban-industrial society was the expanding system of legal poor relief, based upon assessments on property and the recognition of a legal right to relief on the part of the indigent. This legal poor relief, he believed, created barriers between rich and poor, diminished 'natural' benevolence and communal sentiment, undermined the independence of the labouring orders, and threatened to unleash the Malthusian horrors of overpopulation. Thus, the abolition of legal poor relief would be necessary to establish parish-based, communal values in the city.

In 1819, Chalmers convinced the town council and magistrates of Glasgow to give him a free hand to pursue his parish community ideal in a new parish, St. John's, which was being created in a working-class district.[7] Here he developed his celebrated programmes for an urban

[7] For recent discussions of the St. John's experiment, see R.R. Cage and E.O.A. Checkland, 'Thomas Chalmers and Urban Poverty: The St. John's Parish Experiment in Glasgow, 1819–1837', *Philosophical Journal* (Glasgow), **13** (1976), 37–56; and S.J. Brown, *Thomas Chalmers*, op. cit., 116–44.

parish, or 'territorial' ministry. He divided the large parish into twenty-five 'proportions', each with about 400 inhabitants. He recruited an agency of lay officers and teachers from his predominantly middle-class congregation, many of whom had followed him from the Tron parish. The agency included elders, deacons and Sunday school teachers, who were each assigned a proportion and instructed to penetrate the district on the principle of 'aggression', visiting each household on a regular basis. An elder was assigned to each proportion, with responsibility to supervise moral and spiritual discipline and to investigate serious moral infractions such as child-abuse, wife-beating or chronic drunkenness. At least one Sunday school teacher was assigned to each proportion and instructed not only to conduct a district Sunday school, but also to visit the homes regularly to report on the children's progress and endeavour to see that every child received religious instruction and basic primary education at one of the day schools established in the parish.

Further, each proportion was assigned a deacon, who was to oversee the material needs of all the parishioners. To the deacons was given responsibility over the central, and most controversial aspect of the parish experiment – the effort to eliminate all legal poor relief in the parish. Chalmers was convinced that most pauperism could be eliminated by refusing relief to the able-bodied and appealing to each individual's capacity for self-help and desire for the respect of the community. Cases of genuine need could be met through appeals to the needy individual's extended family, neighbours, and, as a last resort, to the private philanthropy of wealthy persons. The deacons were to appeal to self-help and orchestrate communal sharing. They were to visit regularly the families in their respective proportions, and keep written records, or case studies, of those in need. In time, all parishioners would be educated to value both their personal independence and their contributions to the community, while the parish mission societies would encourage them to subordinate private interests to transcendent ideals. Lasting social improvement would come through the nurture of moral character and communal responsibility within the extended family of the parish.

In 1823, Chalmers left the Glasgow parish ministry for a university chair, first at St. Andrews and then, in 1828, at Edinburgh. While much of his work at St. John's was widely praised, there was considerable controversy over his poor relief programmes. Critics viewed them as callous in the treatment of the poor, more concerned to eliminate pauperism than to meet the real needs of the poor. Chalmers, however, was convinced that the entire St. John's experiment had been a success, and he publicized it widely through his writings. As a professor, he lectured regularly on his parish community ideal, and converted a generation of presbyterian ministers to the benefits of the 'territorial' system and the principle of 'aggression'. In his *Political Economy* of 1832, he argued that neither free trade nor social legislation could achieve lasting social improvement. The permanent well-being of society could only be secured by educating people in the communal values of benevolence and co-operation through the parochial structures of the national Church.[8] In the early 1830s, Chalmers emerged as leader of the Evangelical party in the Church of Scotland – in large part because of his comprehensive social vision and his success in defending the established Church against challenges from organised Dissent.

In 1834, the Evangelical party gained a working majority in the General Assembly of the Church of Scotland. Chalmers was now able to organize a Church Extension campaign, which aimed for the realization of his parish community ideal on a national level through the erection of hundreds of new parish churches and schools. He hoped to see the whole population of Scotland organized into parish communities of not more than 2,000 inhabitants. These parish communities would employ the methods developed at St. John's, including subdivision of the parish, regular house-to-house visiting, the replacement of legal poor relief by church-directed communal benevolence, and education through parish day schools and district Sunday schools. Scotland would become a 'godly commonwealth' of small parish communities, preserving Christian social values of benevolence and co-operation against the inevitable human dislocations resulting from the 'natural' laws of political economy. To collect the funds needed for church and school building, Chalmers created a national organisation of local societies, which encouraged popular participation through penny-a-week subscriptions, as well as larger contributions from the middle and upper classes. He sought to arouse the Scottish nation through what was termed a movement of 'spiritual O'Connellism', and by 1841 his campaign had added over 220 new churches to the Establishment.[9]

A key element in Chalmers's plan was a proposed endowment grant from the State. Parliament, he believed, should provide an endowment for each of the new parish churches and schools, in order to eliminate the need for high church seat rents and school fees and thus ensure that the churches and schools would be the common property of the whole community. He promised contributors to Church Extension that once Parliament had felt the moral force of their voluntary giving, it would provide the endowments. He was mistaken. Dissenters and radicals attacked Church Extension as both an unnecessary expense and a threat to religious liberty, and in 1838

---

[8] T. Chalmers, *On Political Economy in Connexion with the Moral State and Moral Prospects of Society* (Glasgow, 1832).
[9] S.J. Brown, *Thomas Chalmers*, op. cit., 233–79.

Melbourne's Whig Government declined to introduce the endowment grant. The result was growing ill-feeling between the Church of Scotland and the British State. When after 1838 the civil law courts declared Church efforts to restrict private patronage over church livings to be illegal, and insisted upon unrestricted patronage, Parliament refused to intervene to defend the Church's claims to spiritual independence. The conflict of civil and religious authority culminated in the Disruption of 1843, when nearly a third of the clergy and perhaps half the lay membership followed Chalmers out of the Established Church to form the Free Church of Scotland.

With the weakening of the Established Church in the late 1830s, the State had also moved to assert control over poor relief. Beginning in 1839, powerful voices, including that of the influential Edinburgh physician, W.P. Alison, urged that State control, an expansion of the system of legal assessments, and greatly increased expenditures were necessary to secure a decent maintenance for the poor.[10] They portrayed Chalmers's parish community ideal as utopian in industrial Scotland, where there was considerable geographic mobility and continuous economic fluctuation. Only through a decent State subsistence for the indigent, Alison maintained, could the masses gain the basic security required before there could be any lasting moral improvement and social progress. In 1843, the Government appointed a Royal Commission of Inquiry into the Scottish poor laws, and in 1845, Parliament passed a New Poor Law for Scotland, which transferred responsibility for maintaining the poor from the Church to elected poor law boards, and which encouraged legal assessments and indoor relief on the English model.

At the Disruption of 1843, Chalmers had hoped that the large majority in the Church of Scotland would sever their connection with the British State and form themselves into a free national establishment – which would continue the campaign to achieve the godly commonwealth in Scotland. In this he was disappointed. The vast majority had not gone out, and it soon became apparent that despite impressive sacrifices to build churches and schools, the new Free Church alone lacked the resources to realize the godly commonwealth. He became convinced that perhaps his ideal of a free and comprehensive national establishment would not be realized until the millennium.[11] In the meantime, as the old Church and the Free Church condemned one another and competed for paying members, much of the urban population seemed to be sinking further into deprivation

[10] O. Checkland, 'Chalmers and William Pulteney Alison: A Conflict of Views on Scottish Social Policy', in A.C. Cheyne (ed.), *The Practical and the Pious*, op. cit., 130–40; S.J. Brown, *Thomas Chalmers*, op. cit., 287–96.
[11] J. MacKenzie, *Dr. Chalmers's Views on Incorporative Union between the Non-Established Presbyterian Churches* (Edinburgh 1871), 17.

and irreligion. The Disruption was destroying all hope for the Christian commonwealth.

Then, in 1844, Chalmers announced the beginning of a new campaign of community-building in the urban environment, conceived for the conditions of post-Disruption Scotland. The new movement was to involve all Protestant churches, encouraging them to compete with one another in the work of reclaiming deprived urban districts to the traditional communal values of rural Scotland. His plan embraced his territorial and aggressive principles. Groups or congregations from the different churches should each map out a territory in a deprived urban area. They would then recruit a missionary and lay agency, subdivide the territory into proportions, assign a visitor and Sunday school teacher to each proportion and instruct them to conduct regular house-to-house visiting. While the missionary conducted Sunday services and week-day prayer meetings, the lay agency would organize day, evening and infant schools, along with a number of other facilities, including savings banks, reading rooms, cooking classes, laundry facilities, and help with finding employment. Poor relief would be left to the secular authorities, but the lay agency would show concern for the material needs of the inhabitants, using their influence to press the city officials for sanitary reforms, clearance of delapidated buildings, and closure of public houses. Their aim, he argued, should be to eliminate as soon as possible the need for outside support and an outside agency of visitors. They should concentrate on creating a self-sustaining territorial Christian community, in which the working-class inhabitants themselves would undertake the work of district visiting, Sunday school teaching, management of the savings bank, reading rooms and other services, support of the minister and teachers, and building of a territorial church, school and hall. They would elevate themselves to self-respect through collective self-help, and eliminate dependence on both outside philanthropy and State poor relief.[12]

With the assistance of a group of Free Church supporters, Chalmers began a territorial operation in the West Port, one of the most deprived districts of Edinburgh. The West Port operation was intended as a model for the proposed community-building operations, and Chalmers devoted his last years to the project. It had considerable success in attracting a working-class congregation, especially after the appointment of a committed minister, William Tasker – though Chalmers's critics argued that it was very costly and that it did not radically transform the surrounding district.

---

[12] For a fuller discussion of this movement, see S.J. Brown, 'The Disruption and Urban Poverty: Thomas Chalmers and the West Port Operation in Edinburgh, 1844–47', *Records of the Scottish Church History Society*, **20**:1 (1978), 65–89.

Chalmers's pleas and example convinced some others, mainly from the Free Church, to begin a few territorial operations in Edinburgh. Chalmers died in 1847. In his final campaign he had managed to adapt his parish community ideal to the new conditions which had developed following the break-up of the Established Church of Scotland and the passing of the New Poor Law of 1845. His territorial community-building scheme raised the possibility that through competition with one another in the work of reclaiming new industrial areas, the Protestant denominations might gradually learn mutual respect and co-operation, then move quietly toward reunion and shared effort for the achievement of the Christian commonwealth in Scotland.

Few Scots, however, were prepared to embrace such a vision of interdenominational co-operation in the mid and late 1840s. The sectarian jealousies raised by the Church Extension controveries and the Disruption remained acute. The Church of Scotland was insecure, and hostile towards those who had walked out in 1843. The Free Church was primarily engaged in the work of building churches, manses and schools for the nearly 800 congregations which had gone out in 1843, and had few resources to spare for Chalmers's ideal of a territorial mission in the urban slums. The other major presbyterian denomination in Victorian Scotland, the United Presbyterian Church, embraced the Voluntary principle and rejected the ideas of an establishment and territorial ministry. Of the four or five Edinburgh operations founded during the mid 1840s in the wake of Chalmers's appeal for an interdenominational territorial mission, only two seem to have been pursued with much vigour: the West Port operation, and a territorial mission established in the Fountainbridge by Robert Candlish's Free St. George's congregation.

Then, in the early 1850s, Chalmers's territorial community ideal was dramatically revived in the Free Church, mainly through the efforts of Robert Buchanan, minister of Glasgow's Free Tron church. In 1847, Buchanan's middle-class congregation had begun a territorial operation on the West Port model in the Wynds district, one of the most deprived areas of Glasgow, with a population of about 12,000. They recruited an agency of district visitors, established district schools, and in 1850 appointed a missionary.[13] Impressed by Buchanan's appeals and the pioneering work in the Wynds, the Free Church General Assembly of 1851 created a special Committee on Glasgow Evangelization, under the convenorship of Andrew Gray, to co-ordinate and encourage territorial operations in deprived areas of Glasgow. The goal was to revive Chalmers's Church

[13] N.L. Walker, *Robert Buchanan* (London, 1877), 300–29.

Extension campaign in Glasgow, and provide an example for other cities and large towns.[14] Within a year, the Committee was supervising four territorial operations, which included salaried missionaries, district visiting, district Sunday schools, day, evening and industrial training schools, savings banks, libraries, lectures in popular science, and clothing societies. In one operation alone, there were sixty-seven district visitors. With the General Assembly's approval, the Committee on Glasgow Evanglization established in 1852 a 'Chalmers Endowments' fund, to provide subsidies to territorial operations in Glasgow. By May 1854, the Committee had collected over £6,000 for the Chalmers Endowments and was supporting ten territorial operations.[15] In 1853, the Glasgow Committee reported that in two of the territorial mission communities, a process of 'self-extension' had begun; that is, working-class men from the new territorial missions were venturing forth into surrounding districts, visiting homes and seeking to lay the foundation for new territorial community-building operations.[16] Independent working-class communities were evidently emerging, which were pursuing their own home missions.

One of the most active figures in the territorial campaign in Glasgow was Dugald MacColl, who began mission work in the Wynds in 1853 while completing his divinity studies, and became the first minister of the Wynds territorial church in 1854. MacColl became convinced that the work of reclaiming the 'sunken masses' to Chalmers's Christian communal ideal would not be achieved by a number of isolated operations, but would need to be pursued comprehensively.[17] As soon as he felt the Wynds church and schools were secure, MacColl turned his attention to a neighbouring district. With the support of a wealthy iron manufacturer, he purchased a site for a church and hall in the Bridgegate, and with a portion of his Wynds congregation as his agency, he began a new territorial operation, which included a medical mission. The Bridgegate territorial church was opened in 1860, and almost immediately young working-class men from his congregation began venturing into surrounding areas for district visiting – laying the foundations for four additional territorial churches and schools at Cadder, Cathcart, Carmunnock and Crossmyloof.[18] The work of MacColl and other territorial missionaries was assisted by the revival of 1859–60.

---

[14] *Proceedings of the General Assembly of the Free Church of Scotland* (1851), 304–32; C.G. Brown, 'Religion and the Development of an Urban Society: Glasgow 1780–1914' (Glasgow Univ. Ph.D., 1981), 412–14.

[15] *Proceedings of the General Assembly of the Free Church of Scotland* (1852), 306–21; *Proceedings* (1854), 280–1; Appendix, 140–5.

[16] *Proceedings of the General Assembly of the Free Church of Scotland* (1853), Appendix, 261–2.

[17] D. MacColl, *Among the Masses; or Work in the Wynds* (London, 1867), 197.

[18] Ibid., 358–62.

Nativist fears of Irish Catholic immigration also encouraged support for territorial operations designed to achieve a Protestant commonwealth. Between 1854 and 1867, the Free Church added twenty territorial churches in Glasgow, with agencies of district visitors, schools, savings banks, clothing societies, temperance societies – intended to create and maintain Christian communities in working-class districts.[19]

In Edinburgh, the Free Church territorial movement initiated by Chalmers in 1844 was revived and strengthened by the example of the Wynds movement in Glasgow. William Tasker, Chalmers's choice as minister of the West Port territorial church, emerged as an impassioned propagandist for the movement. More influential was James Hood Wilson, a close friend of Glasgow's Dugald MacColl, who in 1853 became missionary to the Fountainbridge territorial operation. A 'muscular Christian', Wilson directed his physical strength against abusive husbands and local toughs, while he was fearless in the face of cholera. He treated the inhabitants of the Fountainbridge as his equals and gained their confidence.[20] Becoming the first minister of the Chalmers Territorial Church in the Fountainbridge in 1854, he founded schools, a soup kitchen, and a Chalmers Working Men's Club and Institute, with library, reading room, games room, night classes and public lectures. His working-class congregation then began a territorial mission of its own in a neighbouring district.[21] With a bequest of £10,000 from a Miss Barclay, the magnificent Barclay church was erected for the new territorial community, and Wilson became the minister there in 1864, bringing with him some of the congregation from the overcrowded Fountainbridge church.[22] Almost immediately, his new congregation began still another territorial mission. There was a tone of colonial enthusiasm in these operations, with their language of 'reclaiming' moral waste and expanding Christian 'territory'. In his opening address as moderator of the Free Church General Assembly of 1895, Wilson recalled the excitement which young ministers experienced in the 'territorial Movement' of the 1850s and 1860s. Theological students felt they should devote time to the territorial missions before settling into an ordinary charge. Under Chalmers's continuing influence, 'the Free Church had, in its Home Mission operations, become aggressive as no other church then was', and was 'in the best sense a national Church'.[23]

In 1854, the Home Mission and Church Extension Committee of the Free Church General Assembly began making special grants to encourage and

---

[19] Ibid., 257–306, 320–35, 373.
[20] J. Wells, *The Life of James Hood Wilson* (London, 1905), 36–61.
[21] Ibid., 72–127.
[22] Ibid., 143.
[23] *Proceedings of the General Assembly of the Free Church of Scotland* (1895), 3.

sustain territorial community-building operations in deprived urban areas throughout Scotland. During the first year, grants were made to five new urban territorial operations – two in Edinburgh, two in Dundee, and one in Ayr – which were in addition to the new territorial operations being supported by the Glasgow Committee.[24] Numbers continued to grow, until by 1868, the Free Church was supporting thirty-three territorial operations in urban Scotland. These operations included territorial day, evening, and Sunday schools, savings banks, clothing societies, libraries, reading rooms, temperance societies, as well as hundreds of voluntary workers. Indeed, a single territorial operation at the Pleasance in Edinburgh had alone over 150 voluntary visitors and workers.[25] The territorial operations were viewed as living expressions of Chalmers's godly commonwealth ideal. 'The territorial charges which they now had in their large towns', insisted a speaker at the Free Church Assembly of 1870, 'were all the offspring of Dr. Chalmers' West Port Territorial Mission; and the best monument they could erect to the memory of that distinguished man, would be to erect more'.[26]

The Free Church commitment to the territorial community ideal reached its high point during the late 1860s and early 1870s. There was growing concern over both the rising costs of poor relief and the continuing social misery and unrest. Many became convinced that the Poor Law of 1845 had failed. The total cost of poor relief was estimated to have risen from about £300,000 to over £850,000 per annum, while the New Poor Law had not fulfilled the promise of W.P. Alison and other proponents that a decent and secure State provision for the poor would encourage self-help and moral improvement, and elevate the condition of the labouring poor. Urban deprivation had not been eliminated, and conditions for the urban poor may even have deteriorated. New charitable associations were now created in Scottish cities – including an Edinburgh 'Chalmers Association for Improving the Condition of the Poor' – which embraced Chalmers's criticisms of legal poor relief and employed district visiting and case studies on the St. John's model. Growing criticisms of the Poor Law led to the formation of a Parliamentary Select Committee on the Scottish Poor Laws in 1869.[27] Some in the Free Church feared social unrest and revolutionary ideas among the irreligious 'sunken masses' of the cities,

[24] *Proceedings of the General Assembly of the Free Church of Scotland* (1855), 92–6.
[25] *Proceedings of the General Assembly of the Free Church of Scotland* (1868), 130–2.
[26] *Proceedings and Debates of the General Assembly of the Free Church of Scotland* (1870), 143.
[27] I. Levitt, *Poverty and Welfare in Scotland 1890–1948* (Edinburgh, 1988), 14–18; [A. Richardson], *The Future Church of Scotland* (Edinburgh, 1870), 258.

fears which were greatly increased in early 1871 with the violent events of the Paris Commune.[28] For many, the only answer to the social crisis lay in Chalmers's territorial community ideal. 'As an instrument for overtaking the reclamation of the lapsed masses', the Free Church minister, John Pirie, assured the Glasgow Free Church Presbytery in December 1871, 'I have the most perfect faith in that particular form of missionary organisation known as Dr. Chalmers' Territorial Scheme'.[29] 'The true and only remedy for the irreligion of our City', asserted the Glasgow Free Church minister, James Johnston, in 1871, 'is a return to the old parochial system . . . so eloquently advocated by Dr. Chalmers'.[30]

During the mid 1870s, however, this Free Church enthusiasm for Chalmers's territorial system began to wane. The early 1870s had been the noon tide; after that the Free Church underwent a gradual, but perceptible, movement away from the godly commonwealth ideal. It began ceasing to perceive of itself as a national Church, with responsibility for the spiritual and social welfare of the whole people of Scotland, and increasingly viewed itself as a gathered Church of believers. In part, this was the result of the passing away of the older Free Church leadership, especially Robert Candlish and Thomas Guthrie (strong supporters of the territorial ideal), and the emergence to leadership of Robert Rainy, who embraced the principle of religious Voluntaryism. The Scottish Education Act of 1872 brought presbyterian schools under the management of elected school boards, greatly diminishing the educational functions of the Free Church territorial missions. In 1874, Rainy brought the Free Church into alliance with the United Presbyterians to campaign for the disestablishment and disendowment of the Church of Scotland, and the end of all establishments. The Free Church was strengthened in this new voluntaryist direction by the national revival of 1873–4 associated with Dwight L. Moody and Ira D. Sankey, two professional American revivalists who placed emphasis on personal salvation and the individual decision for Christ. While the Free Church continued to provide grants for territorial operations, the numbers of these operations and the attention given to territorial missions declined. When the Free Church held a great public meeting in Edinburgh in 1880

---

[28] *Proceedings of the General Assembly of the Free Church of Scotland* (1871), 248; See also T. Guthrie, *The Poor and How to Help Them* (London, 1868); J. Johnston, *Religious Destitution in Glasgow* (Glasgow, 1870); J. Begg, *The Ecclesiastical and Social Evils of Scotland, and How to Remedy Them* (Edinburgh, 1871); W.G. Blaikie, *The Future of the Working Classes: God or Mammon?* (Edinburgh, 1872).

[29] J. Pirie, *The Lapsed, with Suggestions as to the Best Means of Raising Them* (Edinburgh, 1871), 21.

[30] J. Johnston, *The Rising Tide of Irreligion, Pauperism, Immorality, and Death in Glasgow, and How to Turn It* (Glasgow, 1871), 43–4.

to mark the centenary of Chalmers's birth, virtually no notice was given to his territorial community ideal.[31] In 1883, the Free Church General Assembly was supporting only twenty-four territorial operations, and the Convener of the Home Missions and Church Extension Committee observed to the Assembly that 'there was a feeling in the Church against extension', including opposition to operations in 'mission districts that were poor, because going there involved a certain amount of liability'. By 1888, the Free Church was supporting only seventeen territorial operations, and by 1889, only twelve.[32] During the third quarter of the nineteenth century, the Free Church had devoted considerable enthusiasm, effort and money to Chalmers's territorial system and the creation of independent urban Christian communities, emphasizing co-operation and fellowship. It had created fifty or sixty urban territorial churches, many with healthy congregations and strong social commitments. These communal operations had reflected the ideal of independence from upper-class patronage and paternalism which had played such an important part in the Disruption of 1843, and which had continued to define the Free Church ethos. The territorial missions had also represented the high point of the Free Church's perception of itself as Scotland's true national Church with a mission to create, through voluntary effort, the godly commonwealth. But during the 1870s, the Free Church increasingly withdrew from its commitment to achieving the Christian commonwealth, and began regarding itself primarily as a gathered Church of Christian individuals, 'holding the fort' in the midst of a sinful, secular society.

While Chalmers's godly commonwealth ideal was waning in the Free Church, however, it was becoming increasingly important within the Established Church, helping to revive that Church's image as Scotland's national Church. The process of restoring Chalmers as a prophet of the Established Church had been a slow one. In the aftermath of the Disruption, Chalmers's reputation had fallen very low in the Establishment. He was the maker of the Disruption, the spoiler of the national Church. His name was scarcely mentioned; indeed, the Church of Scotland General Assembly, though it was meeting at the time of Chalmers's death in 1847, declined even to notice the event. Gradually, however, Churchmen began returning to Chalmers's social ideal and his reputation was quietly restored.

   Much of the credit for reviving Chalmers's communal ideal in the

---

[31] 'Centenary of Dr. Thomas Chalmers: Full Report of Celebration Meeting in Edinburgh', *Daily Review* (Edinburgh), 4 March 1880.
[32] *Proceedings of the General Assembly of the Free Church of Scotland* (1883), 66, and 'Report of the Home Mission and Church Extension Committee', Appendix III; *Proceedings* (1888), Appendix III; *Proceedings* (1890), Appendix III.

Established Church belongs to Professor James Robertson, who had been an Aberdeenshire parish minister and an active member of Chalmers's Church Extension Committee during the 1830s. Robertson had remained in the Establishment in 1843, and was appointed to the Chair of Church History at Edinburgh University. In 1846, he became convener of a General Assembly Endowment Committee, which sought to provide endowments for the 222 Church Extension churches erected between 1834 and 1841 by Chalmers's Church Extension campaign. A great admirer of Chalmers. Robertson revived the idea of an endowed parish system as the means to create a sense of Christian community.[33] He worked to revive the conception of the Established Church as the Church of the poor – the Church that through its endowments was uniquely qualified to reach those who were unable to pay for religious and educational services, and reclaim them for the Christian commonwealth. 'It is by the attention she has thus bestowed on the interests of the poor', Robertson wrote in 1856, 'that the Church has been enabled to rally her broken forces'. He was extremely successful in his appeals for funds, both to endow existing territorial churches and to build new churches: he raised over £400,000 and added some sixty new parishes to the Church before working himself to a premature death in 1860.

His work made a great impression on the young A. H. Charteris, who wrote Robertson's biography. Charteris was a Church of Scotland minister in Glasgow from 1863 to 1868, during the height of the Free Church territorial movement. On moving to Edinburgh to take up an academic appointment, he became a leading proponent of the Church's social mission, and an advocate of Chalmers's ideal of an aggressive urban territorial mission. In 1870, Charteris organized his Edinburgh students into the Tolbooth University Mission, which proceeded on the lines of Chalmers's West Port operation, mapping out a district in Edinburgh's Old Town, conducting house-to-house visiting and establishing district Sunday schools, Bible classes, prayer meetings, mothers' meetings, clothing society, savings bank, reading room, library, games room, musical entertainments, and a work society to provide assistance with employment. The aim was both to create a sense of Christian community in a deprived urban area, and to educate future ministers in the benefits of the parish community ideal.[34] In 1869, on Charteris's recommendation, the Church of Scotland General Assembly created the Christian Life and Work Committee, to promote and co-ordinate the evangelical and pastoral

[33] A.H. Charteris, *The Life of the Rev. James Robertson* (Edinburgh, 1863), 51, 254–69.
[34] A. Gordon, *The Life of Archibald Hamilton Charteris* (London, 1912), 158–63.

work of the Church.[35] Under Charteris's convenorship, the Life and Work Committee advocated the territorial system. 'Had your Committee a thousand tongues', it asserted in its report of 1871, 'they would with them all proclaim that the *territorial home mission*, and it alone . . . is proved by all experience to be the only effectual means of bringing the Gospel to bear on the masses of the population, and raising them'.[36]

Also contributing to the revival of Chalmers's parish community ideal in the established Church were the brothers Norman and Donald Macleod, members of a prominent Scottish clerical family. An admirer of Chalmers and a close friend of James Robertson, Norman Macleod became minister of the Barony parish church, Glasgow, in 1851, and commenced an aggressive territorial operation in his parish in 1852. This included the usual district Sunday schools, several parish day schools, evening classes for adults, a savings bank, a tea and refreshment room, reading room, Young Men's Association and clothing society. His parish church also supported aggressive missionary activity into surrounding districts.[37] Macleod related to his working class parishioners with genuine personal warmth and respect, and treated them as equals. In 1860, he began editing a new popular religious magazine, *Good Words*, which became one of the most successful Christian periodicals in Victorian Britain. *Good Words* did much to popularize Chalmers's social ideal, directing attention in its first issue to the influence of Chalmers's thought on the efficient communal charity operation in the German city of Elberfeld.[38] In a pamphlet published in 1867, based on articles previously published in *Good Words*, Macleod advocated Chalmers's territorial community system as the only effective means to deal with growing urban poverty. 'Whatever may be the fame of Chalmers in the next generation as a theologian or as a Church leader', Macleod maintained, 'he is destined to tell on the future . . . by his wise and sagacious plans . . . for elevating the masses, economically and spiritually'.[39] Following Norman Macleod's early death in 1872, his brother, Donald Macleod of the Park Church, Glasgow, took over as editor of *Good Words* and as a leading proponent of Chalmers's territorial community ideal in the established Church. He rejected as patronizing attempts to reach the urban poor through paid missionaries and

[35] Ibid., 303–12.
[36] *Reports on the Schemes of the Church of Scotland* (1871), 412. See also *Reports* (1872), 446–9. Later in the 1870s, Charteris lost some of his confidence in the territorial system. Lord Sands [Christopher N. Johnston], *Dr. Archibald Scott* (Edinburgh, 1919), 88.
[37] D. Macleod, *Memoir of Norman Macleod*, vol. ii (London, 1876), 1–14.
[38] 'Dr. Chalmers at Elberfeld', *Good Words*, no. I (January 1860).
[39] N. Macleod, *How Can We Best Relieve Our Deserving Poor?* (London, 1867), 31.

mission stations. The masses, he observed, rightly 'stand aloof and refuse to be missionised'. The only means of elevating them, he maintained, was through the creation of autonomous, self-respecting Christian communities on Chalmers's model. Such communities were needed to preserve the fabric of society amid large-scale industrialization and the anonymity of mass society. Chalmers's communal ideal would provide society with a 'deeper foundation than selfish utility or the cold requirements of the social contract'.[40] In the later 1880s, Donald Macleod emerged as a leading advocate of the municipal provision of working-class housing in Glasgow, calling for both increased governmental social legislation and a more efficient territorial system in the Churches.[41] He represented a link between Chalmers's godly commonwealth ideal of the 1830s and 1840s, and the Glasgow municipal collectivism of the later 1880s and 1890s.

The renewed commitment to Chalmers's parish community and godly commonwealth ideals in the Church of Scotland coincided with the remarkable revival of the Establishment, in membership and social outreach, during the 1860s and 1870s. Chalmers's parochial ideal also presented Scottish Churchmen with arguments for Church defence once the campaign for disestablishment began in earnest in Scotland in the early 1870s. In a pamphlet on *Endowed Territorial Work*, published in 1873, the Edinburgh minister and future leader of the Church of Scotland, Archibald Scott, argued that endowments and centralized authority were necessary for the organization of industrial Scotland into territorial communities. Only an endowed, established Church could commit itself to the needs of the whole nation, including the poor who could not afford to pay for church membership; the efforts of voluntary Churches could never achieve Chalmers's godly commonwealth ideal.[42] In his Baird Lectures for 1875, also published under the title *Endowed Territorial Work*, William Smith, minister of North Leith and James Robertson's successor as convener of the Church's Endowment Committee, defined Chalmers's territorial community ideal as 'essential to every rightly constituted Church'. Only a properly endowed territorial Church, he argued, could penetrate deprived urban areas, unite the social classes, reduce the growing burden of legal

---

[40] D. Macleod, 'The Parochial System', in *The Church and the People*, St. Giles Lectures, 6th Series (Edinburgh, 1886), 131, 154. See also, D. Macleod, *Home Missions* (Glasgow, 1883) and D. Macleod, 'Thomas Chalmers', in *Scottish Divines 1505–1872*, St. Giles Lectures, 3rd Series (Edinburgh, 1883), 273–316.

[41] D. Macleod, *Non-Church-Going and Housing of the Poor: Speech delivered in the General Assembly* (Edinburgh, 1888).

[42] A. Scott, *Endowed Territorial Work, the Means of Meeting Spiritual Destitution* (Edinburgh, 1873), esp. 9–33. For Scott's leadership of the Church of Scotland during the 1890s and his continued commitment to the parish community ideal, see Lord Sands, *Dr. Archibald Scott*, op. cit., 76–104.

poor relief and elevate the whole population to communal responsibility.[43]
In a lengthy defence of Chalmers's parish community ideal and the
endowed national Church, published in 1884, the Church of Scotland
minister Robert Milne rejected *laissez faire* policies. 'The better classes',
he observed, 'can take care of themselves; the very poorest cannot'. 'What
is liberty', he asked, 'if it is only liberty to go to ruin?'[44] He advocated close
co-operation between an endowed territorial Church and an interventionist
State. The parish communities of the national Church, he argued, would
end the rootlessness of the urban poor. Such stable communities would
in turn render the State's increasing body of social legislation more
effective in bringing lasting social improvement.[45] By the 1880s, then,
it was increasingly the established Church which claimed the mantle of
Chalmers, while the majority in the Free Church joined with the United
Presbyterians in moving away from Chalmers's territorial system and
campaigning for disestablishment. Chalmers's godly commonwealth ideal
proved important in providing arguments for the intellectual defence of the
established Church, and helping it stave off the threat of disestablishment
during the 1870s and 1880s.

  With the waning of the disestablishment movement in Scotland during
the 1890s, Chalmers's territorial community ideal also began to fade.
Scottish society was changing, with the growth of large-scale industries
and the corresponding development of industry-wide trade unions. Class
consciousness was becoming more acute, as reflected in the emergence of
socialist organizations like the Social Democratic Federation in 1883 and
the formation of the Scottish Labour Party in 1888 and the Independent
Labour Party in 1892. Scottish urban society was also becoming more
religiously pluralistic, with the massive immigration, especially during
the 1870s, of Catholics from Ireland and Italy, and of Jews from Central
Europe. District visitors found the principle of 'aggressive' house-to-
house visiting less and less workable, as they encountered, not simply
the indifference of the lapsed, but real hostility from non-presbyterian
households. The increasing residential segregation of the 1880s and 1890s,
with the middle classes moving to suburban neighbourhoods, decreased
the amount of middle-class effort and money that could be called upon
to initiate community-building operations in deprived urban districts.
Further, as the State assumed a more active role in social welfare
during the 1890s and early 1900s, the idea of rooting welfare in small,

---

[43] W. Smith, *Endowed Territorial Work: Its Supreme Importance to the Church and Country*
(Edinburgh, 1875), 93, 236–72.
[44] R. Milne, *The Problem of the Churchless and Poor in Our Large Towns* (Edinburgh,
1884), 69.
[45] Ibid., 53–95.

Church-based, largely self-contained communities seemed less and less a viable alternative. Chalmers's communal ideal succumbed to what Callum Brown has termed a late nineteenth-century 'crisis for religion' associated with social change and new social visions.[46] In 1901, John Marshall Lang, convener of the Church of Scotland Commission on the Religious Condition of the People from 1890 to 1896, concluded that the territorial schemes of Chalmers and James Robertson had proved sterile. They had failed to reclaim the lapsed urban masses and it was time for the Church to explore new methods of social mission.[47] Chalmers's social ideas were not totally forgotten. His views on the importance of regular visiting and case studies in the distribution of relief continued to influence social workers, such as Helen Kerr, secretary of both the Edinburgh Social Union and the Edinburgh Charity Organisation Society, who was described in 1911 as the 'Octavia Hill of Edinburgh'.[48] But by the end of the Victorian era, Chalmers's communal ideal was no longer inspiring serious effort from the Scottish Churches; it was, as Lord Rosebery had noted, a land of promise that his countrymen were not destined to enter.[49]

Chalmers's social vision had exercised an enduring influence through much of the Victorian era. Through his godly commonwealth ideal, he had contributed to the preservation of the traditional communal values of pre-industrial Scotland amid the rapid social changes of industrialization and urbanization. His godly commonwealth ideal had survived the Disruption of 1843 and had profoundly influenced the mainstream presbyterian Churches throughout the Victorian era. Although its influence was at first most dramatically felt in the impressive urban mission of the Free Church during the 1850s and 1860s, by the 1870s and 1880s it was the established Church of Scotland which increasingly claimed Chalmers's mantle. Indeed, Chalmers's territorial ideal had played a major role in the revival of the established Church and in providing it with an effective defence against the disestablishment campaign. Although Chalmers had taken a leading role

---

[46] C. Brown, *The Social History of Religion in Scotland since 1730* (London, 1987), 169–208.

[47] J. Marshall Lang, *The Church and Its Social Mission*, the Baird Lectures for 1901 (Edinburgh, 1902), 115–33.

[48] H.L. Kerr, *The Path of Social Progress: A Discussion of Old and New Ideas in Social Reform* (Edinburgh, 1912), 1–37. For the comparison of Helen Kerr and Octavia Hill, see *The Churches' Task in Social Reform: Report of the Proceedings of the United Free Church Congress on Social Problems* (Edinburgh, 1912), 68.

[49] In the 1930s, following the presbyterian Church Union of 1929, John White, architect of the Union and leader of the Church of Scotland, sought to revive Chalmers's Church Extension campaign – though with only modest success. See A. Muir, *John White* (London, 1958), 285–95, 321–34. For comparisons of the Church Extension campaigns of White and Chalmers, see 'Thomas Chalmers and John White', *British Weekly*, 24 August 1933.

in the Disruption of 1843, his ideas, as represented by James Robertson, Norman and Donald Macleod and Archibald Scott, may well have later helped to save the Church of Scotland from disestablishment.

Through much of the nineteenth century, a time of weak government and great social tensions in Scotland, the godly commonwealth ideal had helped maintain a sense of social cohesion, especially in the urban environment. The territorial operations had involved thousands of voluntary workers, and affected tens of thousands of urban Scots. They had formed many successful urban churches. These operations, with their careful organization and considerable investment of resources, demonstrated that the Church was seriously concerned with the problems of urban society. They reflected a real effort to overcome the anonymity and fragmentation in the rapidly expanding industrial towns and cities, and to place the Church at the centre of collective life. The continuing Scottish support for the territorial ideal is a reminder of the importance of community in Victorian Scotland. Ideas of social responsibility were strong; many looked upon wealth as held in trust for the general welfare. Although most nineteenth-century Scots accepted the laws of political economy as true and inexorable, they none the less also recognised the human need for a sense of community to set against the effects of economic individualism, the competitive marketplace, and the concentrations of wealth and productive power. While Evangelicalism was the predominant ethos in the Scottish presbyterian Churches between the 1830s and 1880s, concern for individual morality and personal salvation had coexisted beside the desire to organize society into closely-knit communities, independent from upper-class patronage and State paternalism, and embracing the values of corporate responsibility. The effort of the presbyterian Churches to organize Scottish society into small, autonomous communities, recognizing both the individuality of each member and the need for co-operation and benevolence, may have been utopian in an industrial century, increasingly dominated by large-scale firms, international finance capital, industry-wide trade unions, and the military-industrial complex. But many Victorian Scots had found Chalmers's godly commonwealth a compelling ideal, for all that.

Proceedings of the British Academy, **78**, 81–107

'I suppose you are not a Baptist or a Roman Catholic?': Nonconformity's True Conformity

CLYDE BINFIELD

University of Sheffield

'Mrs. THATCHER'S "Victorian Values" are chapel values . . .' Thus Raphael Samuel, at least in abstract.[1] Mr. Samuel is not quite right. Hers would have been the values of many, perhaps very many, in chapel but they are not chapel values. My end, in which no doubt should have been my beginning, may make that distinction clear. My theme, however, which must link both that end and this beginning focuses upon the convergence, brief enough and fortuitous, yet intense and real, between Nonconformity and Mr. Gladstone. That convergence, most exemplary of Victorian moments, is the true celebration of Victorian values. It is Nonconformity's true conformity.

To begin before the beginning, with my title:

> *11 July 1911*: Lunched at 13 Upper Belgrave Street, and took Father up to Lord's to see the Gentlemen v. Players; subsequently dined with him at Boodle's, after his interview with George Lloyd. This seems to have passed off to the complete satisfaction of both parties, and Father likes him very much, I think. George told me last night that they sat for a while in stony silence, broken at last by Father asking him if he was fond of fishing! Which he followed up with: 'I suppose you are not a Baptist or a Roman Catholic?'[2]

Read 13 December 1990. © The British Academy 1992.

[1] R. Samuel, 'Victorian Values and the Lower Classes', *Victorian Values: Abstracts*, p. 1.
[2] D. Hart-Davis (ed.), *The End of An Era: The Letters and Journals of Sir Alan Lascelles 1887–1920* (1988 edn), p. 105.

13 Upper Belgrave Street was the town house of the fifth Earl of Harewood. Father was the earl's younger brother and George was Father's prospective son-in-law. Needless to say, George was neither a Baptist nor a Roman Catholic and Boodle's, Lord's and Upper Belgravia could rest secure in their values; and since the diarist, his father and his future brother-in-law were born and formed in Victorian England, it follows that those values were expressed in a very strong Victorian accent. They were presumably Victorian values.

But 'Victorian values' are very much a triumph of rhetoric. The phrase suggests a complex of values which are known and immutable: thrift, industry, sobriety, respectability, responsibility, order. The word 'value' is a positive word. It has at once a moral and a commercial ring to it, as in that other Thatcherite value plucked from yester-year, 'value for money'. The word 'Victorian' sets limits of chronology and these, being coterminous with both a life and a reign, give the phrase a human face which is also an establishment face. And since the converse of thrift, industry, sobriety, respectability, responsibility and order is fecklessness, laziness, drunkenness, disreputableness, irresponsibility and disorder, these values are socially very conformist indeed.

Yet it is as hard to know of an age which has not placed a premium on these qualities as it is to think of one which has not seen them subverted in the highest places. Certainly the Victorians are no exception. Worse yet, their age is in fact indefinable. The lady herself was the least Victorian of Victorians and 'her' age saw social and religious flux and intellectual, economic, political, industrial and aesthetic turmoil. The Victorian age was stony ground for Victorian values. The ironies are splendid. This indefinable age, racked by fear that it had no distinguishing marks, had yet an intense consciousness of itself as an age. This can be read in its buildings. Victorians were haunted by the dilemma of style.[3] Their buildings were Gothic, classical, Louis XV, Wrenaissance, often beyond perfection and always anything but Victorian. Yet, even to the half-formed eye, each and every one of them is distinctively Victorian.

All this is also caught by the age's Nonconformity. Victorian values are frequently thought in their religious aspect to be those of the Nonconformist Conscience as best expressed by Mr. Gladstone and Queen Victoria. That is a useful nonsense which underlines both the social conformity of religious Nonconformity and the fact that society at most levels was shot through with Nonconformity. Frederick Lascelles was quite right to bark that question at George Lloyd, his Old Etonian and tractarian son-in-law-to-be, since the Lloyds owed their position to the enterprising

---

[3] See J. Mordaunt Crook, *The Dilemma of Style* (1987).

values of their Quaker ancestors.[4] In a world where few people are entirely innocent of Dissenting kinsmen nothing can be quite what it seems; except, of course, that Frederick Lascelles need not have worried.

And that, perhaps, is the point. The coining of that phrase, 'The Nonconformist Conscience', is a classic case of shutting the stable door after the horse has bolted. It emerged at the tail end of 1890 as the carefully staged issue of a carefully planted campaign in and by a newspaper – *The Times* – not immediately or naturally associated with that side of things.[5] It captured the essence of a great disintegrative force which, like classic horror stories, all knew for fact but none had really encountered. Just as we know a Victorian building or a Victorian value when we see one, though there is nothing Victorian about either, so we know a Victorian Nonconformist – until, that is, we meet one.

Where does this leave us? It leaves us with the new social fact of which Victorians were most self-conscious and with its most distinctive religious aspect: the middle classes and the Nonconformity nurtured by them. And it leaves us with that aspect's most characteristic myth: the affinity with Mr. Gladstone.

These can be explored in a reminiscence, a *roman-à-clef* and two sets of diaries. First the reminiscence:

> My father, who was a hot Liberal, had a nephew the same age as himself, who was a hot Tory. During Disraeli's last administration – I think in 1889 [sic] – Gladstone came down to speak in Bedford, and the two Cootes went over to hear him. At the time, some by-elections had gone against the government, and Gladstone's theme was that the days of the ungodly were numbered if only the efforts to unseat them were maintained. He concluded an hour of heady and mesmeric stuff with a peroration somewhat as follows:
>
> > And now, gentlemen, now that the rising sun begins to tinge the hills with golden hope, shall we draw back?
>
> Whereupon the Tory Coote leapt on to his chair, flung both his arms in the air in an ecstasy of approval, and shrieked, 'Never !!!'[6]

It is an identi-kit story, plucked from family lore. It may be *bien trouvé* but it sounds right. Here is the mesmeric Gladstone, the People's Homer straight from Olympus, just to hear whom say 'Ladies and Gentlemen!' is enough in all conscience. Here is the statesman on a state visit to the land of the Russells and the Whitbreads. For Gladstone it is a case of Bootle one day, Bedford the next. For Bedford it is the new Cromwell come to the Cromwell country which is also John Bunyan country which is also John

---

[4] D.B. Windsor, *The Quaker Enterprise: Friends in Business* (1980), esp. ch.3 on 'The Lloyds of Birmingham', p. 28–41.

[5] C. Binfield, 'A Conformist Conscience', *The Times*, 10 December 1990.

[6] C.R. Coote, *Editorial* (1965), p. 243.

Howard country. So who was in that audience? The stalwarts of Bunyan Meeting, founded by Bunyan, ministered over by Bunyan's biographer (who was also Maynard Keynes's grandfather)? Or the stalwarts of Howard Congregational Church, founded by John Howard the prison reformer? Or even the in-laws of Hugh Price Hughes, Katherine Price Hughes's Wesleyan Methodist, manufacturing, Bedford Howard relations? Certainly there was the narrator's father, Howard Coote of Oaklands, The Rookery and Stukeley Hall, Hunts. Like countless other Nonconformist Howards, Coote was named after the prison reformer. The Coote family church was St. Ives Free Church, with a statue of Oliver Cromwell fronting it in the market place. The Cootes collected Cromwelliana. They had a chest of drawers carved with the initials 'O.C.', which Howard Coote would show off, though visitors liked to think that they stood for 'Oward Coote rather than Oliver Cromwell.[7] And, to set the record straight, who is telling the story? Colin Coote, baptised at the Free Church, who became a Coalition Liberal M.P., and ended up as Editor of the *Daily Telegraph*.[8]

Bedford and its Bunyan Meeting were fictionalised by Mark Rutherford. Theirs was a rooted Congregationalism, like that of St. Ives, transplanted (or re-potted) by the Victorians.

For another fiction, this time of a Victorian Congregationalism seeking for roots, come north. Gordon Stowell was a journalist of Colin Coote's generation.[9] His theme, explored in a sociological novel of considerable merit, is Button Hill, a suburb of Fleece:

> Before it swam into the mainstream of history it was just a hill and nothing more. Dairy farms and market gardens upon its slopes helped to feed the populace in the busy valley below; and there were rhubarb-fields too – the world's most succulent rhubarb will ever be grown around Fleece.
>
> Bisecting the hill like a precise centre parting was the main turnpike road between Fleece and Bathwater Spa . . .
>
> In those days Button Hill, as the world came to know it . . . had not even begun to exist. Nor did it even begin to exist in 1885, when the name entered politics as the name given (somewhat fancifully) to one of the four divisions of the borough of Fleece in the new parliamentary register: for

[7] Ibid., p. 75.

[8] For Howard Coote b.1864 see H. Coote, *While I Remember*, (privately, 1937); for Sir Colin Coote 1893–1979 see *The Times*, 23 November 1979, and D. Hart-Davis, *The House the Berrys Built*: if it in fact happened during Disraeli's last ministry it would have to be 21–26 October 1878 when Gladstone was staying at Woburn and Wrest. Then indeed 'Deputation came from Bedford: but I steadily declined to go. Conversation with Mr. Howard'. Tuesday 22 October 1878, H.C.G. Matthew (ed.), *The Gladstone Diaries, Vol. 9* (Oxford, 1986), p. 355.

[9] For Gordon Stowell 1898–1972 see *Who Was Who* 1972–1980. I am grateful to Mr. David Stowell for information about the Stowell family.

though the hill was geographically within the Button Hill division, the bulk of the voters lived in the slum districts of Lambswell and Tannersdale, lying like dirty puddles at the foot of the hill.

The seventh Lord Bentham (grandfather of the present earl) was the real founder of the modern Button Hill. He owned a great chunk of the hillside . . . And he chose to let it fall into the hands of the speculative builder . . .

By the census of 1891 there were more than three hundred thousand people penned within the city boundaries, and the housing problem was becoming troublesome. The prime difficulty was not the housing of the working-class population . . . For them only too many houses had been provided . . . The people who were hardest hit were the really nice people, the people with nice ideas and aspirations who . . . could afford to send their children to the Grammar School or to the new Modern School.[10]

To such as these the new suburb of Button Hill was in the nature of a godsend:

Builders were turned loose on the estate. It was split into gaping rectangles. Water, gas and drains were laid. And presently a dozen rows of desirable villa-residences shot up as if by magic, and all the contours of the hill were permanently changed. The old turnpike was cleared away, and the Fleece Tramways Company, extending its track, put on a new service of horse-trams out to the Bentham Arms. Removal vans became a familiar sight up Bathwater Road as the best people in Fleece moved themselves and their furniture to a more worthy setting.

Lord Bentham in his wisdom had decreed that the builders were to restrict themselves to villas of a superior type. Retail shops and licensed premises were barred. From the outset the new suburb could not help but feel itself exclusive and superior. Its modestly imposing houses were manifestly designed with some pretensions to that subtle quality known as 'class' . . .

With the coming of the terraces, Button Hill was no longer the name . . . of a hill. It had become a place-name . . .[11]

Its *History* describes Button Hill's first three suburban generations from 1894 to 1929. It begins brick-new and hopeful, upper-lower-middle class aspiring to middle-middle class, clerkly, professional and piano-playing. It ends inner-suburban and immigrant, with its bricks spatched. The sequence is suggested by the chapter headings: 'Button Hill Acquires a Mind', 'Button Hill Acquires a Voice', 'Button Hill Drifts with the Tide', 'Button Hill is Knocked Sideways', 'Button Hill in Eclipse'.

The suburb's focal points are its churches, especially its Congregational church, gothic and clocktowered, and the novel's lens is a chapel lens. Consequently Button Hill's mind and voice are Congregational and Liberal.

[10] G. Stowell, *The History of Button Hill* (1929), pp. 11–13.
[11] Ibid., pp. 13–14.

The drifting with the tide is marked by the break up of the Bible Class. The knocking sideways is the decimation of the Fleece Pals, too many of them from the Bible Class, in France in 1916. The eclipse comes with the minister's farewell. The perceptions are from the pew rather than the pulpit, chiefly the pew of Alfred Ellersby. Ellersby is a leather merchant from Bootle. He is 'a teetotaller, a non-smoker, and a vegetarian, all on principle. He also believed in universal disarmament and Home Rule and women's rights and fresh air, and a host of other rebellious and unpopular things'.[12] He eventually dies from kidney failure brought on by pneumonia caught while zeppelin-watching from the tower of Fleece Town Hall. In a way necessary to novels but which real life can seldom afford, there is a sequence of high points. They are predictable: the Boer War, with mobs on Mafeking Night when Fleece's Pro-Boers have their backs to the wall; Passive Resistance and a heroic by-election; the Somme; the end. The underlying theme is the steady dilution of what began as the fresh distillation of Gladstonianism (or was it Congregationalism?) of purest essence. Here are five quotations to illustrate this:

1   The ubiquitous portrait of *Mr. Gladstone as he is Today* was in Mr. Mendip's hall [Mr. Mendip was in provisions. He rose as poor Ellersby sank], hanging in the place of honour between the hat-stand and the front-door, and it transpired that in support of Mr. Gladstone he had written several letters to the *Fleece Argus*.[13]

2   When Eric was born, his father wanted him to be called William Ewart Gladstone Ellersby. On the other hand his mother favoured the name of Edward . . . They fell back on 'Eric' as a compromise . . . 1893 and 1894 were vintage years for Erics.[14]

3   The general election of 1895 gave Button Hill its first opportunity for a general display of local patriotism.
Always, the seat had been held by a Liberal. But in the year 1895, lifelong devotees of Mr. Gladstone found themselves hesitating [when faced by] Lord Rosebery . . . Mr. Ellersby was only one of many devout Liberals who could not bring themselves to trust a leader who had been busy winning the Derby when he ought to have been wooing votes, and who in so many other ways was emphatically *not* Mr. Gladstone. And in the Button Hill division the local Conservatives made an astute move when they persuaded Sir Matthew Phelps of Gledmere to contest the seat for them, the more so as the Liberal candidate was an importation from the south of England.
Sir Matthew romped home. 'A Button Hill man for Button Hill', the blue

---

[12] Ibid., p. 23.
[13] Ibid., p. 26.
[14] Ibid., p. 30.

placards had cried; and the appeal had been irresistible . . . And afterwards the sight of Sir Matthew's carriage in Bathwater Road gave the suburb new thrills of pride. He was Button Hill's very own M.P. A man who might even at that moment be on his way to the station to travel up to Westminster, there to rub shoulders with the greatest in the land. And yet here he was among them, returning the salutes of his neighbours and constituents with as genial a smile as he had worn on polling-day. And on Sunday he would be back at St. Michael's, going round with the collection bag and taking an unostentatious place with his fellow-sidesmen, just like an ordinary human being.

He cut a good figure in the House, too – he spoke on the Deceased Wife's Sister Bill when it came up, and was mentioned in the newspapers . . .[15]

4   [But Liberalism is not quite dead in Button Hill. In 1899 Alfred Ellersby for fifteen shillings places an advertisement in the *Fleece Argus*. It takes the form of an open letter to Campbell-Bannerman, 'the last hope of true Liberalism, who was still sitting on the fence in a state of beatific Liberal hesitation'].

1, Algernon Terrace,
Button Hill,
Fleece.

Sir, – The Tory Imperialists, who think this war right in principle and purpose, are mistaken, but at least their position is honourable. This cannot be said of those puny Liberals who go about saying, 'We don't agree with the war, but, having begun, we must go on with it.' That is like saying, 'It is wrong to murder, but, having murdered one man, we must murder many.' If that is the Liberal policy, it is a weak, wicked policy, and it spells immediate and final death to the party I have hitherto been proud to support.

Rosebery methods will end in ruin. True Liberals will not want to profit by the shedding of innocent blood. The only true Liberal policy is to stop the war, to refuse all supplies, and to appeal to the country on a traditional, sound, wise, economic, Christian, Gladstonian programme. You, sir, have the chance now, take it.

I am sir, your obedient, humble servant,

Alfred Ellersby.[16]

5   [It is 1929, give or take a year. Alfred's son (and Mendip's son-in-law) Eric, who teaches English at an L.C.C. secondary school, has briefly returned. He reflects on the suburb that he knew, and is now history]:

For the villas of Button Hill had been constitutionally solid. Like their occupants, they had made a bold bid for permanence. They thought they were not made to die. They had an air about them, those houses, an air of conscious moral weight. They were Gladstonian houses. Whereas the new houses assumed neither eternity nor finality, being frivolous, ephemeral affairs of stucco and pebble-dash. They seemed to know that they were

---

[15] Ibid., pp. 56–7.
[16] Ibid., pp. 73–4.

built to enshrine a restless and shifting generation, the jazz generation. Incidentally they were smaller houses than of old – three or four bedrooms and a garage. Marie Stopes, and all that.[17]

They were Baldwin houses. There you have it. In broad, comfortably predictable brush strokes the Nonconformists' Mr. Gladstone is sketched in for the middle-brow, post-Gladstonian, post-chapel novel reader: Gladstone as icon, Gladstone as *man* – man for others and man for us, Gladstone as programme, Gladstone as moral value, Gladstone, in sum, as myth.

The History of Button Hill is fiction, not history but, to mix metaphors, there is nothing wrong in broad brush strokes, nuanced more by literary contrivance than by real life complexity, if the architecture is right. The architecture of this novel is right.

Although its author's name is now best known through that of a family firm, Stowell's of Chelsea, the wine merchants (who lived in Ealing), it was better known in the last century through its parsons. Five generations of Stowells in two branches produced at least eleven clergymen. Four of them were Anglicans, one of them that portentous Evangelical, Hugh of Salford.[18] Six of them were Congregationalists, one of them a college principal. The seventh was both, since he was a Congregational minister who became an Anglican priest. Gordon's father was one of the six.[19] He ministered for forty-one years at the Newton Park Union Church (Congregational and Baptist), Chapeltown Road, Leeds, gothic and clocktowered on the way to Harrogate. It is now a Sikh temple.

Fleece is Leeds. Bathwater is Harrogate. Button Hill is Newton Park and its minister, Arthur Samuel Knight, is Arthur Knight Stowell, a man whose four children, says an obituary referring to the 'palmy days of the suburb', 'have attained distinction in either educational, literary or other artistic respects'.[20] The seventh Earl of Bentham, unless he is the Earl of Mexborough, must be the fifth Earl of Harewood, with luncheon in whose town house this paper began.[21] Sir Matthew Phelps of Gledmere must be

[17] Ibid., p. 430.

[18] For Hugh Stowell 1799–1865 see *Dictionary of National Biography*.

[19] For Arthur Knight Stowell, 1854–1932, first cousin twice removed of Hugh Stowell, see *Congregational Year Book* 1933, p. 246.

[20] *Yorkshire Congregational Year Book* 1932, p. 53.

[21] This is more conjectural. The aristocratic ground landlords for the Headingley and Potternewton districts of Leeds were the Earl of Cardigan (his title subsumed in that of Marquess of Ailesbury by 1894) for Headingley and the Earl of Mexborough and Earl Cowper for Potternewton. The streetnames of Potternewton are Mexborough and Cowper family names and in 1894 the reigning Earl Cowper was the 7th Earl: but it is Harewood which is the consistent, resident, county presence – Mexborough and Cowper were antiquarian associations by the 1890s. See M. Beresford, 'The Face of Leeds 1780–1914', D. Fraser (ed.), *A History of Modern Leeds* (Manchester University Press, 1980), p. 100.

W.L. Jackson of Allerton Hall, later Lord Allerton;[22] and, although the electoral geography and history of Button Hill are at significant variance with that of Newton Park, there can be no doubt as to the 1902 by-election when Rowland Barran (in the novel transmogrified into Everard Sympath from Ipswich, a sort of secular Charles Sylvester Horne), son of Sir John Barran of Chapel Allerton Hall, swept in on the shoulders of the righteous indignation of passive registers and voters who *knew* about education.[23]

Now to push this *roman-á-clef* further towards its Leeds reality, first at its lynch point, Button Hill Congregational Church, in the shape of Newton Park Union Church.[24]

Its building was a model of nonconforming conformity, standing not so much back to front as apse to front to the road, flying-buttressed and gabletted and clockfaced and gas lit ('supplied free by the Leeds Corporation' for the clock's illumination). It struck a Bradford newspaper as 'one of the most picturesque and pleasing erections in the borough . . . quite an ornament to the neighbourhood', 'charmingly picturesque', its promoters to be 'congratulated on their public spirit in the erection of this comparatively small but beautiful specimen of Gothic architecture.' It was in fourteenth-century decorated gothic, with features 'not seen in any other church in Leeds . . . convenient and comfortable to the worshippers'. These included a spacious narthex, 'as it is styled in church architecture', an octagonal nave, 'boldly conceived arcading', 'a handsome dome', carving 'sparingly but tastefully used', the whole making for 'a very fine effect', and 'the general appearance is refined and pleasing, the church having quite a cathedral aspect.' Its stone had been laid in a year of loyal jubilee, 1887, by two grandees, Edward Crossley, the Halifax Congregationalist and Liberal M.P., and John Barran, the Leeds Baptist and M.P. It had been opened in April 1889 to sermons by Guinness Rogers of Clapham.[25] Theirs was a suggestive convergence of names. They may serve to prepare us for the Leeds reality, diary-slanted and feminine this time, of the generation of Howard Coote, Alfred Ellersby, A.S. Knight and A.K. Stowell.

The diaries cover the years 1874–6 and 1880. They describe the doings of Katharine Roubiliac Conder, a thoroughly normal girl of the professional classes anywhere.[26]

---

[22] For W.L. Jackson 1840–1917 see M. Stenton and S. Lees, *Who's Who of British Members of Parliament* Vol. II 1886–1918, (Hassocks, 1978), pp. 189–90.

[23] For Sir Rowland Barran 1858–1949 and Sir John Barran 1821–1905 see ibid., pp. 22–3; for C.S. Horne 1865–1914 see ibid., p. 180.

[24] This account is from *Bradford Observer* quoted in *Congregational Year Book*, 1891, pp. 218–19.

[25] *Leeds Congregational Year Book* 1901 (Leeds, 1901), p. 70.

[26] Katharine Roubiliac Conder (Mrs. Rayner Batten) 1860–1948. I am indebted to Mr. R.J. Simpson for access to her ms. diary.

Katharine Conder was educated first at home by governesses and mama, then at Cheltenham Ladies College, with a finishing of sorts at Leeds High School. Mama was really step-mama and moving through her late thirties. Cheltenham was 'dear old College', with Miss Belcher who was 'a perfect darling' and, even nicer and dearer, 'Miss Kennedy, who teaches us Arithmetic'. It was a life of examinations and competitions and flirting with college boys at the Philharmonic Concert, its horizons enlarged by a much-loved older sister at Girton, a hugely extended family and a round of quietly prosperous doings. There is vicarious pleasure at the new Duchess of Edinburgh's entry to London, marking a general admiration for the whole of the royal family. There is dinner at Sudeley Castle, with its antique oak memories of Katherine Parr, Henry VIII's Protestant queen, and its chatelaine, their hostess, surely so like Queen Katherine. There are readings of Macaulay or Browning or Ruskin or Carlyle or Kingsley or Dickens. There is a dose of scarlet fever, which means hanging the carpets and bedcoverings out of the window. It is a life in which rail travel is normally first class and there is no Evangelical nonsense about *walking* to church. Church is reached by tramcar or the carriage of some family friend or connexion. And church, of course, is chapel, either in the town centre, on East Parade, or close at hand, in the dual-purpose school-chapel served by students which preceded the domed and narthexed fourteenth-century picturesqueness of Newton Park. For this suburban Leeds reality is in fact the fictional Button Hill's prehistory. Sometimes, it has to be said, church is Church, Leeds Parish Church: 'Had the pleasure of hearing the curate, Mr. Knaggs, a fearful specimen . . .'

This prosperous normalcy, a cut or three above the Ellersbys needs to be placed so representative is it. Here it must be placed politically. It is March 1880.

> *1880 : 11 March Thursday* Had our final French class at the Barrans . . . We did nothing at French . . . but talk about the Dissolution. All immensely excited . . .

> *27th March Saturday* Received from good Uncle Jem a packet of yellow leaflets with our song ['The Despot! Lord B!' to the tune of Bonnie Dundee] printed thereon. Took them down to the Mercury Office to be used for the Cause! Went to see Millais' portrait of 'Our chief of Men', which is truly grand.

> *31 March Wednesday* Went down to town, and got some gorgeous yellow ribband for favours tomorrow . . . Came home, worked and made us each a rosette. Read a capital placard on my way home on the 'Strange Disappearance' of 'A Young Person named National Prosperity' . . .

> *1 April Thursday* Ethel and I, largely decorated, started off for Headingley.

Our favours drew forth various remarks, chiefly of approval, such as 'That's the colour! Stick to it!' etc. . . . to Aunt Louie's to tea. Found the children all much excited, disporting themselves in yellow. Then went up to St. Ann's; . . . Had hoped Papa would take us to the Town Hall, to hear the Declaration of the Poll, but when we did not appear at Chapel, he imagined we must have gone with Mr. Willans. All we cld do was to 'tram it' home . . . A little before 11 [Laurie] came in with the grand news:

1. Gladstone 24,600
2. Barran 23,600
3. Jackson
4. Wheelhouse

We went to bed in a state of mighty exultation!

2 April Friday Drenching with rain. Heard from Louie Barran, regretfully giving up the work-house. Wrote to her, sending our heartiest congratulations . . .

3 April Saturday . . . meeting the Scattergoods . . . Gloated over the victory.
Papa and Mamma called at the Barrans to congratulate them.

5 April Monday Drenched with rain and hail, also saw thunder and lightning . . . had to shelter for about half an-hour in a little grocer's shop, had some very amusing political discussions with the owner . . . Grand victories of Midlothian and our West Riding!

17 April Saturday . . . down to see Mr. Gladstone's portrait . . . it rained.

30 April Friday Lucky Laurie has got his ticket for the meeting at the Mechanics, and is gone to hear Mr. Herbert Gladstone . . .

May Day Saturday Laurie was delighted with Mr. Herbert Gladstone last night. The meeting was most enthusiastic. Maggie has been reading the account of it aloud this morning. *Mrs.* Gladstone spoke a few words! Papa has promised to take us to the 'Mass Meeting' at the Coloured Cloth Hall Yard this afternoon! They say that over 30,000 tickets have been issued for it. I do hope we shall be able to get in . . .

We went to the meeting and enjoyed it immensely, all agreeing it was one of the greatest treats we have ever had . . . Papa got some extra tickets from Mr. Willans . . . The huge yard was already crowded near the stairs, though we got there one and a quarter hours before the time. Mr. W. most kindly got us tickets for the barricaded area round the stairs, where we could see and hear splendidly. A small balcony had been erected in front of the steps, with chairs for Mrs. Gladstone, Mr. Herbert Gladstone and Mr. Kitson. The Barrans had chairs just behind these: of course every one else stood. Great Liberal processions soon came pouring in, with bands and banners, and long before 4 o'clock the whole vast hall was densely crowded, except just in one furthest corner. We were in a tremendous jam, but are not the least the worse for it . . . Papa . . . got a 'platform ticket'. At 10 minutes to 4 they arrived, being greeted with tremendous enthusiasm. The cheers then, and at every mention of the name of Gladstone were something to remember all one's life. Mr. Herbert Gladstone is very good looking, and very clever-looking, with a most intelligent, wide-awake expression, and a very lively pleasant smile. He made a capital speech, without the slightest hesitation for one moment, and it seemed wonderfully little exertion to him. He has a very nice voice and capital delivery, and forms all his words with beautiful distinction. There were about 30,000 people there, and he seemed to be heard perfectly all over. It was most amusing to hear the remarks of the people round us: 'Good lad!' 'Eh, he's a nice lad!' 'Stick to it, my lad!' etc. and the enthusiastic cries of 'No! No!' when he said anything about his 'own unworthiness'. Once he spoke of the 'far greater men who had stood upon that platform', and was interrupted with loud shouts of 'No! No!' whereupon he seemed much amused, shook his head, and said laughing 'No, No. You won't quite make *that* go down with me'. After his speech, a good many questions were sent up in writing, which Mr. Kitson read, and the tact and readiness with which Mr. Herbert Gladstone answered them delighted everyone. In fact, he really has taken everyone by storm, and has completely stolen our hearts!

Then Mr. Kitson asked whether any one wished to propose any other candidate, whereupon, amidst tremendous hooting and howling and roars of laughter, a dirty, toothless, disreputable-looking workman mounted the platform, and (after daring to drink out of Herbert's glass of water!) proposed John de Morgan! The hooting and howling made it often quite impossible for him to speak, though the horn was blown two or three times for silence, and Mr. Kitson besought the people to 'give this gentleman two little minutes'. The man declared 'he was a good Liberal and '(waving his hand in Mr. Gladstone's face) 'I've noothing to say against this'ere yoong mon. I daresay he's a very good yoong mon!' upon which Mr. Gladstone raised his hat, and made him a most polite bow! No one was forthcoming to second the amendment, which of course fell through and the resolution adopting Mr. Herbert Gladstone was carried with immense enthusiasm, only 3 out of the 30,000 hands being held up against it. Then 'Archie Sear' started 'For he's a jolly good fellow!' which was roared out by the whole crowd, all of us doing our little best to swell the chorus. Mr. E. Wilson, Mr. L. Gain, Mr. McCheane, Mr. Barran and Mr. Kitson also spoke. Mr. Carter made the one bad-taste speech, raking up the disestablishment question, and receiving very little sympathy. Mrs. Gladstone authorised Mr. Kitson to say that 'Mr. Gladstone was the youngest member of his family and Herbert was the youngest of hers', and also 'that young gentleman had taken upon himself to select Downing St. as the place of his birth!' – remarks which were received with much laughter and applause, and considered as arguing that we are now electing our future Premier. When the meeting was over they made their way along a raised passage which had been erected all along the side of the yard, and as they did so, hundreds of not-over-clean hands were stretched up for a shake! Mrs. Gladstone bore it for some time and then she had to leave off; but we thought Mr. Herbert's hand would be pretty nearly wrung off, as it was grasped by about 8 or 10 hands at a time the whole way along, while he gave them all hearty shakes, laughing the whole time. All the road was thronged with an enthusiastic crowd, and every available window crammed with spectators.

We got home at about 7, perfectly wild with admiration of our new hero. I wrote a four-sheet description of it all to Grandmamma. The weather yesterday and today has been all that could be desired – 'Gladstone weather', we call it.

May 3 Monday into town . . . and bought a capital cabinet of Mr. Herbert Gladstone, Lilly doing the same.

May 4 Tuesday Finished 'Waverley' . . . read 'Modern Painters'.

May 5 Wednesday Alice and Marian Butler came to tea, and we took them there in the evening and finding them enthusiastic Gladstonians, raved about 'Herbert' (whom they had not yet seen) the whole time!

May 6 Thursday Read aloud Mr. Reid's lecture on Mr. Gladstone. Mamma went to the lunch at S.Ann's, taking Eddie to Aunt Louie's, in hopes of his seeing the young hero . . . Mamma came home almost as enthusiastic as we are about Herbert. Says, 'she fell in love with him at once', 'he's a dear boy', 'perfectly charming and fascinating', 'one of the sweetest faces she ever saw', etc! Three cheers for the worthy son of a noble sire! . . .

May 7 Friday We talked, and read a pamphlet on Lord Beaconsfield aloud by turns. What a contrast to our Heroes!

May 8 Saturday A most lovely day. Armed ourselves with Tennyson, and went to Mr. Jowitt's where we read 'Maud' . . . At 2 o'clock, Mrs. S[cattergood], Lilly, Nelly, Louie and I, presented ourselves at Rice's, where we had been promised seats opposite the plat-form from which Mr. Gladstone was to address the crowd. He was nominated, and returned unopposed, to everyone's great joy. A huge crowd filled the square, and we were dreadfully afraid we should not be able to hear a word, but Mr. Gladstone's splendid clear voice was heard all over without any difficulty. He looked as charming as ever, and spoke so nicely. The show of hands was a sight to remember. Mr. Barran disgusted us with a horribly conceited, patronising speech, talking of himself and Herbert as 'one man'!!

Afterwards we went round to the back of the Town Hall in hopes of seeing Herbert drive away; but the crush was so great that we could only see the top of his hat waving, and the carriage . . .

9 May Sunday Cold and dull. Walked down to E.[ast] P.[arade] C.[hapel] with Miss Shaw, who told me that she was in the Great Northern hotel on the night of Mr. Herbert Gladstone's first arrival, and that he shook hands with her, all of his own accord! She was in one of the windows near the Cloth Hall Yard that Saturday, and took an active share in showering down primroses on the carriage after the meeting. She also threw down a handful of hot-house flowers, which he caught, and drove away holding them in his hand. Everyone seems to have shaken hands with him except our unhappy selves! A poor woman in the crowd yesterday told us that *she* had – wretch! . . .

Pyp preached a very original and striking sermon (I thought) this morning, from Job II.10: 'Shall we receive good at the hand of God, and shall we not receive evil?'

10 May Monday . . . met Rose Henderson and Emily Pollock, who said they sat opposite Mr. Herbert Gladstone in Church yesterday. Being prejudiced and ignorant Tories, they did not admire him! . . . Read 'Alton Locke', darned, and read aloud a 'Spectator' article on the Indian appointments. (Lords Ripon and Hartington).

12 May Wednesday Received by post this morning our Hero's autograph! I started the idea of asking him for it, in fun: Nellie took it up in ernest [sic], and insisted on writing, enclosing stamped and addressed envelope. Then we concocted a note, signed with all our initials, saying that 'Four enthusiastic young Liberals' (we were afraid to say 'admirers') 'would consider it the greatest possible favour if Mr. Herbert Gladstone would send them his autograph'. So now behold the reward of cheek – one for each of us! . . .

It is important to be reminded that life is seriously to be enjoyed, that responsibility can be assumed, matter of course, and not be burdensome; that politics is part of life, its froth and passion too; and that women are part of politics, as life. This is of course the world of Midlothian's Leeds side. In 1880 Gladstone ran for Leeds as well as Midlothian, as was then not unusual and entirely prudent. On assuming office he surrendered both seats without the embarrassment, as he charmingly put it, of having to opt for either just yet, and Herbert, in his late twenties and a history don at Keble who had made a brave but quite unavailing showing in Middlesex, stepped in at Leeds where he remained for thirty years. Button Hill, that is to say, had an oblique but real family investment in Gladstonianism. It was more than flavour of the month or spirit of the age. And as for Lilly, Nellie, Maggie, Laurie, Eddie, Ethel, Papa, Mamma, Aunt Janie, Aunt Louie, Uncle J. Willans, Cousin Manwaring, and deaf grandpapa isolated at St. Ann's, it was heart-beat, or at least heart-throb. There is nothing special in Katharine Conder's election account. Nothing, that is to say, that may not be more acutely or immediately found, for example, about Yorkshire elections in Lady Frederick Cavendish's diaries, or Lady Amberley's journals – the one from the angle of an intelligent Anglican, the other more intelligentsia than intelligent, noblewomen both, daily in political circles.[27] But that there is nothing special makes it entirely special.

Note the names in that diary. Most, as in most diaries, are related, or at least connected: not indeed Grosvenor, Lyttelton, Leveson-Gower, Cavendish, but Lupton, Rücker, Conder, Baines, Barran, Crossley, Willans, Scattergood, Jowitt, Crewdson, Reed, Batten, Winterbotham, Heaton, Marchetti, Whitley. Translate them religiously. They are Congregational, Baptist, Quaker, Unitarian. Translate them socially and economically. They are carpets, textiles, newsprint, rag trade, medicine, law, banking. Translate them geographically. They are Leeds, Manchester, Cheltenham, Halifax, Huddersfield, and beyond for Sheffield, Bradford, Liverpool, London, Norwich, Edinburgh, swim easily in. Translate them politically. They are shades of Liberal with a strong municipal accent – but of these names Rücker and Willans had produced or would produce parliamentary candidates, and Baines, Barran, Reed, Crossley, Whitley, Winterbotham had produced, would produce or were producing candidates who became M.P.'s. These are the election-platform, aldermanic-bench, back-bench classes. Translate not so much into another language as into a dialect. This is the *Leeds Mercury* world of the Bainesocracy in its late Indian Summer. Its grand old man is poor, deaf, soon-to-be-Sir Edward Baines up at St. Anne's, who had been ousted in 1874 by the Barranage, whose big new man was rich soon-to-be-Sir John up at Chapel Allerton.[28] But the Baineses and the Barrans are the same sort, East Parade Chapel to South Parade Chapel: and Edward Baines's step-granddaughter's greatest friend, Lily Scattergood, daughter of Leeds's leading physician and East Parade's senior deacon, is shortly to marry Alfred Barran of South Parade, brother of the Rowland Barran whose by-election victory in the new century will be the last victory of Bainesocracy, Barranage, and Button Hill alike.

The diary's pivot is Papa. Inasmuch as the cousinhood's religious accent was Congregational, papa was their pivot too. He is Eustace Rogers Conder, minister of East Parade Chapel and old Edward Baines's son-in-law.[29] The *gravitas* of such a man, whether concentrated on one local congregation or mediated through a national network into several such congregations each represented by a string of such men, is not now easily apprehended. But an understanding of men like Conder is the key to this chapel garden walled around in the pleasure grounds of the Victorian

[27] J. Bailey (ed.), *The Diary of Lady Frederick Cavendish*, 2 vols (1927): B. and Patricia Russell (eds) *The Amberley Papers*, 2 vols (1937).

[28] For the context of the Baines family see C. Binfield, *So Down to Prayers* (1977), pp. 54–100.

[29] For Eustace Rogers Conder 1820–92 see *Congregational Year Book* 1893, pp. 214–16.

political nation. It is a key which Gladstone had his finger on, and which he came closest to turning in the late 1870s.

So from the Gladstone of reminiscence, a novel and a girl's diary to the Gladstone of his own *Diaries*, out of power, out of office, out of official connection with his party, but not out of mind for he was still a British senator and therefore a public man.

A feature of Gladstone's earlier *Diaries* is the extent to which, in his male-menopausal 1850s, he built up an exceptionally wide potential, perhaps actual, power base, simply because he got about. He became known. In large part of course this was the consequence of his personality – his charm, indeed his allure, his stamina, and his incorrigible noseyness. To a degree it was consequent upon the life of any major and serious politician in a society which was still a federation of country houses and Gladstone's own family connexions (and of course his wife's) helped that on famously: Wales, England, Scotland; Hawarden, Fasque, Hagley; an infinite Saturday-to-Monday elasticity, springing to and from that hearth and home of all true country households, London. The Gladstonian dimension to this, however, is less such elasticity (which any Cavendish, Grosvenor, Russell or Leveson-Gower could have worked on, given the temperament) than an interaction with more areas, that is to say more networks, of the British political nation than any other prime politician, certainly any other prime minister, had cared to make. Such interaction was not in itself novel but the Gladstonian intensity of it and the thoroughness were entirely novel. So, to London, Country and Celtic Fringe add Church, 'Oxford' and 'Manchester'; add do-goodery too. Such intersecting is severely constrained if you head an administration. It is the stuff of life if you are in opposition and especially so in a railway age. The federation of country houses worked because each was a carriage drive away from the next. Now the carriage drive away was a railway carriage drive. Gladstone's was the first generation to work this to a fine art. Midlothian is the symbol of this.

In the Midlothian decade, moreover, this Gladstonian intersection was signally enhanced by the Nonconformist network, and if that were still more Bainesocracy and Barranage than Button Hill, the Bainesocracy operated nonetheless in Button Hill. This enhancement was neither new nor uniform but now it came of age. In these years Nonconformists were politically and socially blooded as members of a network integral to the political nation. They were also bloodied. That is not our present concern. Our real concern is that they were more obviously around, socially, professionally, educationally and therefore politically. It would have been unnatural for any Liberal politician with a feel for the political nation to avoid them. Their convergence with Gladstone was as sensibly inevitable as Gladstone's reconvergence with the Liberal leadership.

This is where Gladstone's diaries must be called as evidence. It is not that references to Nonconformists are disproportionate, although their proportion has grown, neither is it that the links thus demonstrated were carefully engineered, though of course they were (Gladstone was too canny not to know what they were after, and who can resist rubbing shoulders, or at least correspondences, with a former Prime Minister and a present statesman?). It is that they were natural. Each party had interests which converged.

Colin Matthew encapsulates Gladstone's style in these years as 'High Church in conception, Evangelical in conviction, and Broad Church in presentation.'[30] No wonder he is so ready a reader of *The Catholic Presbyterian*. It is marvellously encompassed by that famous reflection on the Sunday after Christmas, 1879, as he writes 'in the last minutes of the seventh decade' of his life:-

> *28 December 1879:* . . . For the last 3¹/2 years I have been passing through a political experience which is I believe without example in our Parliamentary history. I profess it to believe it has been an occasion, when the battle to be fought was a battle of justice, humanity, freedom, law, all in their first elements from the very root, and all on a gigantic scale. The word spoken was a word for millions, and for millions who themselves cannot speak. If I really believe this then I should regard my having been morally forced into this work as a great and high election of God . . . But alas the poor little garden of my soul remains uncultivated, unweeded, and defaced. So then while I am bound to accept this election for the time, may I not be permitted to pray that the term shall be short? Three things I would ask of God over and above all the bounty which surrounds me. This first that I may escape into retirement. This second that I may speedily be enabled to divest myself of everything resembling wealth. And the third – if I may – that when God calls me He may call me speedily. To die in Church appears to be a great *euthanasia* but not a time to disturb worshippers. Such are some of the old man's thoughts, in whom there is still something that consents not to be old . . .
>
> . . . All this I ought to have written on my knees: from which were I *never* to rise.
> Last among the last
>   Least among the least
> Can there be a place for me
>   At the marriage feast?[31]

There is the High Churchman whose true home is The Church. There is the Broad Churchman determined not to be a nuisance and a distraction.

---

[30] H.C.G. Matthew (ed.), *The Gladstone Diaries*, Volume IX January 1875–December 1880 (Oxford, 1986), p. XXXVII.
[31] Ibid., pp. 470–1.

There is the Evangelical redeemed, yet in his own true estimation irre-
deemable. But there is more. All this is the very essence of that particular
Nonconformist temper whose dominant accent is Congregational. Here is
true extempore prayer, not the artless spontaneity of unthinking innocence,
but the natural issue of spiritual, disciplined, wrestling. Here is election,
great and high. Here is the Puritan's garden walled around. Here is the
Word – Word as words in the world.

This is the temper in concentrate which informs these diaries. And this is
the temper of those Nonconformists – who are also in all other respects the
weightiest representatives of their churches – most frequently mentioned
in the diaries. Here is a temper shared. Here are men grown aware of a
spiritual, indeed churchly, inheritance held in common.

Like the Nonconformist cousinhood – or the Whig Great-Grandmotherhood
– Gladstone's encounters of the Nonconforming kind are geographically
and denominationally pervasive. There is Principal Rainy for example.
Presbyterianism has to be a fascination for any intelligent Scotchman at
however many removes. No M.P. for a Lowland constituency could ignore
Free Church Presbyterianism, since, were he a Liberal, his committees
increasingly depended on Free Church networks. Gladstone's Midlothian
constituency chairman, John Cowan, the Penicuik papermaker, was such
a man. No representative of Edinburghshire could be blind to the Free
Church's dominating New College, or to the stringpulling power of its
manse-placing Principal; and when its Principal also professes Church
History, could a mere Gladstone hold out?[32]

Dr. Rigg, the Wesleyan, might be viewed in an equally strategic light.[33]
Wesleyanism must be a fascination and a bafflement for an intelligently
nosey passionate English churchman. Hence the Gladstone who ruins a
dinner party by asking 'Imperial' Perks to explain to him the Wesleyan
Methodist 'Body', and smiles politely when Perks corrects 'Body' to
'Church'.[34] Hence too the Gladstone who carefully notes the views of
the Wesleyan barrister and manse son, briefly a Sheffield MP, Samuel
Danks Waddy: 'Found Mr. Waddy under a tenacious conviction that I
am the coming man' (*28 October 1879*); and has then to write six months
later to explain to Waddy why no Wesleyans figure in the coming man's
now come administration: (*21 May 1880*).

If among them there is no member of the Wesleyans I sincerely regret it. I

---

[32] For Robert Rainy 1826–1906 see P. Carnegie Simpson, *The Life of Principal Rainy*, 2
vols (1909); for Sir John Cowan Bt., 1814–1900 see F. Boase, *Modern English Biography*
(1897, reprint 1965), Vol. iv.

[33] For J.H. Rigg 1821–1909 see *Dictionary of National Biography*.

[34] D. Crane, *The Life-Story of Sir Robert W. Perks Baronet, M.P.* n.d. [1909] pp. 111–14.

need not assure you that the circumstance is not due to any prejudice against them in any quarter. Appointments to civil office cannot be substantively governed by religious profession, yet I should be glad, for better knowledge, if you could confidentially supply me with a list of the Wesleyans now in the House of Commons.[35]

But the core of this convergence is Congregational: Henry Allon, J. Guinness Rogers, Newman Hall, Baldwin Brown, all of London; R.W. Dale of Birmingham; A.M. Fairbairn of Bradford, soon to be of Oxford; and Eustace Rogers Conder.[36]

John Parry has amply analysed a complex of reasons for their convergence with Gladstone (and their occasional divergence from him) in the earlier 1870s.[37] I would here for the later 1870s suggest three further dimensions to this: its context of the Word; its aesthetic context; its structural context.

Each of these weighty, intelligent men was a wire puller and an accomplished communicator on a regular basis to sizeable audiences drawn largely from the political nation. That dimension of words needs urgently to be recaptured. 'The word spoken was a word for millions, and for millions who themselves cannot speak', Gladstone mused at the end of the Midlothian year, a fortnight after calculating that in twelve days he had spoken on thirty occasions to 86,930 men and women, for fifteen and a half hours.[38] No wonder the Midlothian years were also years of watching Henry Irving (whose knighthood was a Gladstonian one), of reading, sampling, comparing like any provincial sermon taster:

> *20 July 1879*: the Rector [of St. Marylebone] perfectly complacent delivered a sermon which I can only call pious chatter, perfectly effete, on a grand text . . . which he did nothing to open. In the evening I read Spurgeon's vivid and noble Sermon of last Sunday on the Crisis and the Wars: what a contrast![39]

The pervasive power of such words uttered and published is not to be ignored. This is a culture in which Spurgeon merged into Dickens and Dale into Browning for countless Sunday congregations and weekday

[35] Poor Waddy was not now one of them: he had lost his seat. *Gladstone Diaries*, op.cit., pp. 454, 512. For Waddy 1830–1902 see Stenton and Lees, op.cit., p. 360.
[36] For Henry Allon 1818–92, J. Guinness Rogers 1822–1911, C. Newman Hall 1816–1902, J. Baldwin Brown 1820–84, R.W. Dale 1829–95, A.M. Fairbairn 1838–1912, E.R. Conder 1820–92 see A. Peel, *The Congregational Two Hundred 1530–1948* (1948), pp. 188, 200, 185, 192, 205, 221, 135.
[37] J.P. Parry, *Democracy and Religion: Gladstone and the Liberal Party 1867–1875* (C.U.P., 1986), esp. pp. 200–29.
[38] *Gladstone Diaries*, op.cit., pp. 471, 466.
[39] Ibid., p. 430. For C. H. Spurgeon 1834–92 see *Autobiography*, 2 vols (rev. ed., Banner of Truth Trust, 1973).

reading circles. It is the culture in which 'the best type of Methodist sermon met their desire for knowledge as well as for grace, and if the minister had the sense not to omit the long words but to explain them, so much the better' and in which, when Robert Perks stood for Louth in 1892, he found a large party organisation to all intents and purposes ready made in the eight hundred or so local preachers of his constituency's Wesleyan and Primitive circuits.[40]

The twin contexts for this culture of the Word celebrated in such torrents of words were aesthetic and churchly.

The Nonconformity which Gladstone encountered was culturally in the Victorian mainstream. It was Ruskinian or Pre-Raphaelite and it was very Cook's Tour:

> *5 December 1877*; Went to the opening service of Dr. Allon's Independent Chapel. A notable Sermon from Dr. Dale; and striking music.[41]

Union Chapel, Islington, is one of Victorian Protestant architecture's most catholic triumphs. It is a Gladstone among chapels, at once High, Broad and Evangelical. Its architect, the son of a tutor at Spurgeon's Pastors' College, submitted his design under the name 'Torcello', for here in Islington must be one of the finest Stones of Venice, Santa Fosca rediviva.[42]

When Gladstone visited the real Torcello for himself two years later, he found it all 'tending to modify the received views.'[7 October 1879].[43]

Between 'Torcello' and Torcello there was a visit to another grand chapel, Newman Hall's Christ Church, Westminster Bridge Road. It too announced old values in a new and audacious way, with its combination of octagonal meeting house and Ely Cathedral and its spire in commemoration of Abraham Lincoln. Christ Church was equidistant from Lambeth Palace, Waterloo Station and Bedlam:

> *2 June 1878*: I attended Mr. Newman Hall's remarkable service. He preached a Sermon some part of which would at Oxford 35 years back have brought him into the clutches of Chancellor Winter. It was very brave.[44]

The Gladstonian infrastructure for such visits was usually a barrage of letters, notes and cards. These were more than preparatory courtesies for they were the getting within the skin of the experience which must

---

[40] [Grace Hunter] *Maud Mary McAulay: A Memoir* (1939), p. 57; Crane, op.cit., pp. 172 *et.seq.*

[41] *Glastone Diaries*, op.cit., p. 273.

[42] C. Binfield, 'A Chapel and its Architect: James Cubitt and Union Chapel, Islington, 1879–1899', Diana Wood ed. *The Church and its Arts*, Studies in Church History, 28, Oxford: Blackwell, 1992, pp. 417–448

[43] *Gladstone Diaries*, op.cit., p. 448.

[44] Ibid., p. 319.

be a vital part of any orator's armoury and which was Gladstone's forte. At Union Islington no hearer is out of sight, one to one, eye to eye, soul to soul, of the man in the pulpit. Each hearer is at once individualised and welded into the worshipping community. Union is an ideal arena for any orator or preacher or actor, for whom there can be no communication without rapport. Gladstone spent that June day at Union from 11.30 in the morning to 3.30 in the afternoon. On another June day two years later he was at Mill Hill School, this time from 4 p.m. to 8.15 p.m. Mill Hill was a Free Church boarding school. Its recent past had been bumpy and its great days (a knighted headmaster and membership of the Headmasters' Conference) were not yet, but there were few prominent Dissenting families without Mill-Hillian links. Dr. Weymouth, the headmaster, was a Baptist. Gladstone's preparatory letters to him began on 28 May. On 10 June he noted: 'Dr. Weymouth's Address: read.' Next day:

> To Mill Hill. Went over the buildings and delivered an Address of perhaps three-quarters of an hour after distributing the prizes. An institution strikingly *alive*. Read Mill Mill Magazine and worked on papers about the School.[45]

Such an address at such a time to such an audience, with its promise of bright futurity, could not fail politically; and here too it was mind speaking to mind, Gladstone expressed something of this when he wrote to F.H.C. Doyle in May 1880:

> My fears are excited by the manner in which a large proportion of the educated community is wheedling itself out of the greatest and brightest of all its possessions, the 'jewel of great price'. That great divide between the actual Christian religion and the trained human reason, which has long marked most countries of the continent, has during the past twenty-five years been too perceptible in this country, and is producing its natural fruit in the declining morality of the upper portion of society . . . [and he added] my life has certainly been remarkable for the mass of continuous and searching experience it has brought me.[46]

Value to value; mind to mind, culture to culture; voice to voice. And structure to structure.

The word which best describes the Nonconformist structure – its 'churchmanship' to use a concept which would have teased Gladstone – is 'representative'. The Nonconformist denominations, none of them democratic, each of them representative, were models of what the British political system might become. Each chapel housed not so much Sunday

---

[45] Ibid., p. 420. For R.F. Weymouth 1822–1902 see E. Hampden–Cook, *The Register of Mill Hill School 1807–1926* (priv., 1926), p. 455.
[46] *Gladstone Diaries*, op.cit., pp. 519–20.

sermon-tasters who might on weekdays vote Liberal, as a daily community of interests (almost in the old political sense of the word), each distinct within the one community, their totality fuelling the activities of dozens, perhaps hundreds, of men and women, offering each one a 'continuous and searching experience', rippling out into the wider community. All of them – Sunday school, Mission auxiliary, choir, Bible class – were within the pale of the congregational constitution, as a chapel Gladstone might have put it.

Well within that pale is the political nation proper, the Christian elec-torate, the Methodist Society or the Baptist or Congregational Church, men and women whose mere adherence has turned into membership. Their membership was a commitment consciously taken in obedience to a religious experience duly recognised by others of like experience. Only they constitute the church. They alone attend the meetings which legislate for the church's well-being. They alone elect their officers, call their minister. Those officers, the deacons of a Baptist or a Congregational Church form a House of Lords to church meeting's Commons. Or rather they form a cabinet, with a prime minister, who is the minister. The two fused easily. 'We want theological Mr. Gladstones', cried Thomas Coote, Howard Coote's father, up in Rotherham for the opening of its rebuilt Congregational theological college in 1876.[47] Their call, like Gladstone's, was to serve. It was also to lead. It was to liberate the dynamic which is the motor of that collective known as chapel.

That dynamic explains what made Button Hill for Gordon Stowell. It makes sense of Katharine Conder's otherwise pleasingly unexceptionable family circle. It charges a network which a Gladstone might mentally and politically intersect. That intersection is at once a conscious strategy and quite natural.

Take, for example, the closing months of 1878 and the opening months of 1879. They saw the round of Hawarden, Harley Street and the country houses: Betteshanger in East Kent, Mentmore in Rothschildia and Clumber in the Dukeries. They saw the socialisings of a serious public man: dinner with the Bishop of Winchester followed by the Duchess of Edinburgh's reception. And woven into these higher normalities are the reading of John Stoughton on Religion in the Reigns of Anne and the Georges,[48] or writing on the Evangelical Movement for Henry Allon's *British Quarterly Review* and corresponding with him accordingly. Stoughton and Allon were ecclesiastics in cousinhood and the *Review* was an organ of cousinhood. Herbert Asquith, a nephew of Katharine Conder's uncle Willans, cut his literary teeth on Allon's *Review*, and in his London days uncle

---

[47] *Rotherham and Masbro' Advertiser* 23 September 1876.
[48] For John Stoughton 1807–97 see Peel, op.cit., p. 167.

Willans had been one of Allon's deacons. And Allon's co-editor, H.R. Reynolds,[49] was grandpapa Baines's brother-in-law and had been E.R. Conder's predecessor at East Parade Chapel (he was also the successor of Gordon Stowell's great grandfather as President of Cheshunt College). At the turn of the year Leeds was in Gladstone's mind in the shape of the life of Dean Hook. ('What a man – what a husband!')[50] whose Leeds Parish Church was increasingly tugging at the loyalties of the younger Baineses.

There were further consequences. When Gladstone read about 'The Water Supply of London' in *Fraser's*, he was reading a piece by F.R. Conder, Eustace's civil engineer brother.[51] When he wrote on 30 December 1878 to the Episcopalian incumbent of Fraserburgh to acknowledge his *The Real Character of the Early Records of Genesis* (which he dutifully looked at before turning to Dean Hook and chopping down a beech tree) he was writing to an apostate cousin of Eustace Conder's first wife.[52] When, on 8 January 1879, he was formally invited to stand for Midlothian, the invitation came from an association whose chairman, as we have seen, was (Sir) John Cowan.[53] Cowan's niece, Charlotte Cowan (herself an M.P.'s daughter), was married to H.J. Wilson, the precious metal smelter and future M.P. whose family increasingly ran Sheffield Liberalism.[54] The Wilsons and their kinsmen, the Leaders and Pye-Smiths, were the very pattern of Sheffield Congregationalism and Sheffield's Leadership was a faint yet distinct reflection of the Leeds Bainesocracy, to which of course the Leaders, Pye-Smiths and Wilsons were closely connected by marriage.

Sheffield furnishes the ultimate naturalness in the Gladstonian-Nonconformist convergence of these years. When the Gladstones grudgingly gave up 11 Carlton House Terrace for 73 Harley Street, their neighbour was Mrs. Birks. Gladstone enjoyed her hospitality and frequently dined there. Colin Matthew has discovered that Mrs. Birks was locketed, ringleted and Pre-Raphaelite and suspects that her money came from brewing since Gladstone wrote to her about the malt tax.[55] It did. No Laura Thistlethwayte or Mme Novikov she, Judith Ann Birks was the widow of Thomas Birks, a Sheffield brewer and former mayor. Samuel Plimsoll had been one of his clerks.[56]

---

[49] For H.R. Reynolds 1825–96 see ibid., p. 203.

[50] *Gladstone Diaries*, op.cit., p. 380.

[51] Francis Roubiliac Conder 1815–89. Ibid., p. 489.

[52] Ibid., p. 374.

[53] Ibid., p. 381.

[54] For H.J. Wilson 1837–1914 see Stenton and Lees, op.cit., p. 377.

[55] *Gladstone Diaries*, op.cit., p. LXXX.

[56] Judith Anne Elam was the second wife of Thomas Birks, d.1861, brewer and mayor of Sheffield in 1849. For the Plimsoll link see G.H. Peters *The Plimsoll Line* (1975), pp. 11, 14.

Birks's family, the brewery notwithstanding, were active at two, perhaps three, Sheffield Congregational churches. Katharine Conder's great uncle, Thomas Smith, had ministered at one of them. Thomas Rawson Birks, Old Mill Hillian and Knightsbridge Professor at Cambridge, was Thomas Birks's first cousin.[57] There were other connexions. Mrs. Birks's daughter was Mrs. Louis Crossley of Moorside, Halifax, whom Katharine Conder visited in 1880 and with whom Lady Frederick Cavendish, Mrs. Gladstone's niece, stayed for the 1880 election.[58] Louis Crossley was the brother of Mrs. Marchetti and the first cousin of Edward Crossley also mentioned in Katharine Conder's diaries. He was the uncle of the future Mrs. Speaker Whitley. This was the very purple of Congregationalism. As for Mrs. Birks, her own Congregationalism had survived Sheffield at least to February 1876, since she was until then a member of Westminster Chapel.[59] There she had sat under Samuel Martin, which might explain her Pre-Raphaelite air since Westminster Chapel was where the art-collecting Glasgow M.P., William Graham, had worshipped when in Town.[60]

Whatever the state of Mrs. Birks's churchmanship at the time of her dinners for Mr. Gladstone its *context* – whether expressed as something to be reacted against or developed from or not mentioned at all (being taken for granted) – cannot have been wholly unknown to him. (*22 March 1878* 'Spent the forenoon at a breakfast of Nonconformists around Mrs. Birks's table: much interesting conversation').[61] It completes my case for the naturalness of such links between Dissent's thinking classes, even if at their chattering edge, and the Westminster classes as concentrated so memorably on this one man, representative because outsize. He was the first Prime Minister whom they could easily see and quite likely meet and come to feel that they knew, without ever having to dethrone him from his necessary pedestal. Hence the importance of such myths as the thirtyfold chewing of each mouthful: outsize, grand, yet down-to-earth – and given the state of the nation's bowels, not least Gladstone's own (at the turn of 1879 he was a martyr to 'internal insecurity'),[62] those myths were not entirely implausible.

The convergence between Gladstone and Dissent was unique. No other politician could have retained that response once elicited, or been so

[57] For T.R. Birks 1810–83 see *Dictionary of National Biography*.

[58] J. Bailey (ed.), op.cit., vol. II, p. 247.

[59] Judith Birks was a member of Westminster Chapel 1870–6. Her daughter Hannah was a member 1862–6, transferring her membership from the chapel at the time of her marriage to Louis Crossley. Members List, Westminster Chapel 1849–66, 1866–1908.

[60] For Samuel Martin 1817–78 see Peel, op.cit., p. 187; for William Graham 1817–85 see Stenton, op.cit., vol. I (1832–85), p. 163.

[61] *Gladstone Diaries*, op.cit., p. 300.

[62] Ibid., p. 386.

interested in it, or indeed would have wished to or needed to. Of Gladstone's prime ministerial predecessors, Russell could have been the only serious candidate and he is easily ruled out. Gladstone's successors in theory furnish several candidates but it is only theory. Asquith is the one who belongs most securely to the Nonconformist cousinhood. His was Katharine Conder's world.[63] But Asquith made little active and no consistent use of them after 1890, although they did not let him slip away quite as easily as the biographers make out. Though for a while a church member, Asquith was not in the old sense a serious person. The form never ceased to interest him, and it marked him. The reality was irrelevant to him.

There is of course a generational dimension to this. After 1918, increasingly no doubt after 1885, that Congregational representativeness which was so consonant with how things seemed to be going constitutionally ceased to march with the van of progress. Regardless of any spiritual affinity, the intellectual allure was vanishing and the political attraction was visibly diminishing. Votes are not easily deployed to best advantage in a system of universal suffrage, especially if it has in fact never really been possible to take their uniformity for granted. As for that artefact of the years after 1885, the 'Nonconformist Conscience', it was more of a smokescreen than anything else, real (since smoke is real enough) but misleading. Behind it lay Nonconformist influences in almost bewildering diversity and among them was the Gladstonian *rapport*, but they were influences only, increasingly more memory than reality.

Yet influences have their power. For was not Gladstonianism after the mid-1870s one person's prejudices elevated to a system, like Thatcherism? And like Thatcherism it caught hold because it seized on the prejudices (though for Gladstone 'sympathies' is a fairer word) of all men of push and go; and since people of push and go end often in the Establishment so they became assimilated.

The theme of *The History of Button Hill* is less its dissolution, even its dilution, than its diffusion. That is also the theme of the Conder cousinhood. Ethel Mary, Katharine's admired elder sister, transmitted its values as headmistress of a school for ministers' daughters, proud of its links with the women at Cambridge.[64] Katharine married an opthalmic surgeon in Kensington. Her brother Laurie became an architect in Buenos Aires. Little Eddie became an Anglican parson.[65] Cousin Talbot, not mentioned in these extracts but frequently mentioned nonetheless in the diaries, married

[63] See C. Binfield 'Asquith: The Formation of a Prime Minister', *The Journal of the United Reformed Church History Society*, vol. 2, No. 7, April 1981, pp. 204–42.
[64] Ethel Mary Conder 1859–1942 second headmistress of Milton Mount College 1889–1906.
[65] For Canon Edward Baines Conder 1872–1936 see *Who Was Who* 1929–1940, p. 279.

en second noces a niece of Lady Frederick Cavendish, and a great-niece by marriage, therefore, of Mrs. Gladstone: more to the point she was at once a Tory M.P.'s daughter and a niece of one of Dean Hook's successors as Vicar of Leeds.[66]

This suggests less the failure of Nonconformity's politics, theology or nerve than their success. It suggests values as much assimilated as overturned or jettisoned, the values of a representative 'churchmanship', broad but freely elected, which is to say *élite*; the values of order as opposed to anarchy; of trust rather than democracy. These are the natural values of sound establishments, and they have been open to much question by the grocer's daughter who would herself have been nowhere without their formative powers.

I began with an identikit story, Colin Coote's family lore of the mesmeric Gladstone. Here, to end, is another. The scene is Scotch baronial, Glen Tana. The action is a late Victorian conversation between the old laird and his landscape architect, whose story it is:

> I remember . . . telling . . . a story about Gladstone . . . describing how the veteran statesman, with his personal charm, won the Midlothian election. 'I believe every word of that story', said Sir William, 'for I have experienced the fascination of his evil eye. One night' he continued, 'when a very important discussion was on, Gladstone fixed me with his eye and literally dragged me into the Government lobby; but just then he transfixed another victim, and the spell being broken, I bolted!'[67]

Sir William was a banker, Tory, Anglican, house in Grosvenor Square, patron of two livings, father-in-law of a Marquess and of a Marquess's younger son, such a father-in-law indeed as a Lascelles might approve. He was, nonetheless, the son-in-law of a Stockport Wesleyan and the son of a Manchester Congregationalist whose money had made possible the theological college whose first principal was the founder editor of Henry Allon's and H.R. Reynolds's *British Quarterly Review*. And the landscape architect embellishing Sir William's traditionary carapace was Thomas Mawson, an admirable choice for a landowner who wished to shape his countryside as if it had ever been thus.[68] Mawson, who had a Gladstone for a client, was a lifelong Congregationalist. That is to say, he was not just an individual who happened to be a Congregationalist rather than a New Connexion Methodist or a Baptist, so much as a member of a church, or

---

[66] For Talbot Baines 1852–1927 see C. Binfield, *So Down to Prayers* (1977), pp. 99–100.

[67] T.H. Mawson, *The Life and Work of an English Landscape Architect* n.d. (*c*.1927) p. 51; for Sir William Cunliffe-Brooks 1819–1900 see Stenton and Lees, op.cit., vol. II, pp. 46–7; for the family background see L.H. Grindon, *Manchester Banks and Bankers* (Manchester, 1878), pp. 202–18. I am indebted to Dr. Douglas Farnie for this reference.

[68] Thomas H. Mawson 1861–1933 see Mawson, op.cit.

society, such as that described in the *Manual* of Purley's Congregational Church, newer than Button Hill's, Southern and more select, but just as set on making its way with some integrity:

> A society has a soul of its own which far exceeds the sum total of the individual souls who compose it. Thought, emotion, enthusiasm and strength come to an individual from an inspired community which he could not realise without it. The soul-life of each is enhanced by the general soul . . . the power of the corporate life acts upon the individual . . . A church whose atmosphere is charged with spirituality of a healthy and practical, as well as richly spiritual kind, will draw men irresistibly into the sweep of its power . . .[69]

That is the crucible for chapel values. However 'Victorian' they cannot be Mrs. Thatcher's 'Victorian values' since for all her Wesleyan childhood and her husband's Free Church schooling,[70] she has no room for such society, but they are the values of the Cromwell country and Button Hill and Mr. Gladstone respected them.

[69] Purley Congregational Church, *Manual 1914*, p. 1.
[70] Sir Denis Thatcher was educated at Mill Hill School.

Proceedings of the British Academy, **78**, 109–127

Goodness and Goods:
Victorian Literature and Values
for the Middle Class Reader

VALENTINE CUNNINGHAM
Corpus Christi College, Oxford

'WE are a commercial people', said Matthew Arnold in one of his late essays, 'The Incompatibles'.[1] And readers of Arnold are familiar with his devoted problematising of Victorian materialism. In a typical passage of *Culture and Anarchy*, where once again he was attacking the spirit of 'our free-trading Liberal friends', he declared that his target was the mechanical worship of the 'fetish of the production of wealth and of the increase of manufactures and population'.[2] On this view, materialism – the pursuit of ever-expanding money prosperity, conspicuous consumption, the uninhibited growth of commerce – was false religion, a sort of paganism more appropriate to darkest Africa than Christian England, and thus bad morals. What Arnold was trying to do was to drive a wedge into the common equation – an equation built into the English language – between the good and (material) goods: what Mrs. Bulstrode in *Middlemarch* (Ch. 61) called 'perishable good'.

'Perishable good': the echo in the phrase of Christ's words about not laying up treasure on earth where moth and rust corrupt and thieves break through and steal, was clear. And Arnold's answer to those who thought that 'Business is Civilization' was also to resort to Biblical words

Read 13 December 1990. © The British Academy 1992.
[1] Matthew Arnold, 'The Incompatibles', *Irish Essays and Others* (1882; Popular Edition, Smith, Elder, and Co., 1891), 1–58.
[2] Matthew Arnold, 'Our Liberal Practitioners', *Culture and Anarchy* (1869), ed. J. Dover Wilson (Cambridge University Press, 1963), 195.

and Christianised moral imperatives. He used the words of Christ in reply
to the temptation of Satan: 'It is written: *Man doeth not live by bread
alone*'. This was, again, in 'The Incompatibles' essay. Equally striking
about this essay is that it also calls in aid a novelist and a novel, Charles
Dickens and *David Copperfield*. Dickens gets invoked because, Arnold
declares, he knew the middle class 'intimately' ('he was bone of its bone
and flesh of its flesh. Intimately he knew its bringing up'). Salem House,
the ghastly school to which little David is sent in *David Copperfield*, is
taken as representative of middle-class schooling. The awful Murdstones,
who take over David's early life, hard, calculating, grasping, puritanical
people, are read by Arnold as characteristic of a wide middle-class faith
in the morality, the virtue, of commercial activity. And Arnold's use of
Dickens was not at all casual. He was carefully drawing support for his
polemic from a chief representative of what was a huge contemporary
writing army of men and women who offered repeated literary critiques
of crude economic advantage and of a shoddy ethical confusion between
moral goodness and the possession of material things.

Nor was it distortive of Dickens and the whole anti-materialist school
of literary thought to frame that body of writing in Biblical quotation and
reference, for Dickens and the rest were steeped in the New Testament's
habit of siding with the poor.

Victorian writing is full of Good Samaritans – Cheerybles, a Brownlow,
a Dorothea Brooke, a Jane Eyre – personal benefactors who share their
material goods with the less well-off. 'The Good Samaritan was a Bad
Economist': that, we're told in *Hard Times* (Ch. 12), is what Mr. Gradgrind,
northern manufacturer, Liberal MP and devotee of *laissez faire* economic
principles, is seeking to prove in his writings. Biblically inspired sympathy
for the poor ran directly counter to the self-advantaging doctrines of
Political Economy – what *Hard Times* labels as 'the fictions of Coketown',
the untruths promoted by Gradgrind's friend and ally Josiah Bounderby.
This Biblicised body of fictional writings is the one that has given the
English Language the name Scrooge as the title of all selfish, miserly
persons, the opposites of Good Samaritans. 'You all know the parable of
the Good Samaritan', Charles Kingsley told his Liverpool audience in June
1870, when he preached his famous 'Human Soot' sermon on behalf of the
Kirkdale Ragged School.[3] And acting the true Good Samaritan, declared
Kingsley, would involve far more than simply contributing to the funds of a
Ragged School. There were great armies of destitute children on the streets
of northern cities who were crying out for quite radical assistance.

---

[3] *Charles Kingsley, His Letters and Memories of His Life*, ed. By His Wife (Henry S. King
and Co, 1877), II, 322–6.

Kingsley particularly appeals to women, the wives and daughters of the commercial men of Liverpool. And women writers, people like George Eliot, Mrs. Gaskell, Charlotte Brontë, were particularly moved to express this sort of Christian sympathy in their texts. George Eliot, her atheism totally moulded by Christian ethics, proposed sympathy for ordinary people, which should be provoked by realistic portraits in realistic fictions, as the very essence of art: 'a picture of human life such as a great artist can give, surprises even the trivial and the selfish into that attention to what is apart from themselves, which may be called the raw material of moral sentiment. . . . Art is the nearest thing to life; it is a mode of amplifying experience and extending our contact with our fellow-men beyond the bounds of our personal lot. All the more sacred is the task of the artist when he undertakes to paint the life of the People.'[4]

But the Biblically based, Christian appeal on behalf of the poor was not limited to females. 'The Good Samaritan', Kingsley declared in the Human Soot sermon, 'would have known what his duty was; and I trust that you will know, in like case, what your duty is'; and he meant to include men too. Men and women had the same Lord, and so the same responsibilities. 'For is not this . . . your relation to these children in your streets? ragged, dirty, profligate, untaught, perishing – of whom our Lord has said, "It is not the will of your Father in Heaven that one of these little ones should perish".' And it's in agreement with this Biblical approach that Dickens has the dying crossing-sweeper of *Bleak House*, the London waif Joe, coached in the Lord's Prayer by the good Doctor Woodcourt before the Dickensian text rounds angrily on Christian England: 'Dead, Right Reverends and Wrong Reverends of every order. Dead, men and women, born with Heavenly compassion in your hearts. And dying thus around us every day' (Ch. 49). When this kind of fiction thinks of the homeless, it's prayerfully – like Copperfield, once he's safely rescued from his spell of tramping: 'and how I prayed that I never might be homeless any more, and never forget the houseless' (Ch. 13).

Admittedly, respectable Victorian fiction is happiest with the virtuous and educable poor, the honest labourer, the picturesquely Rembrandtesque worker – Stephen Blackpool, Joe Gargery, Adam and Seth Bede, Caleb Garth, Jude the quiet and obscure, Mr. Toodles – many of whom get named ostentatiously for Bible characters and

---

[4] George Eliot, 'The Natural History of German Life', *Westminster Review* (July 1856); *Selected Essays, Poems and Other Writings*, ed. A.S. Byatt and Nicholas Warren (Penguin, 1990), 110.

well-known Christian saints, and who will prove worthy candidates for the role of Christ in the Carpenter's Shop. Admittedly, too, this fiction is commonly discomfited by more marginal labourers, such as the river-men and dust-men of *Our Mutual Friend*, the brick-workers of *Bleak House*, the likes of Matthew Arnold's Zephaniah Diggs – 'my poor old poaching friend . . . who, between his hare-snaring and his gin-drinking, has got his powers of sympathy quite dulled and his powers of action in any great movement of his class hopelessly impaired'.[5] But however disturbed by what Arnold called the 'festering masses' of East London – 'children eaten up with dis-ease, half-sized, half-fed, half-clothed, neglected by their parents, without health, without home, without hope'[6] – these Christian and Christianised writers could not help recalling that these were just the people for whom Christ had become poor, homeless, marginal, a consorter with outcasts and rejects, the demented, lepers, Samari-tans, a woman with an issue of blood. These were the very ones Christ had died for outside the City Wall in the Jerusalem garbage tip.

Theological considerations of this kind animate Charles Kingsley's extra-ordinary Liverpool indictment of the manufacturing systems of Britain as being designed explicitly and consciously to produce a calculated quantity of Human Soot, wasted trash people, a filthy discarded human by-product that is as much a built-in and accepted part of the economics of manufactures as the certain by-product of smoke, soot, ashes. This particular economic analysis, buttressing a theological allegation and solution, is, of course, what provided the imaginative drive and stimulus for Kingsley's novel about the Human Soot of Britain, *The Water Babies* (1863). A not dissimilar theology of Christ's wasted people likewise spurred Robert Browning. His poem 'Fra Lippo Lippi' (1855), for example, is the story of a street arab compelled to live at the social margin on waste matters, the chucked-away trash of the city: 'On fig-skins, melon-parings, rinds and shucks/Refuse and rubbish'. This lad 'learns the look of things' by keeping an eye out for which person is likely to let him keep a bit of discarded 'half-stripped grape-bunch', which dog is likely to yield up 'His bone from the heap of offal in the street', which gentleman in church will 'let him lift a plate and catch/The droppings of wax to sell again'. (George Eliot quoted extensively from just these passages of 'Fra Lippo Lippi' in her approving review of Browning's *Men and Women* volume in *The Westminster Review* of

---

[5] *Culture and Anarchy*, ed. cit., p. 100.
[6] *Culture and Anarchy*, ed. cit., p. 194.

January 1856.)[7] Mrs. Gaskell's presentation of the grisly existence of the cellar-dwellers of Manchester in *Mary Barton* (1848) comes out of precisely the same sort of theological calculations. So, again, does the picture of Jane Eyre's destitution after she has fled from a bigamous marriage to Rochester, when the starving girl eagerly eats up 'a mess of cold porridge' intended for pigs (*Jane Eyre*, 1847, Ch. 28). Biblically minded readers would know they were to compassionate with this unwillingly prodigal-like, wandering daughter who would 'fain have filled her belly with the husks that the swine did eat.' The economic arrangements of Britain were being condemned because of their obviously inhuman tactics, their evil management of the circulation of wealth and resources, in these presented acts of desperate recycling – the wax droppings, the pig food – and the cruel fate of these wasted human beings, the Human Soot, compelled to live like trash upon trash. And the empowering of this criticism of a malevolent economy was Biblical theology.

Conversely, but still Biblically, the love of money is repeatedly demonstrated in Victorian literature to be the root of all evil. Again and again the plots of Victorian novels are arranged to demonstrate that the craving for money, the desire to get far on the upgrade of prosperity, simply corrupts. Eliot's Silas Marner, *Middlemarch*'s Bulstrode, *Bleak House*'s Richard Jarndyce, *Great Expectations*' Pip are all examples of the corrupting power of greed. Great financial expectations rot the self. In a telling passage of *The Mill on the Floss* (Bk. 4, Ch. 3) George Eliot contrasts 'good society', that is wealthy people, adversely with the 'unfashionable lives' that she would persuade her readers are morally superior both as people and as subjects for fiction. This moralised aesthetic seeks to invert snobbish assumptions about the value of 'good society'. This fiction will be on the side of the huge underclass, however over-earnest and emphatic (Eliot's wry adjectives) that it might be about gin or religious enthusiasm, because of its economic wastedness. This despised class *spends* itself to keep the fashionable, the subjects of fashionable fiction, in their leisure. George Eliot arranges *Silas Marner* precisely as a miniature allegory of the alienating power of cash. Cash cuts you off from human company. Silas is saved when he loses his gold and finds the golden-haired little child Eppie who leads him, in sound Biblical fashion, back into the society of his fellow-villagers (a little child leading the erstwhile miser back into a secular version of the Kingdom of Heaven). According to Kingsley (in his pamphlet about the sweating trades, *Cheap Clothes and Nasty*, 1850), capitalism is cannibalistic; it eats up its own wage-slaves. Again and again Dickens demonstrates that the cash-nexus is

---

[7] George Eliot, *Westminster Review* (January 1856); *Selected Essays*, ed. cit., 349–57.

destructive of fellow-feeling, humanity, family, loving relationships. This is
what divides Pip from Joe Gargery, Mr. Dombey from his family and his
employees, indeed from the whole world of the non-rich. Ch. 20 of *Dombey
and Son*, the famous railway station encounter between Mr. Dombey and
Mr. Toodles, stoker of the train, has rightly been seized on by critics as
central to Dickens's vision of the relative moral weight of the rich and
the artisan class. Toodles is filthy, covered in the dust and ashes of his
profession, a piece of Human Soot no less. Mr. Dombey looks at him
'as if a man like that would make his eyesight dirty'. Dombey would
shrug off Toodles's personal interest in his grief – Toodles's wife was
wet-nurse to Paul Dombey who has recently died. Dombey wants no
personal engagement with such people: when Polly Toodles worked for
him she was renamed Richards as part of a casually cruel but carefully
contrived depersonalising process. It's particularly gruelling to Dombey,
then, to perceive that the piece of new black crepe in Toodles's stoker's
cap is a mark of mourning for Paul Dombey. What's more, Toodles will
not take charity: handing out cash haughtily is Dombey's usual way, and
Toodles, a 'professional' man now, in railway employ, will have none of
it. His claim is on a fellow-feeling that gold has nothing to do with, and the
rich man is upset as well as morally condemned by his resistance to that:

> To think of this presumptuous raker among coals and ashes going on before
> there, with his sign of mourning! To think that he dared to enter, even by
> a common show like that, into the trial and disappointment of a proud
> gentleman's secret heart! To think that this lost child, who was to have
> divided with him his riches, and his projects, and his power, and allied
> with whom he was to have shut out all the world as with a double door of
> gold, should have let in such a herd to insult him with their knowledge of
> his defeated hopes, and their boasts of claiming community of feeling with
> himself . . . .

The cash-connection, which is the only one that the rich man – even the
proudly charitable one like Dombey – will allow, has to be physically
annihilated, as in the extraordinary ritual burning of the two one-pound
notes that Pip at first supposes to be the only connection between himself
and the returned convict Magwitch (Ch. 39):

> He watched me as I laid my purse upon the table and opened it, and he
> watched me as I separated two one-pound notes from its contents. They
> were clean and new, and I spread them out and handed them over to him.
> Still watching me, he laid them one upon the other, folded them long-wise,
> gave them a twist, set fire to them at the lamp, and dropped the ashes into
> the tray.

There's more in human relations and obligations than can be dissolved by
the simple paying back of an old bit of charity – the two greasy pound notes

that Magwitch contrived to have sent to Pip as reward for the stolen pie and metal file and the small human contact out on the marshes years before. What's more, there are further lessons for Magwitch to learn. His mistake is to believe that all the cash he's lavished from the distance of Australia on making Pip into a gentleman will buy him the affection of the now well-off youth. It takes some time before true affection grows between the orphan and his surrogate father.

What both parties in the Pip-Magwitch relationship have to learn is that money dehumanises. Money relationships turn the parties to them into things, absorb flesh and blood into the fetishised object world where people are simply one more possessable item in a scene of mere possessions. Pip had a glimpse of this quite early in his career, when (Ch. 19), ready cash in hand, he went along to Trabb the tailor and found himself to have become an object in a world of things and numbers. Trabb calls for rolls of cloth by their numbers; he touches Pip possessively; he measures him 'as if I were an estate'. Money is the immediate cause of Pip's being metamorphosed into the mere stuff of the materialist world of the Victorian capitalist imagination. It's the world of Mr. Podsnap who (*Our Mutual Friend*, Ch. 11) plumes himself 'in the midst of his possessions', which include his daughter and the guests at his dinner-table , who are all put away at night like so many items of the Podsnap plate:

> Certain big, heavy vehicles, built on the model of the Podsnap plate, took away the heavy articles of guests weighing ever so much; and the less valuable articles got away after their various manners; and the Podsnap plate was put to bed.

People as mere articles to be disposed of by rich possessors: it's a constant theme of Henry James's sharp reflections on parents and lovers and husbands. Pansy Osmond in *The Portrait of a Lady* (1881), is so treated by her father and by the suitor, Rosier. Rosier's appreciation of Pansy is all one with his appreciation of Madame Merle's 'jolly good things'. Gilbert Osmond greatly resents it when another suitor, Warburton, rejects his daughter as one might turn down a 'suite of apartments' after having got a month's lodging there for nothing. And it's not the idea that a daughter on the marriage market should be treated like an apartment up for sale or rent that's offensive to this father, only the eventual spurning of a prospective deal. 'I want a great woman', declares Christopher Newman of James's *The American* (1877, Ch. 3):

> What else have I toiled and struggled for all these years? I have succeeded, and now what am I to do with success? To make it perfect, as I see it, there must be a beautiful woman perched on the pile, like a statue on a monument. . . . She shall have everything a woman can desire; I shall not

even object to her being too good for me; she may be cleverer and wiser than I can understand, and I shall only be the better pleased. I want to possess, in a word, the best article in the market.

Newman is only putting bluntly and crudely the attitude that prompts Mr. Dombey, or Rochester in *Jane Eyre* or, *mutatis mutandis*, Casaubon in *Middlemarch*. Women are particularly focused on in Victorian writing in their role as tradeable articles in the bourgeois marriage market. But the depersonalising, materialising, fetishising effect that enslaves them to the ownership of their husbands is only a particular example of an inclusive materialising effect that the literature of the time is widely anxious to satirise.

Victorian plots are obsessively hostile to what Tennyson in his long poem *Maud* (1855) called, in yet another Biblically inspired accusation, 'Mammonism'. Mammonites are the greedy, like Bella Wilfer in *Our Mutual Friend*, hardened by her desire 'to be r-r-rich'. They're the crudely, ostentatiously well-off, like Maud's Sultan-like brother, or Mr. Dombey, or the Veneerings of *Our Mutual Friend*, or the elegantly got-up Brocklehurst women and Rochester's house-guests in *Jane Eyre*. They're the easy-money people – the women who marry or are married off for money (the likes of Edith Dombey); the relatives who jostle greedily for inheritances (such as the Featherstone family and friends in *Middlemarch*); the chisellers, cheats and swindlers who populate Victorian novels in such numbers, like Uriah Heep (*David Copperfield*), Carker (*Dombey*), the Chadbands (*Bleak House*), Bulstrode (*Middlemarch*), the Bumbles (*Oliver Twist*); gamblers like Gwendolen Harleth in *Daniel Deronda* and Lydgate and Fred Vincy in *Middlemarch*; investors, especially those involved in stock-market scams, like the Lammles in *Our Mutual Friend* or Merdle in *Little Dorrit*.

And the filthy rich are – well – filthy. Acquiring money is connected again and again in Victorian fiction with some sort of moral blackness, and that evil's physical emblems and analogues – with crime, darkness, filth, trash, with the lower places of the city, the world and the self, with madness and with particular kinds of exile and alienation (as in *Oliver Twist* where the slums are the haunts of the fearful Irish and Jews as well as of criminals). Becoming rich is linked with the fears and anxieties provoked by a terrifying sense of otherness. Mad, jilted Miss Havisham in *Great Expectations* is the emblem of such awful estrangement. The narrator of *Maud*, a Victorian update of Hamlet, is driven insane by his encounters with the Mammonism, both public and private, of Victorian England – a dementing congeries of money-making wickedness that Tennyson approaches in a whole clutch of references to other literacy accusers of the age, including Kingsley's *Alton Locke* and Dickens's *The Old Curiosity Shop*. Magwitch, the outcast from the prison hulks who makes money down-under in criminalised Australia, is just one representative of this sense of the darkly alienating filthiness of lucre. So is Mr. Boffin, the Golden Dustman of *Our Mutual Friend*, his wealth accumulated from his trade in the waste of London, the accumulated trash-heaps of the city: 'Coal-dust, vegetable-dust, bone-dust, crockery dust, rough dust and sifted dust, – all manner of Dust' (Ch. 2).

And this filth is hard to wash off or clean up. There are ritually arranged baptisms or cleansing operations in the fiction, but redemption for this particular kind of corruption is difficult to come by. The two clean one-pound notes that Pip offers in exchange for the filthy pair he originally received from Magwitch aren't accepted by Magwitch, or by the text, as in any way a recuperation into purity. In the same novel the lawyer Jaggers may be able to get the dirt of Newgate out of his fingernails, by dint of his obsessive hand-washings and persistent use of his pen-knife as a nail-file, but he can't get the dirt of Newgate – a criminal association which enriches both him and his portable-property accumulating assistant Wemmick – out of his life. Ritual washings are simply not regenerative enough. The very water of washing or pseudo-baptism that Gaffer Hexam employs in the opening pages of *Our Mutual Friend* is after all the slimy ooze of the Thames, and the cash he's seeking to sanctify remains spoil taken from dead bodies:

> It was not until now that the upper half of the man came back into the boat. His arms were wet and dirty, and he washed them over the side. In his right hand he held something, and he washed that in the river too. It was money. He chinked it once, and he blew upon it once, and spat upon it once, – 'for luck', he hoarsely said – before he put it in his pocket.

'There's some things that I never found among the dust', said Boffin: not everything in the world 'wears to rags'. Love, for instance, isn't such trashy stuff. But everything is trash in what *Household Words* called 'The City of Unlimited Paper', the world of stock-jobbing fortunes, paper affluence, greedy stock-market bubbles, the new financial Babylonia, a moral and spiritual wasteland presided over by such financial houses as Strawboy and Rag of Fustian Lane, or Chaos, Rotbill and Clay of Bankside.[8] And the financial smashes, scams and bankruptcies that result from doings in that surrealistic materialist nightmare zone are essentially of moral significance:

> Next day it was noised abroad that Dombey and Son had stopped, and next night there was a List of Bankrupts published, headed by that name.
> The world was very busy now, in sooth, and had a deal to say. It was an innocently credulous and a much ill used world. It was a world in which there was no other sort of bankruptcy whatever. There were no

---

[8] 'The City of Unlimited Paper', *Household Words* (19 December 1857), 1–4.

conspicuous people in it trading far and wide on rotten banks of religion, patriotism, virtue, honour. There was no amount worth mentioning of mere paper in circulation, on which anybody lived pretty handsomely, promising to pay great sums of goodness with no effects. There were no short-comings anywhere, in anything but money. The world was very angry indeed; and the people especially, who, in a worse world, might have been supposed to be bankrupt traders themselves in shows and pretences, were observed to be mightily indignant.

The overt oppositions in play here – virtuous poor versus immoral rich; honest, though ill-paid worker versus dishonest but richly rewarded financier; sympathetic human trash versus unsympathetic filthy lucre – are in some senses clear and in almost every sense morally impressive. The oppositions are not, though, absolutely clear-cut, and Victorian literature finds it difficult to think about them straightforwardly much of the time. The trouble begins, I think, in that symbiosis within money-generating capitalist enterprise that Kingsley dwelt on so powerfully: the complete fit he observes between the filthy wealth-creating mechanisms of Victorian commerce and industry and the Human Soot that both produced the wealth and was wasted by it. For Kingsley supports both sides of the commercial operation, both parties to the opposition. He believes that the country's economy needs its foul industries and also needs to rescue the humans who are trashed by those industries. And it's clearly hard to be welcoming to both, hard to have your heavy industrial cake and also deplore its human effects. And this is characteristic of Victorian literature.

For a start, the moralised language of darkness, depravity, filthiness carries on sticking to the poor. However much the poor are sympathised with, and the causes and causers of the filthy conditions are satirised, the blackness remains as offensive as ever. The dark places of the earth remain dismayingly dark. Slums remain noxious places to the outsider's nostrils and imagination. Cellars go on being fearful places in a fearful underground. And how could this not be, since the immediate motor of the analysis is a Christian discourse in which sin is after all sin, and utter darkness utter darkness? Which must be part of the reason why Victorian fiction seems largely incapable of effecting much of an imaginative compromise between, on the one hand, a dementing living death – as in *Maud* where the narrating victim of financiers and speculators is buried alive in a private nightmare – or actual death (Stephen Blackpool of *Hard Times*, Joe the crossing-sweeper, Jude, Magwitch), as the final fate of victims of the world of English wealth, fashion, ownership, and on the other hand, fixing upon some kind of far-off, far-fetched, utopian escape as the solution for the poor to England's economic problems. It's better, one supposes, to be shipped out to the Colonies, as in *Mary Barton* or *David Copperfield*, than to be put sacrificially to death, an exemplary martyr upon the altar of a novel's critique of mammonism. Better still to be ratcheted onto a fantasy plot of personal wealth-making, the so-called 'plot of fortune' that is Victorian literature's commonest final solution to the economic and moral ills of the modern world that it keeps making its prime concern. But these individual utopias are no real answer at all; they certainly do nothing for the great mass of Human Trash so sympathetically, but problematically, defined as such by the troupes of writing Samaritans.

For all of literature's Good Samaritan intentions – in fact, it might be said, because of them – the living slum-dweller, the one who didn't get away, the one not 'picked out from the rubbish' (as Jaggers puts it) by courtesy of benefactor or plot as the likes of Oliver Twist and Great Expectations' Estella are, the one who has to carry on living in Coketown or the East End, remains troublingly Other, still sunken, diseased, infectious, dark, and fearfully stigmatised as mob, trades-unionist, artisan, Jewish, Irish, criminal.

> It was a foul, chilly, foggy Saturday night. From the butchers' and green-grocers' shops the gas lights flared and flickered, wild and ghastly, over haggard groups of slip-shod dirty women, bargaining for scraps of stale meat and frost-bitten vegetables, wrangling about short weight and bad quality. Fish-stalls and fruit-stalls lined the edge of the greasy pavement, sending up odours as foul as the language of sellers and buyers. Blood and sewer-water crawled from under doors and out of spouts, and reeked down the gutters among offal, animal and vegetable, in every stage of putrefaction. Foul vapours rose from cowsheds and slaughter houses, and the doorways of undrained alleys, where the inhabitants carried the filth out on their shoes from the back-yard into the court, and from the court up into the main street; while above, hanging like cliffs over the streets – those narrow, brawling torrents of filth, and poverty, and sin, – the houses with their teeming load of life were piled up into the dingy, choking night. A ghastly, deafening, sickening sight it was. Go, scented Belgravian! and see what London is!

That's from Kingsley's *Alton Locke* (Ch. 8), a fiction intensely sympathetic to the plight of the poor, especially the inhabitants of the awful and notorious London parish of St. Giles. But the mixed feelings even of the reformist evangelist for clean streets, clean air and efficient sewer systems, are obvious. These people are horrifying unclean. So are the denizens of the London slums in the reform-minded novel of yet one more of Victorian fiction's major reformer-satirists, *Oliver Twist*. Playing the part of an awed Dante to the Artful Dodger's Virgil, little Oliver is initiated into the terrors of London's Field Lane, yet another notorious slum region of the time:

A dirtier or more wretched place he had never seen. The street was very
narrow and muddy, and the air was impregnated with filthy odours. There
were a good many small shops; but the only stock in trade appeared to be
heaps of children, who, even at that time of night, were crawling in and out
at the doors, or screaming from the inside. The sole places that seemed
to prosper amid the general blight of the place, were the public-houses;
and in them, the lowest orders of Irish were wrangling with might and
main. Covered ways and yards, which here and there diverged from the
main street, disclosed little houses, where drunken men and women were
positively wallowing in filth; and from several of the door-ways, great
ill-looking fellows were cautiously emerging, bound, to all appearance, on
no very well-disposed or harmless errands (Ch. 8).

The lowest orders of the Irish, these drunken wallowers in filth, comprise a
human stage-set for the even greater horrors of the even darker population
they frame – the Jew Fagin (known, to the vexation of Jewish readers, most
usually throughout the first versions of the novel simply as 'the Jew'), and
his household of thieves and thugs and whores. What's being approached
thus nightmarishly – and it must be stressed again that these are texts
that in principle side with the wretches they're presenting – is a kind
of internal alien body, uncannily dark and sooty, an internal infection
in the land, as fearfully troubling as the dark people of the colonial
edge, the colonial sources of British wealth, that keep intruding as the
worrying, guilty frame of so many Victorian fictions and texts produced
within the prosperous classes for the enjoyment of prosperous readers.
The Jews, Irish and criminals of *Oliver Twist*, stoker Toodles of *Dombey
and Son*, are the native equivalents of Bertha Mason, the mad Creole
woman in the attic of *Jane Eyre*, or Joey Bagstock's Native manservant
who is somewhere on the fringes of the Dombey–Toodles encounter on
the railway platform, or the Africans of Conrad's *Heart of Darkness*.
The Belgian Congo of Conrad's 1899 nouvelle is far away, like the
India of *David Copperfield*, the Canada of *Mary Barton*, the Australia
of *Great Expectations*. But the dark inhabitants, and dark truths, of those
margins have a way of invading the centre. Magwitch turns up in London;
what Bertha Mason represents can't stay locked up in the attic. Britons,
of course, infect the colonial place with their British values (Matthew
Arnold thinks inevitably, in his meditations on British Puritanism in his
'Incompatibles' essay, of the Tranvaalers, the 'commercial gentlemen' and
their wives, who carry 'a kind of odour of Salem House all round the
globe'), but the darkness of colonial places returns with more subtly
infectious powers. The imperialist adventure in the Crimean frames
Tennyson's *Maud* and conditions all of Kingsley's, and Gerard Manley
Hopkins's, thoughts about the poor of England's great cities. But, still,
the Crimean, like the Congo, is out there, a long way off. How troubling,

then, the sense that 'this too', as Conrad's narrator has it in *Heart of Darkness*, i.e. London, might be 'one of the dark places of the earth' – a darkness to be found witnessed to on the slightest excursion into St. Giles or Field Lane.

And if the darkness remains uncanny – *unheimlich*, literally out of place at home – and so unthinkable even to the sympathetic Victorian novelist, there is some case for suggesting that this might not be unconnected, *inter alia* no doubt, with the fact that all Victorian writers are steeped in, infected, compromised by the necessary commercialism of their own writing trade. What novelists do in their fictions with swindlers, for instance, is clearly conditioned by their own daily experience of swindling publishers. Victorian novelists had themselves to become sharp financial operators or go under. Theirs was often a case of choosing between being financially masterful or being financially mastered. Writing and publication in Victorian England were obviously a kind of gambling. Losing novelists were often as hooked on loss-making writing ventures as losing gamblers are. Great fortunes were to be got, of course, by writing. Dickens's *Our Mutual Friend* earned £10,000; so did George Eliot's *Romola*. The tough negotiations of George Eliot and George Henry Lewes over *Middlemarch* reminded its publishers of the ways of the two swindling lawyers in *Copperfield* who acquired Pip's services for nothing. George Eliot's faith should have been called *Countism* rather than *Comteism*: that was the bitter jest of those who ran up against her manoeuvrings for the large and steady buck.[9] And all of this kind of entrepreneurial financial wizardry was conducted on behalf of texts, such as *Our Mutual Friend*, *Middlemarch*, *Great Expectations*, that are greatly agitated by the morally distorting power of pelf. It's not the least irony of this situation that, for example, *Great Expectations* should have been hurriedly put into the pages of Dickens's periodical *All The Year Round* to boost its flagging circulation. The allegory of money's filth would itself be a best-selling source of major revenue. The novel that satirised the notion that acquisitions of cash somehow expanded the physique of the owner – which is the satirical reason, perhaps, why Mr. Trabb has to take Pip's measurements again now he has a large sum of ready money – is the means of substantially fattening Dickens's bank account.

It's very noticeable indeed that some of the strongest dramas of money and property in Victorian literature are centred on the anxieties of the loss of cash, material thinning, the denuding of property – for

[9] I am indebted to J.A. Sutherland's wonderfully informative *Victorian Novelists and Publishers* (The Athlone Press, 1979) for these informations.

example, the confiscation of Magwitch's money that land Pip in the hands of the debt-collectors, the Marshalsea episodes of *Little Dorrit*, the terrible stripping bare of the Tullivers' home in *The Mill on the Floss*. Dickens's whole approach to life and writing was, of course, famously affected by his own father's financial problems which landed the father in debtor's prison and the son in the Blacking Factory. Financial deprivation was intimately linked in Dickens's imagination and nightmares with the plunge he thus made into the black zones of the urban poor. His texts fear for, and with, all those who must lose their property. The stripping and wasting of the Dombey house after the crash (Ch. 59) becomes a litany of terrifying material loss populated by a filthy-handed vampire crew of Jews (and Christians), the grasping agents of commerce and trade at their most predatorily fearful and dark:

> The house stands, large and weather-proof, in the long dull street; but it is a ruin, and the rats fly from it.
>
> The men in the carpet caps go on tumbling the furniture about; and the gentlemen with the pens and ink make out inventories of it, and sit upon pieces of furniture never made to be sat upon, and eat bread and cheese from the public-house on other pieces of furniture never made to be eaten on, and seem to have a delight in appropriating precious articles to strange uses. Chaotic combinations of furniture also take place. Mattresses and bedding appear in the dining-room; the glass and china get into the conservatory; the great dinner service is set out in heaps on the long divan in the large drawing-room; and the stair-wires, made into fasces, decorate the marble chimney-pieces. Finally, a rug, with a printed bill upon it, is hung from the balcony; and a similar appendage graces either side of the hall door.
>
> Then, all day long, there is a retinue of mouldy gigs and chaise-carts in the street; and herds of shabby vampires, Jew and Christian, over-run the house, sounding the plate-glass mirrors with their knuckles, striking discordant octaves on the Grand Piano, drawing wet forefingers over the pictures, breathing on the blades of the best dinner-knives, punching the squabs of chairs and sofas with their dirty fists, touzling the feather beds, opening and shutting all the drawers, balancing the silver spoons and forks, looking into the very threads of the drapery and linen, and disparaging everything. There is not a secret place in the whole house. Fluffy and snuffy strangers stare into the kitchen-range as curiously as into the attic clothes-press. Stout men with napless hats on, look out of the bedroom windows, and cut jokes with friends in the street. Quiet, calculating spirits withdraw into the dressing-rooms with catalogues, and make marginal notes thereon, with stumps of pencils. Two brokers invade the very fire-escape, and take a panoramic survey of the neighbourhood from the top of the house. The swarm and buzz, and going up and down, endure for days. The Capital Modern Household Furniture, &c., is on view.
>
> Then there is a palisade of tables made in the best drawing-room; and

on the capital, french-polished, extending, telescopic range of Spanish mahogany dining-tables with turned legs, the pulpit of the Auctioneer is erected; and the herds of shabby vampires, Jew and Christian, the strangers fluffy and snuffy, and the stout men with the napless hats, congregate about it and sit upon everything within reach, mantel-pieces included, and begin to bid. Hot, humming, and dusty are the rooms all day; and – high above the heat, hum, and dust – the head and shoulders, voice and hammer, of the Auctioneer, are ever at work. The men in the carpet-caps get flustered and vicious with tumbling the Lots about, and still the Lots are going, going, gone; still coming on. Sometimes there is joking and a general roar. This lasts all day and three days following. The Capital Modern Household Furniture, &c., is on sale.

Then the mouldy gigs and chaise-carts re-appear; and with them come spring-vans and waggons, and an army of porters with knots. All day long, the men with carpet-caps are screwing at screw-drivers and bed-winches, or staggering by the dozen together on the staircase under heavy burdens, or upheaving perfect rocks of Spanish mahogany, best rosewood, or plate-glass, into the gigs and chaise-carts, vans and waggons. All sorts of vehicles of burden are in attendance, from a tilted waggon to a wheel-barrow. Poor Paul's little bedstead is carried off in a donkey-tandem. For nearly a whole week, the Capital Modern Household Furniture, &c., is in course of removal.

At last it is all gone. Nothing is left about the house but scattered leaves of catalogues, littered scraps of straw and hay, and a battery of pewter pots behind the hall-door. The men with the carpet-caps gather up their screw-drivers and bed-winches into bags, shoulder them, and walk off. One of the pen and ink gentlemen goes over the house as a last attention; sticking up bills in the windows respecting the lease of this desirable family mansion, and shutting the shutters. At length he follows the men with the carpet-caps. None of the invaders remain. The house is a ruin, and the rats fly from it.

To be sure, moral lessons are drawn and satirical questions are asked of these rituals of negated materialism. In the bare sparseness of the family mill, sans linen, sans crockery, sans carpets, sans nearly everything material, George Eliot's Maggie Tulliver learns life-altering lessons of resignation, assisted by the little copy of Thomas à Kempis that Bob Jakin lovingly provides her with. The material downfall of the House of Dombey is a lesson in the hubris of materialism. Henry James's *The Spoils of Poynton* (1897) offers a richly satirical comedy of upper-class greed as its Mrs. Gereth carts her rare and beautiful *objets* back and forth across the south of England in pantechnicons hired in the Tottenham Court Road: hers is Jamesian moral self-disgrace by furniture removal. But for all their carefully orchestrated moralised responses, it's easy to perceive that these writings are themselves steeped in the Tullivers' dismay at the loss of their things, and the Dombey horror at having the outward and visible manifestations of wealth unsentimentally stripped away. These texts seem all at once to find Mrs. Gereth's incomprehension morally deplorable and to share it: 'She could at a stretch imagine people's not having, but she couldn't imagine their not wanting and not missing'. For '"Things" were of course the sum of the world' (Ch. 3).

What is present in large measure, then, in Victorian writing about money and possessions is the great bourgeois problematic of the English novel: that flawed equation which has so sustained English fiction, the link that began in Puritanism and was amply kept up in our novels, the felt connection between salvation (moral being, moral health) and (commercial) prospering, between selfhood and ownership, between being right with God and being blessed by God with houses, lands, goods. The problematic famously began with Defoe's *Robinson Crusoe*. The English novel has been, in these regards, one long *Robinsonade* (as the German language has it) ever since. The writers and their audience – heirs to the Puritans all – were heirs to this dire equation, the connected twin concerns of Arnold's Philistine as exemplified by the tragic case, alluded to in the 'Porro Unum Est Necessarium' chapter of *Culture and Anarchy*, of Mr. Smith, an insurance company secretary who had committed suicide because he 'laboured under the apprehension that he would come to poverty, and that he was eternally lost'. Protestant writers – and most Victorian fictionists are Protestant – are stuck with the fact that the bourgeois Protestantism that has shaped the age's dominant form of writing, the novel, and that has inspired their Good Samaritanism and their moral deploring of the deleterious effects of filthy lucre, is the very same bourgeois Protestantism that is quite visibly infected with the very commercialism they deplore. In other words, 'our serious middle class', as Arnold called it, produces both George Eliot, the critic of commercial fiddling and financial grasping, and also her character Bulstrode, *Middlemarch*'s London Dissenter and banker whose theological suppleness about where the so-called divine leadings are taking him, whose expert inventing of good ends for bad commercial practices, are the ground of his terrible and rightly deplored corruption. Dickens and Chadband, the crooked loud-mouthed preacher of righteousness, and the Murdstones, and Mrs. Clennam, the ruthless mother in *Little Dorrit* who sits graspingly behind her iron-bound copy of the Scriptures, and, for that matter, both Matthew Arnold and his invented horror of a Philistine, the northern Liberal dissenting manufacturer 'Mr. Bottles Esquire of *Friendship's Garland*, all come out of the same Protestant matrix. Representatively, Arnold deplores, in *St. Paul and Protestantism*, the 'bargain' theology of Calvinism. But some kind of bargain-mindedness informs all the activities of writers like him.

It's an impasse, and a guilty one. Some sense of it is perhaps one reason why Dickens labels the doctrines of Political Economy, as lampooned in

Hard Times, the 'fictions of Coketown'. The commercially aggressive and corrupted factory apologists and the novelists who satirise them are all fictionists together, just as, like Mrs. Gaskell and the factory owner W.R. Greg who publicly deplored her *Mary Barton*, they are all Protestants together.

Dickens is particularly troubled by the convergence between literacy and criminality, between forgery, swindling, illegitimate acquisitions of wealth, and what he himself is about as a writer. This convergence appears nowhere more succinctly than in that article that appeared in Dickens's paper *Household Words* in December 1857, entitled 'The City of Unlimited Paper'. A very Dickensian piece indeed, it was actually by John Hollingshead. It was written to satirise City scams and commercial fraudulence that put honest investors' moneys at great risk through the kind of bankruptcies that had occurred in great numbers in the City crisis of 1857. The piece caused, apparently, a great sensation. Thackerary, for one, greatly admired it and he tried to get Hollingshead to write for his journal *The Cornhill*. The central bankruptcy concerns of the article looked back to the Bundelcund Banking Co. swindle in Thackeray's *The Newcomes* (1853–5) and forward to the ruin of Philip Firmin in *The Adventures of Philip* (1861–2). And there are plenty of ironies hereabouts apart from the Dickensian ones. Hollingshead, for example, received the regular *Household Words* contributor's fee of £3.13s.6d for his article, whereas Thackeray was in receipt of £600 a month for his editorship of *The Cornhill*.[10] But the Dickensian ironies are even more arresting.

The article sets up many hintful associations with Dickens's fictional money dealings as Hollingshead jeeringly refers to the corrupt dealings of City institutions and companies. There are Messrs. Ignes, Fatui and Company who trade fraudulently with Australia via the Australian mail. In Bullion Alley there is the dubious house of Fossil, Ingot and Bagstock. During the South Sea Bubble collapse Mr. Fossil staved off a run on his bank by standing at his door and shovelling gold sovereigns 'into baskets out of a dust-cart'. The Australian mail, Mr. Bagstock, dust-carts: these names and features all throw out lines of communication to Dickens's own sharpest fictional attacks on the corruptions of money and commerce. Pip's cash comes via the Australian mail; Bagstock is the name of Dombey's awful ex-colonial sidekick; Mr. Boffin the Golden Dustman's fortune came out of his dust-carts. Even closer to home, though, are the misleading pictures

[10] G.N. Ray, ed., *The Letters And Private Papers of William Makepeace Thackeray*, 4 Vols (Oxford University Press, London, 1945–46), IV, *1857–63*, p. 157; 'John Hollingshead', *Household Words: A Weekly Journal 1850–1859 Conducted by Charlts Dickens: Table of Contents, List of Contributors and Their Contributions*, compiled by Ann Lohrli (Univ. of Toronto Press, 1973), 305–8.

of non-existent factories and mills engraved as letter-heads and on invoices – such as the portrait of the Scottish Mills complex allegedly owned by Lacker, Crane and Company of Packingcase Yard, Lower Thames Street. For such lying engravings are 'works of the imagination':

> The premises in Packingcase Yard are modest enough, and would not seem to indicate a business of very extensive character; but, in this instance the art of the engraver is called in, and we are presented upon invoices and bill-stamps with a flattering and highly suggestive view of the important and busy Dunmist Mills, of which the small office in London is only one of the numerous agencies. There are water-power and steam-power; high chimneys sending forth volumes of smoke; long ranges of out-buildings with groups of busy work-people, and large, solid bales of merchandise; bridges and tramways, and waggons loaded with raw material, drawn by struggling horses of the Flemish breed, towards the crowded gates of this industrial settlement. The whole is a work of the imagination of the highest order alike creditable to the designer and the engraver. When, in the usual course of things, the house of Lacker, Crane and Company is compelled to call its creditors together, and an inspection of the magnificent factory, outworks, and plant, takes place by the order of the assignees, the dissolving view of the industrial hive, with its active work-people and its din and clatter of machinery, gradually recedes, and in its place stands the pastoral simplicity of a couple of barns, and a kilted shepherd tending his flocks.

In *Great Expectations* lower-class forgers, such as rough coiners and swindlers, end up in Newgate. The satiric point of the *Household Words* article is that the smart London swindlers get off scot-free. Dickens's novel is less tolerant than the world is. Pip is presented to us in the wake of Joe's London visit (Ch. 28), as a demoralised self-swindler, a man passing off nutshells upon himself for bank notes, and when in the same chapter Pip travels down to see Joe and Biddy we're not too surprised that in the same coach there should be a pair of convicts discussing Magwitch and that one of them should be the man who brought Magwitch's two one-pound notes to Pip, nor that these two villains should eat nuts and spit the shells about. Convicts are, like the poor, always with Pip, and so is Newgate prison. The presence of the prison is kept up by the novel as an accusation of the respectable. The prison haunts Pip's respectable life as a trainee lawyer; it's the source of Jaggers's income; it's where Jaggers's strong-wristed servant Molly, Estella's mother, comes from; it's the gold-mine of Wemmick's stash of portable property; it's the contaminated centre of the lives of Miss Havisham and her jilting lover Compeyson, the secret at the heart of Estella's glamorous life and Pip's expectations; it's where Jaggers has his potentially lucrative brushes with dubious Jews and other criminal types like Abraham Lazarus and his brother (Ch. 20). And the accusatory criminal connections of Newgate, so significantly bound up with the financial and social expectations of Pip and the respectability of the rest, are also crucially allied with the world of the Blacking Factory. In Ch. 27, Joe Gargery and Wopsle, up from the country, went off straightaway to have a look at a 'Blacking Ware'us.' '"But we didn't find that it come up to its likeness in the red bills at the shop doors; which I meantersay", added Joe, in an explanatory manner, "as it is there drawd too architectooralooral"'.

Dickens's worry about writing matters and what matters in his own writing could scarcely be clearer. Sticking the labels on the blacking bottles was Dickens's own traumatic childhood occupation. Blacking became for him the lifelong emblem of the hellish, criminal, darkened depths of London poverty and a lowering existence in the lower commercial depths of the city that had once threatened to engulf him for life. A measure of his distaste, and his relief at having escaped, is the fact that he gave the name Fagin to the attractive-repulsive father of slum criminality in *Oliver Twist* – the name of the one boy who befriended him in the Blacking Factory and so the one, ironically, likeliest to make life there passable and endurable. And Joe's comment on the misleading architectooraloorality of blacking manufacturers' publicity materials ('the red bills at the shop doors') links them accusingly with the lying paperwork put about in the City of Unlimited Paper. They're all 'works of the imagination'. And so Dickens's own trade, the textual and imaginative means of the Good Samaritan, the fictional instrument of moral protest, the very vehicle of high moral values and moral goods, is being felt to be uncomfortably close to the works of commercial darkness that had threatened to seal the boy Charles Dickens as a scared and victimised piece of Human Soot. Respectable writing was, on this reckoning, only as sullied as what it was seeking to clean up. It's a consideration that understandably belonged rather to the nightmare un- or sub-consciousness of Dickens' writing than to its daylight consciousness. But, it might be thought, in these anxious self-reflections, the unconscious life of Dickens's texts was thus confronting the moral problematic of the fictional medium in bourgeois Victorian England with greater honesty than most fully conscious discussions ever managed.

Proceedings of the British Academy, **78**, 129–147

Darwinism and Victorian Values:
Threat or Opportunity?

PETER J. BOWLER

The Queen's University of Belfast

POPULAR understanding of the 'Darwinian Revolution' is dominated by the metaphor of a war between science and religion. We are used to being told that Darwin's theory was perceived as a threat to the religious values that most Victorians accepted as the moral foundations of their society. The claim that we had evolved from the apes would undermine the assumption that the world of moral and spiritual values existed independently of material nature. The most popular expression of this image of conflict is the confrontation between 'Darwin's bulldog,' Thomas Henry Huxley, and Bishop Samuel Wilberforce at the Oxford meeting of the British Association for the Advancement of Science in 1860. Huxley is supposed to have triumphed over the bishop's efforts to discredit Darwinism and thus hold back the march of scientific rationalism. From the viewpoint of a rationalist, of course, this was a good thing – yet our interpretation of late-Victorian thought is also influenced by another image of conflict which paints a less rosy picture of Darwin's impact. It is claimed that for some Victorians, at least, the philosophy of 'social Darwinism' legitimized the replacement of traditional values with the worship of brute force and success at any price.

The vested interests which underlie these conflicting interpretations are obvious enough. Scientists want to see Darwinism as a symbol of modern humanity's ability to throw off the shackles of outdated superstition and face up to the harsh realities of nature. Some religious thinkers want to

Read 13 December 1990. © The British Academy 1992.

brand the theory as a symptom of the materialism that is undermining
the traditional fabric of society. But as with most cases in which historical
myths are used to support modern values, the familiar images begin to
blur when the past is studied in more detail. The history of science is a
relatively new discipline, but it has taken upon itself the task of exposing the
mythological dimension of the classic stories about the 'heroes of discovery.'
At the same time, a growing awareness of the ideological divisions within
Victorian society has allowed us to see that there were many different
ways of responding to the challenge of evolutionism. Historians of science
have uncovered the ideological dimensions of the Victorian debate over
Darwinism with as much gusto as they have explored the details of Darwin's
biological work.[1]

In this paper I want to survey the results of a decade or more's
work both by the 'Darwin industry' and by social historians seeking to
create a more sophisticated picture of the complex process by which
evolutionism acquired its role as one of the most powerful themes
in late-Victorian thought. I shall argue that, far from being merely a
threat to conservative values or an opportunity for the exponents of
ruthless capitalism, evolutionism was taken up in many different ways
and used for many different purposes. Instead of looking for a monolithic
'Darwinism' which had to be either rejected or accepted as a whole, we must
recognize that *evolutionism* succeeded precisely because it could be adapted
to many different social purposes. There were several different varieties of
Darwinism, and also many non-Darwinian versions of evolutionism, each
with its own set of moral and social consequences. In some cases, models
of evolutionary progress that owed very little to Darwin's thought were able
to exploit the idea of the 'struggle for existence' to create what looks like a
form of social Darwinism.

One casualty of the historians' efforts to undermine traditional myths
has been the Huxley-Wilberforce debate of 1860. Several studies have now
shown that the popular image of Huxley wiping the floor with the bishop
is a product of the scientists' wishful thinking.[2] In fact many of those who
attended the debate did not think that the evolutionists had carried the
day. But this cautionary tale should not mislead us into overestimating

[1] For surveys of recent developments in the history of evolutionism see Peter J.
Bowler, *Evolution: The History of an Idea* (Berkeley: University of California Press,
2nd edn 1989); for a reassessment of the 'Darwinian Revolution' see Bowler, *The
Non-Darwinian Revolution: Reinterpreting a Historical Myth* (Baltimore: Johns Hopkins
University Press, 1988).
[2] See for instance J. R. Lucas, 'Huxley and Wilberforce: A Legendary Encounter', *Historical
Journal*, **22** (1979), 313–30 and J. V. Jensen, 'Return to the Wilberforce-Huxley Debate',
British Journal for the History of Science, **21** (1988), 161–80.

the long-term opposition to the general idea of evolution. There are many surveys of the debate both in science and in society at large, and they almost all agree that by the late 1860s the tide had set very firmly in the evolutionists' favour.[3] Whatever their initial doubts, most Victorians – including those of more conservative opinions – gradually came to accept the general concept of evolutionism.

Whether they accepted Huxley's version of Darwinism is, however, another matter. There now seems little doubt that Huxley used Darwin's theory as a weapon in his campaign to take control of the scientific community. At the same time he was able to forge an alliance with the liberal social evolutionism being promoted by Herbert Spencer, which corresponds to the classic image of social Darwinism. Since this invoked many aspects of the Protestant work ethic as the driving force of progress, some religious thinkers were able to accommodate themselves to evolutionism by following its lead. We now know that neither Huxley nor Spencer were good Darwinians as measured by their acceptance of Darwin's most innovative ideas – yet their efforts to publicize evolutionism determined what most people thought 'Darwinism' ought to be. At the same time there were several efforts being made to create non-Darwinian versions of evolutionism that would salvage some aspects of the traditional world view. These have often been dismissed as blind-alleys in the development of science, but we now know that they played an important role in late-Victorian evolutionary thought.

The Evolutionists' Challenge

The traditional story of the Darwinian revolution is based on the assumption that the *Origin of Species* assaulted Victorian sensibilities like a bolt from the blue. There was no warning, because there had been no serious attempt to float a theory of biological evolution in the earlier decades of the nineteenth century. The work of scholars such as Adrian Desmond and James Secord has exploded this myth by showing that evolutionism *was* debated both inside and outside science in the decades before Darwin. It is appropriate in a paper delivered originally in Edinburgh to record that the leading figures in the pre-Darwinian evolutionary movement were the

---

[3] See especially Alvar Ellegård, *Darwin and the General Reader: The Reception of Darwin's Theory of Evolution in the British Periodical Press. 1859–1872* (Göteburg: Acta Universitatis Gothenburgensis, 1957, reprinted Chicago: University of Chicago Press, 1990).

Scots anatomist Robert Edmond Grant and the publisher and writer Robert Chambers. In the 1820s and 30s, Grant promoted radical evolutionism as part of a campaign to reform both the medical profession and society at large.[4] The new transformism pioneered by French biologists such as J. B. Lamarck and Etienne Geoffroy Saint-Hilaire exposed the outdatedness of establishment science and provided a model of natural development which could be used to justify demands for social progress through the removal of an outdated power structure. When Grant moved to London in 1827, the English medical establishment took great pains to isolate him. The anatomist Richard Owen rose to prominence because he was able to 'modernize' the old natural theology and use the discontinuity of the fossil record to block Grant's claims.

Grant fell into obscurity, but it is possible to see Robert Chambers' anonymously published *Vestiges of the Natural History of Creation* of 1844 as an attempt to popularize radical transformism south of the border.[5] To make it seem more palatable to an audience used to thinking in terms of design by God, Chambers presented evolution as the progressive unfolding of a divine plan of creation, advancing steadily toward ever higher states of development. His theory was certainly not an anticipation of Darwin's: it took progress rather than adaptation as its starting point, and made no attempt to suggest a naturalistic mechanism of change. Even so, Secord has shown that Chambers saw the idea of progress as part of a political campaign. He wanted to throw off the shackles of traditional authority so that active, middle-class entrepreneurs could push society toward new levels of activity.

If the conventional story of the Darwinian revolution mentions Chambers at all, it is as an amateur whose wild speculations were shunned by the scientific community. It is true that many conservative naturalists spoke out against *Vestiges*, but the evidence suggests that the book had a much greater impact than was once supposed. Even Owen refused to criticize it in print, and in the late 1840s wrote vaguely about a law of creation operating by natural rather than supernatural means:

> To what natural laws or secondary causes the orderly succession and
> progression of such organic phenomena may have been committed we

---

[4] See Adrian Desmond, *The Politics of Evolution: Medicine, Morphology, and Reform in Radical London* (Chicago: University of Chicago Press, 1989).

[5] See James Secord, 'Behind the Veil: Robert Chambers and the Genesis of the *Vestiges of Creation*', in J. R. Moore (ed.), *History, Humanity and Evolution: Essays for John C. Greene* (Cambridge: Cambridge University Press, 1989), pp. 165–94. On the non-Darwinian character of Chambers' theory see M. J. S. Hodge, 'The Universal Gestation of Nature: Chambers' Vestiges and *Explanations*', *Journal of the History of Biology* 5 (1972), 127–52.

are as yet ignorant. But if, without derogation of the Divine power, we may conceive the existence of such ministers, and personify them by the term 'Nature,' we learn from the past history of our globe that she has advanced with slow and stately steps, guided by the archetypical light, amidst the wreck of worlds, from the first embodiment of the Vertebrate idea under its Ichthyic vestment, until it became arrayed in the glorious garb of the human form.[6]

Owen did not follow this suggestion up in the years before the *Origin of Species* appeared, and when he did begin to speak openly about transmutation, it was in a distinctly non-Darwinian form (see below). But his brief concession suggests that long before Darwin published, conservative attitudes were beginning to soften.

This is confirmed by Pietro Corsi's recent study of the Oxford mathematician and philosopher of science Baden Powell.[7] In his *Essays on the Spirit of the Inductive Philosophy* of 1855, Powell argued that God's influence over nature was demonstated more effectively through the laws He had imposed than through any miraculous interference with those laws – and explicitly extended the argument to the appearance of new species. His comments suggest that liberal Anglicans had begun to think seriously about the idea of evolution in the 1850s. At one level, Chambers had spiked his opponents' guns by showing that transmutation could indeed become part of natural theology; God might create new species by a predetermined law rather than by miracle. What was *not* acceptable to the Anglican establishment was the linear progressionism of Chambers' theory, which reduced mankind to the last step in the continuous ascent of the animal kingdom. Evolution would be acceptable only if it could be divorced from the idea of continuous progress – a topic I shall return to later.

From the perspective of the radical exponents of free-enterprise individualism, however, Chambers' had abandoned a vital component of the evolutionary model. For them, progress had to be the cumulative result of many individual acts of self-improvement, not a preordained law imposed from on high. The man who did most to develop this model of evolution was, of course, Herbert Spencer. Already in the early 1850s Spencer was advocating both *laissez-faire* individualism as the key to social progress and

[6] Richard Owen, *On the Nature of Limbs* (London: van Voorst, 1849), p. 89. On Owen's attitude to evolution see Evelleen Richards, 'A Question of Property Rights: Richard Owen's Evolutionism Reassessed', *British Journal for the History of Science*, **20** (1987), 129–72. See also Adrian Desmond, *Archetypes and Ancestors: Palaeontology in Victorian London, 1850–1875* (London: Blond and Briggs, 1982).

[7] Pietro Corsi, *Science and Religion: Baden Powell and the Anglican Debate, 1800–1860* (Cambridge: Cambridge University Press, 1988); see Baden Powell, *Essays on the Spirit of the Inductive Philosophy, The Unity of Worlds, and the Philosophy of Creation* (London: Longmans, 1855).

biological evolution based on the Lamarckian mechanism of the inheritance of acquired characteristics.[8] Lamarckism had always been associated with progressionism, and Spencer seems to have realized that it offered the perfect parallel to the individualist model of social progress. Animals (and human beings) acquired new habits to cope with new environments, the new habits generated new bodily structures through exercise and effort, and these acquired characters were inherited to become the foundation for the species' evolution. Progress was inevitable in the long run because animals were always having to develop their intelligence and initiative in order to cope with an ever more challenging environment.

This was the model for biological and social evolution that Spencer was already promoting in the late 1850s. Although he has been presented as a leading 'social Darwinist'[9] Spencer was really a Lamarckian and he defended this theory vigorously in the biological debates of the late nineteenth century.[10] He certainly adopted Darwin's mechanism of natural selection once it was published – indeed it was Spencer who coined the term 'survival of the fittest' – but for him this was always a secondary mechanism, removing those individuals who were incapable of self-development. The emphasis was on struggle as the spur to self-improvement, not primarily as a means of eliminating the congenitally unfit. I suspect that many people actually found it very difficult to distinguish between the two processes of Lamarckism and natural selection, at least until the biological developments of the late nineteenth century began to focus much more attention on to the problem of heredity. Much of what has passed for 'social Darwinism' was actually Spencerianism, in which the Darwinian mechanism played only a subsidiary part. The term 'Darwinism' was attached to it because it was Darwin, not Spencer, who had actually converted the scientists to evolutionism.

The problem with Spencer's philosophy was that it offered no new initiative on the scientific front. Lamarckism had been blacklisted in the earlier debates, and few scientists were prepared to see it as the basis for rethinking the whole framework of biology. Some preferred to talk vaguely about 'creation by law,' but those of a more radical disposition

---

[8] See J. D. Y. Peel, *Herbert Spencer: The Evolution of a Sociologist* (London: Heinemann, 1971). There is no good modern account of Spencer's biological evolutionism, but for an amplification of the point made here see Bowler, *The Non-Darwinian Revolution* (note 1), pp. 38–40 and 64–6.

[9] Spencer is presented as a social Darwinism in Richard Hofstadter's *Social Darwinism in American Thought* (revised edn, Boston: Beacon Press, 1959); for a contrary view see Robert Bannister, *Social Darwinism: Science and Myth in Anglo-American Social Thought* (Philadelphia: Temple University Press, 1979).

[10] For Spencer's defence of Lamarckism see his *Factors of Organic Evolution* (London: Williams and Norgate, 1887).

felt that the whole situation had become deadlocked. This is very clear in the attitude of the young T. H. Huxley, desperately trying to find himself a niche in the very small world of professional science in the 1850s. Huxley was determined to promote science as a key component of the new industrialized society, and he despised those who used natural theology to keep science subservient to religion. He attacked Chambers' *Vestiges* savagely because he regarded its appeal to a divinely-implanted law of progress as mere pseudo-science.[11] Yet he could see no way of developing a truly naturalistic evolutionism. The *Origin of Species* was a revelation to him, not because he accepted the idea of natural selection unreservedly (indeed he had major reservations about it), but because it showed that science could enter the hitherto restricted area of theorizing about natural relationships.[12]

Meanwhile, what of Darwin himself? It is impossible to summarize here the vast amount of scholarly analysis that has been devoted to uncovering the path by which he developed his theory.[13] Almost all commentators now agree that his notebooks reveal a theory emerging from a dialogue between his scientific interests in biogeography and reproduction, and his concerns about the human implications of his ideas.[14] Darwin's theory became much more sophisticated in the course of the 1840s and 50s, but he realized that to make it acceptable to the general public, he must give it a gloss that would neutralize the prevailing moral concerns. This was particularly important because natural selection emphasized the harshness of nature and provided no obvious means by which the Creator could be said to guide evolution along a chosen path.

There has been much controversy on the question of whether or not

[11] See [T. H. Huxley], 'Vestiges of the Natural History of Creation', *British and Foreign Medico-Chirurgical Review*, **13** (1854), 332–43.

[12] For Huxley's own assessment of his response to Darwinism see his 'On the Reception of the "Origin of Species"', in Francis Darwin, (ed.), *The Life and Letters of Charles Darwin* (London: John Murray, 1887, 3 vols), vol. 2, 179–204. See Desmond, *Archetypes and Ancestors* (note 6) and Mario T. Di Gregorio, *T. H. Huxley's Place in Natural Science* (New Haven: Yale University Press, 1984).

[13] For a survey see David Oldroyd, 'How Did Darwin Arrive at his Theory?', *History of Science*, **22** (1985), 325–74. The best collection of modern Darwin scholarship is David Kohn (ed.), *The Darwinian Heritage* (Princeton: Princeton University Press, 1985). See also Peter J. Bowler, *Charles Darwin: The Man and his Influence* (Oxford: Basil Blackwell, 1990).

[14] There is now a splendid edition of the notebooks edited by Paul H. Barrett *et al.*, *Charles Darwin's Notebooks, 1836–1844* (London: British Museum (Natural History) and Cambridge: Cambridge University Press, 1987). At the time of writing, the project to reprint Darwin's correspondence has reached its sixth volume: Frederick Burckhardt and Sydney Smith (eds), *The Correspondence of Charles Darwin* (Cambridge: Cambridge University Press, 1984–90).

Darwin was a progressionist in the Spencerian mould. As modern biologists understand his theory, its concentration on migration and adaptation as the driving forces of evolution makes it the very antithesis of linear progressionism. For Darwin, evolution had to be a tree rather than a ladder, and each branch of the tree had to be seen as evolving in its own particular way. To measure progress in one branch by standards based on another was inappropriate. When Darwin was wearing his biologist's hat he recognized these implications, and much of his later scientific work was devoted to studying the minute details of adaptation. But when he became a social philosopher Darwin was much more likely to talk in progressionist terms. He realized that it was important for him to present the *Origin of Species* both as a new initiative in science and as a contribution to progressionism. This is evident from the optimistic message of its closing passages:

> Thus, from the war of nature, from famine and death, the most exalted object which we are capable of conceiving, namely, the production of the higher animals, directly follows. There is a grandeur in this view of life, with its several powers, having been originally breathed into a few forms or into one; and that, whilst this planet has gone cycling on according to the fixed law of gravity, from so simple a beginning endless forms most beautiful and most wonderful have been, and are being, evolved.[16]

The *Origin of Species* had an immediate impact. Darwin offered new lines of evidence for adaptive evolution as well as a new mechanism of change, and it seems that these were both important in convincing many biologists that it was now time to take the general idea of evolution seriously. Whatever the strength of feelings raised by the debates of the early 1860s, surveys of both the scientific and popular literature suggest that by the end of the decade evolutionism was being taken largely for granted. The scientific breakthrough catalysed a dramatic change in popular opinion on the question – which had already been primed by writers such as Chambers and Spencer.

But we now know that Darwin's particular theory of natural selection did not gain a firm foothold even within science. Some biogeographers took it very seriously, including the botanist J. D. Hooker and the co-discoverer of the selection mechanism A. R. Wallace. But the most active area of evolutionary science was the reconstruction of the ancestral tree of life, and here natural selection was of little relevance. This was Huxley's field, and thanks to the work of Mario Di Gregorio, Adrian

---

[16] Charles Darwin, *On the Origin of Species by Means of Natural Selection* (London: John Murray, 1859), p. 490.

Desmond and others, we now know just how complex Huxley's reaction to Darwinism was.[17] He saw natural selection as merely an interesting suggestion that might be worth following up, and preferred to believe that transmutation occurred through predetermined variations forcing a species in a fixed direction.[18] As a scientist, Huxley was certainly not a very good Darwinian.

Why, then, did he champion Darwin's cause so actively? The answer to this question lies in Huxley's determination to use evolutionism as a vehicle for galvanizing the scientific community into activity. By throwing off the shackles of natural theology, science would take its place as a leading force in a progressive, industrialized society. Evolutionism based on the assumption that development was a natural process would symbolize science's bid to replace religion as the source of authority in the modern world. It was *evolutionism* that Huxley really wanted – and he was prepared to call himself a 'Darwinian' despite his reservations about natural selection because he realized that the *Origin of Species* served as the movement's figurehead. He was immensely successful in playing the political game within the scientific community which ensured that suporters of the new approach were placed in positions of power and influence.

At the same time, Huxley was concerned about social reform and saw evolution in biology as a useful model upon which to base his assurances that the machinery of government would be steadily improved. He was thus able to throw in his lot with Spencer and the advocates of social evolutionism. Spencer was also a member of the informal 'X-club,' the group which masterminded the Darwinian takeover of the scientific community.[19] For the time being, at least, Huxley's scientific Darwinism went hand in hand with Spencer's social evolutionism – although Huxley would turn against Spencer's optimistic philosophy in the 1890s.[20] Advocates of the free-enterprise system were thus able to climb aboard the Darwinian bandwaggon – although the term 'social Darwinism' would not be invented for several decades yet. As Jim Moore has shown in his survey of the religious debates, many nonconformists were able to absorb Spencer's evolutionary philosophy because it represented merely a

---

[17] See note 10.

[18] See Huxley's 1871 article, 'Mr. Darwin's Critics', reprinted in Huxley, *Collected Essays* (London: Macmillan, 1893–94, 9 vols), vol. 2, *Darwiniana*, 120–86, pp. 181–2 and his 1878 'Evolution in Biology', reprinted ibid., 187–226, p. 223.

[19] See Roy MacLeod, 'The X-Club: A Scientific Network in Late-Victorian England', *Notes and Records of the Royal Society*, **24** (1970), 305–22.

[20] Huxley's later opposition to Spencer's progressionism was developed in his 1893 lecture 'Evolution and Ethics', reprinted in *Collected Essays* (note 18), vol. 9, *Evolution and Ethics*. 46–116.

naturalistic interpretation of the Protestant work ethic.[21] In the new scheme of things, thrift and initiative would be rewarded in this world as well as the next, as part of nature's steady advance toward higher things.

The model of development along a progressive scale brought about by the accumulated effects of individual effort was used throughout the social and natural sciences. Darwin's emphasis on the branching character of evolution was suppressed by implying that the tree of life had a central trunk defining the ladder of progress toward mankind. In archaeology, the linear scale of stone-age cultures erected by Gabriel De Mortillet dominated the study of prehistory.[22] Anthropologists followed Edward B. Tylor in postulating a scale of cultural evolution to be seen among living societies.[23] The most primitive savages corresponded to the early stages in the evolution of higher cultures – they were frozen relics of the past, preserved because they had never been exposed to the more stimulating environment of the temperate regions. The belief that progress only occured in response to an environmental challenge fitted Spencer's Lamarckian view of evolution as an extension of self-development. It also offered an easy way of explaining why the lower points on the scale could still be seen in the world today. Where geographical diversity had pushed Darwin towards the model of an open-ended tree, here it was subordinated to the notion of a historical scale.

In biology these themes can be seen in the work of one of Huxley's protégés, the zoologist E. Ray Lankester.[24] Although ostensibly a Darwinian, Lankester's view on variation and heredity were vague enough to leave room for a Lamarckian interpretation. And although he warned about the dangers of picturing evolution as a ladder rather than a tree, he defined the grade of all the major groups of animals in terms of the point at which they branched off a main trunk leading toward mankind. Lankester did, however, modify the concept of progress through

---

[21] See James R. Moore, *The Post-Darwinian Controversies: A Study of the Protestant Struggle to Come to Terms with Darwin in Great Britain and America, 1870–1900* (New York and Cambridge: Cambridge University Press, 1979) and Moore, 'Herbert Spencer's Henchmen: The Evolution of Protestant Liberals in Late-Nineteenth-Century America', in J. Durant (ed.), *Darwinism and Divinity* (Oxford: Basil Blackwell, 1985), pp. 76–100.

[22] Gabriel De Mortillet, *Le Préhistorique* (Paris: Reinwald, 1883). On De Mortillet's influence see Peter J. Bowler, *Theories of Human Evolution: A Century of Debate, 1844–1944* (Baltimore: Johns Hopkins University Press and Oxford: Basil Blackwell,. 1986), part 1 and Bowler, *The Invention of Progress: The Victorians and the Past* (Oxford: Basil Blackwell, 1989), part 2.

[23] On evolutionism in anthropology see J. W. Burrow, *Evolution and Society: A Study in Victorian Social Theory* (Cambridge: Cambridge University Press, 1966); and George W. Stocking, *Victorian Anthropology* (New York, Free Press, 1987).

[24] On Lankester's work see Peter J. Bowler, 'Development and Adaptation: Evolutionary Concepts in British Morphology, 1870–1914', *British Journal for the History of Science*, **22** (1989), 283–97.

struggle in an interesting way. As a biologist he was aware that some simple animals are not primitive relics of early stages in evolution. They are, in fact, the end-products of lines of evolution which have degenerated because they have adopted a softer, less challenging lifestyle. In an address given to the British Association for the Advancement of Science in 1879 he compared this process with the degeneration of human cultures when they had dominated their surroundings too effectively and had removed the stimulus for further progress.[25] It is probable that Lankester's ideas formed the basis for the picture of future human degeneration in H. G. Wells' story *The Time Machine* of 1895.[26]

The notion of progress through struggle thus had a darker side that could be brought out by anyone who realized that the relaxation of struggle would produce the reverse effect. But for Lankester and most of his contemporaries this was only an occasional aberration from the main theme of progress. From this point of view, evolutionism offered an opportunity to present progress as the cumulative effect of individual effort. The fact that this missed what modern biologists see as the most crucial insights in Darwin's thinking should not blind us to the fact that to the Victorian mind, 'Darwinism' almost inevitably carried this progressionist implication. Darwin's ideas about the struggle for existence were close enough to Spencer's mechanism for them to be absorbed – with Darwin's connivance – into the ideology by which the middle classes hoped to justify their rise to power. Darwin became the figurehead of popular evolutionism because his theory catalysed the transformation of the scientific community, and could also be adapted to popular tastes. It is one of the ironies of history that this process of adaptation concealed what modern biologists regard as the most important implications of his theory.

The Conservative Response

The Huxley-Wilberforce confrontation may easily mislead us into thinking that the conservative opponents of *laissez-faire* progressionism found the idea of evolution unacceptable. They certainly found the model of progress by the accumulation of individual effort unacceptable, but Chambers had

[25] E. Ray Lankester, *Degeneration: A Chapter in Darwinism* (London: Macmillan, 1880), pp. 59–61.

[26] Shortly before beginning work on *The Time Machine*, Wells wrote a popular article on 'Zoological Retrogression' which borrows many of Lankester's themes; it is reprinted in R. M. Philmus and D. Y. Hughes, (eds), *H. G. Wells: Early Writings in Science and Science Fiction* (Berkeley: University of California Press, 1975), pp. 158–68. See Peter J. Bowler, 'Holding Your Head Up High: Degeneration and Orthogenesis in Theories of Human Evolution', in Moore (ed.), *History, Humanity and Evolution* (note 5), pp. 329–53.

already shown how it was possible for transmutation to be seen as the unfolding of a divine plan. If evolution were subject to built-in trends that pushed it in a certain direction whatever the behaviour of the individual organisms, the Darwinian-Spencerian interpretation would be undermined. If the element of continuity in this model of change could also be undermined, it might be possible to create a theory of evolution in which progress was confined to occasional episodes during which life advanced suddenly on to an entirely new plane. This would have the advantage of preserving a gap between the human race and the rest of the animal kingdom. Progress would occur in cycles, each one beginning with the injection of something new into the world, and then continuing along its own inexorable path until replaced by the next upward step.

The analogy between this cyclic theory of evolution and certain models of human history is obvious enough – and I believe that the similarity is not accidental. Those biologists who rejected the Darwinian initiative were exploiting an alternative model of historical development that was already well-developed outside science. They were thus able to create non-Darwinian theories of evolution which preserved the view that the world is governed by something more than individual acts of selfishness.

We can well appreciate how the cyclic model of progress could be revived in the late-Victorian era as the foundation for a more self-conscious imperialism based on the idea of racial or national destiny. What is less well-known is that the equivalent non-Darwinian model of evolution gained considerable strength within biology in the later decades of the nineteenth century. Far from continuing its domination of science, Huxley's Darwinism was gradually overtaken by rival theories. During what Julian Huxley (T. H.'s grandson) called the 'eclipse of Darwinism' at the turn of the century, theories of nonadaptive evolution were widely endorsed.[28] In the early years of the twentieth century they were extended into human prehistory to become the basis for an ideology of racial struggle which is often, somewhat confusingly, referred to as yet another version of 'social Darwinism.' In fact, these theories were the product of an interlude separating the original Spencerian version of Darwinism from the synthesis of natural selection and Mendelian genetics in the 1920s and 30s which created modern Darwinism.

---

[28] See Bowler, *The Eclipse of Darwinism: Anti-Darwinian Evolution Theories in the Decades around 1900* (Baltimore: Johns Hopkins University Press, 1983).

In the early Victorian era, the cyclic model of development was incorporated into what has been called the 'liberal Anglican' view of history developed by Thomas Arnold.[29] For Arnold, each civilization goes through a cycle of progress through to maturity, followed by decline and decay. If there was overall progress, this was because certain civilizations were able to build on cultural foundations established by their predecessors. As developed by Charles Kingsley, this became the basis for the claim that modern Christianity represents the outcome of a unique sequence of events planned by God. Greece and Rome each went through its cycle of maturity and decline in order to pass on to Western Europe certain traditions that could only be fully developed when combined with the Teutonic love of freedom.[30] A similar model was proposed by philologists such as Max Müller, who saw the development of European languages as the product of successive waves of Aryan invaders coming in from the East.[31] Archaeologists too saw bronze and iron technologies as the products of new and more highly-civilized peoples invading Europe from a souce of inspiration in central Asia. Progress was not the result of continuous self-development within single cultures, it occured through a series of waves, each representing the unique contribution of a particular race.[32]

This approach to history evaded the question of the true source of new cultures so as to give the impression that higher powers were somehow involved. The internal history of each nation or culture was bound by rigid laws of development that could not be used to predict the character of the next upward step. It is less well-known that similar models were used to interpret the fossil record as an alternative to the linear progressionism of Grant and Chambers. Richard Owen coined the term 'dinosaur' in his 1841 address on 'British Fossil Reptiles' to the British Association, and at the same time he emphasized the fact that the dinosaurs, although the earliest reptiles, were also the most advanced. The subsequent history of the class was a decline not a

[29] See Arnold's essay 'The Social Progress of States', which appears as appendix 1 to his edition of Thucydides, *History of the Peloponnesian War* (Oxford: S. Collingwood, 1830–35, 3 vols), vol. 1. More generally see Duncan Forbes, *The Liberal Anglican Idea of History* (Cambridge: Cambridge University Press, 1952) and J. W. Burrow, *A Liberal Descent: Victorian Historians and the English Past* (Cambridge: Cambridge University Press, 1981).

[30] See for instance Kingsley's *The Roman and the Teuton* (new edn, London: Macmillan, 1895).

[31] See J. W. Burrow, 'The Uses of Philology in Victorian England', in Robert Robson (ed.), *Ideas and Institutions of Victorian Britain: Essays in Honour of George Kitson Clark* (London: G. Bell, 1967), pp. 180–204.

[32] For more details on these developments see Bowler, *The Invention of Progress* (note 22), chap. 2.

progression.[33] In the 1840s similar ideas were used against Chambers'
Vestiges by critics such as Hugh Miller: gradual progress was obviously
wrong because the fossil record showed a series of sudden advances each
followed by a decline:

> The general advance in creation has been incalculably great. The lower
> divisions of the vertebrata precede the higher; – the fish preceded the
> reptile, the reptile preceded the bird, and the bird preceded the mammiferous
> quadruped. And yet, is there one of these great divisions in which, in at
> least some prominent feature, the present, through this mysterious element
> of degradation, is not inferior to the past?[34]

For Miller, this irregular pattern of development suggested that the sudden
appearance of each new class must be by miracle. But we have already
noted that by the 1850s even Owen was beginning to suspect that the
existence of law-like trends in the fossil record must imply preordained
patterns of development. These were of divine origin, but they worked
without the need for miraculous intervention. They also worked through
a series of discontinuous cycles, making it clear that something more than
mere individual effort was involved. In the 1860s Owen naturally took up
an anti-Darwinian stance, but he was not – as has often been claimed –
an outright opponent of evolution. Now that the general idea of natural
development was becoming popular, Owen supported it, but made it clear
that he saw evolution as the unfolding of built-in trends rather than the
adaptation of individuals (or populations) to their environment.[35] On the
question of human origins, he insisted that there was no simple linear trend
leading to mankind. These points were developed further by St. George
Jackson Mivart in his *Genesis of Species* of 1870 – one of the most powerful
sources of anti-Darwinian arguments in biology.[36]

There can be no doubt that Owen and Mivart were outmanoeuvred
by Huxley and the Darwinians, so that the scientific community was for
a time dominated by a view of evolution that made fewer concessions
to the idea of divine predestination. But in the later decades of the
century the non-Darwinian view of evolution modernized itself to create
a framework for a theory in which the cyclic model of development

[33] Richard Owen, 'Report on British Fossil Reptiles, Part 2', *Report of the British Association
for the Advancement of Science*, 1841 meeting, 60–204. See Adrian Desmond, 'Designing the
Dinosaurs: Richard Owen's Response to Robert Edmund Grant', *Isis.* **70** (1979), 224–34.
More generally see Desmond's *Archetypes and Ancestors* (note 6) and Bowler, *The Invention
of Progress* (note 22), chap. 6.
[34] Hugh Miller, *Footprints of the Creator: Or the Asterolepis of Stromness* (3rd edn, London:
Johnston and Hunter, 1850), p. 179.
[35] For further details see Richards, 'A Question of Property Rights' (note 6), Desmond,
Archetypes and Ancestors (note 6).
[36] On Mivart and his influence see Bowler, *The Eclipse of Darwinism* (note 28), chap. 3.

figured very strongly. Somewhat paradoxically, the supporters of this model appealed to Lamarckism as an alternative to natural selection when explaining adaptive evolution. Once dismissed as a radical heresy, Lamarckism now became acceptable to conservatives because it offered an alternative to the materialism of natural selection.

There is a sense in which the opponents of Darwinism, including the writer Samuel Butler, had a clearer idea of the implications lying behind selectionism than the pseudo-Darwinians of the Spencerian school. Butler's *Evolution, Old and New* of 1879 began a campaign against Darwinian materialism that would last into the 1890s.[37] Like Owen and Mivart, Butler was marginalized by the Darwinian group that had taken over science – but it is significant that his Lamarckian ideas were taken much more seriously in the later decades of the century. August Weismann's attack on Lamarckism, often seen as a prelude to modern genetics, was highly controversial during the 1890s. Somewhat paradoxically, Herbert Spencer and Samuel Butler spoke with once voice, at least in opposition to Weismann. For profoundly different reasons, they both wanted to preserve a role for individual effort and initiative in evolution. For Spencer, this corresponded to the activity of the individual humans who contributed to social progress, for Butler it represented a divine spark of creativity implanted in nature.

More directly relevant to my present theme is the preference of many anti-Darwinians for theories which assumed that the evolution of each group runs through a predetermined cycle paralleling the life-cycle of the individual organism. Instead of invoking divinely-implanted trends, palaeontologists assumed that the fossil record gave evidence of regularities that could not be explained in terms of random variation and adaptation to the local environment. The theory of 'orthogenesis' had its origins in the work of American palaeontologists such as Alpheus Hyatt. In studying the pattern of evolution in the Ammonites and other cephalopods, Hyatt was sure that he could detect an initial phase of progressive evolution (which he explained in Lamarckian terms) followed by a decline toward bizarre nonadaptive structures as a prelude to extinction. The origin of each new group was essentially mysterious, but once established each went through a predictable life-cycle of growth, maturity, senility and death.[38]

[37] See Samuel Butler, *Evolution, Old and New* (London: Harwick and Bogue, 1879). On Butler and the growing interest in Lamarckism toward the end of the century see Bowler, *The Eclipse of Darwinism* (note 28), chap. 4.

[38] Hyatt's earliest statement of his theory is his 'On the Parallelism between the Different Stages of Life in the Individual and Those in the Entire Group of the Molluscous Order Tetrabranchiata', *Memoirs of the Boston Society of Natural History*. **1** (1866), 193–209. On his version of the recapitulation theory see Stephen Jay Gould, *Ontogeny and Phylogeny* (Cambridge, Mass.: Harvard University Press, 1977), chap. 4; see also Bowler, *The Eclipse of Darwinism*, chaps 6 and 7, and *The Invention of Progress* (note 19), chap. 6.

By the end of the century this model of evolution was routinely being applied to the rise and fall of the dinosaurs and other groups. Far from portraying evolution as a linear process, it emphasized the existence of many parallel lines of development, each undergoing its own pattern of progress and decline. The origin of each new line was left unexplained, although it was clearly the result of a process quite unrelated to the normal trends exhibited by established groups. The fact that many lines of development had become exhausted and been replaced by younger, more vigorous types provided a parallel with the older cyclic model of history.

Although the link with natural theology was severed in the late Victorian era, this model of evolution provided a foundation for the vision of human history exploited by conservative imperialists. Those who saw the Anglo-Saxon nations as having a unique mission to dominate the world were naturally inclined to think in terms of the human races as having distinct origins. Instead of treating the races as stages in the evolution of a single type, they preferred to see each race as having its own origin, its own pattern of development, and its own destiny.

This view of race had gained ground among physical anthropologists in the 1860s and 70s, causing a rift with Tylor and the cultural anthropologists who favoured the linear model. There was a similar split in archaeology. Study of the palaeolithic (the old stone age) was dominated by advocates of De Mortillet's scheme of linear, indigenous cultural evolution, while the introduction of neolithic, bronze and iron technologies was attributed to the invasion of more developed races from the East. William Boyd Dawkins of Manchester was one of the few who challenged De Mortillet's scheme and insisted that the various palaeolithic toolmaking cultures were specific to distinct racial types. He explicitly invoked the philologists' image of a mysterious centre of progress in central Asia from which all the higher types of mankind had radiated one after another: '. . . the origin of domestic animals, as well as of the cereals, proves that the Neolithic peoples migrated into Europe from the South-east, from the mysterious birthplace of successive races, the Eden of mankind, Central Asia.'[39]

By the end of the century this more extreme view of racial differences was gaining ground in some quarters as a foundation for the ideology of imperial domination. By moving slightly beyond our designated period, we can see that it was extended to give a complete theory of human origins in the early years of the twentieth century. Boyd Dawkin's approach was revived in William Sollas' book *Ancient Hunters* of 1911 to provide an alternative to the linear model of development. According to Sollas, each

---

[39] W. Boyd Dawkins, *Early Man in Britain and his Place in the Tertiary Period* (London: Macmillan, 1880), p. 306; see Bowler *The Invention of Progress* (note 19), chap. 4.

palaeolithic culture belongs to a distinct race, the races constituting parallel and distinct branches of the human family tree. The pattern of human prehistory could be explained as a series of racial takeovers in which the more highly developed types of humanity expanded across the globe, marginalizing or exterminating the earlier types that preceded them.

I believe that this new interpretation of human evolution was an application of the cyclic model of development then gaining ground in palaeontology. One of the most enthusiastic advocates of the theory of orthogenetic evolution in the realm of biological evolution was Arthur Smith Woodward, a palaeontologist at the Natural History Museum in London. But Smith Woodward is best remembered as the dupe in the notorious Piltdown fraud of 1912: it was he who described these deliberately 'planted' remains as belonging to a distinct species of early humanity, *Eoanthropus dawsoni*. Most of the scientists who took Piltdown seriously were, in fact, advocates of evolutionary parallelism, and some of them linked this theory directly to the claim that the modern races are not closely connected. Arthur Keith, for instance, disputed Smith Woodward's reconstruction of 'Piltdown man' – but only because he wanted to extend the evolutionary parallelism in the human family tree even further back in time.[40]

The significance of Piltdown was that it seemed to confirm the existence of parallel branches within the human family tree, each line having its own pattern of development. Where the brutish Neanderthal type had once been treated as a step in the progression from ape to modern human, now the Neanderthals were dismissed as a separate branch of humanity which had been wiped out by our own ancestors invading Europe from central Asia. This whole episode in the history of palaeoanthropology can thus be interpreted as an extension of the cyclic model of evolution that had existed as an alternative to Darwinism thoughout the Victorian era.

For Sollas race conflict was an important feature of human evolution. Whatever the process that generated the new lines of evolution (certainly not Darwinian natural selection), it was essential that newly evolved types displaced their predecessors The implications of this theory for the imperialist view of race relations is obvious enough – Sollas welcomed the

---

[40] Keith has, in fact, been suggested as the chief architect of the Piltdown fraud in the latest of the many attempts to unravel the mystery, although I find the case against him less than convincing if only because it is not clear *why* Keith would have wanted to 'plant' an ape jaw along with human remains; see Frank Spencer, *Piltdown: A Scientific Forgery* (London: Natural History Museum / Oxford: Oxford University Press, 1990). For background to the Piltdown affair, including the theories of Sollas, Keith and Woodward, see Bowler, *Theories of Human Evolution* (note 22).

extermination of races which could not properly exploit the territory they occupied:

> What part is to be assigned to justice in the government of human affairs? So far as the facts are clear, they teach in no equivocal terms that there is no right which is not founded on might. Justice belongs to the strong, and has been meted out to each race according to its strength; each has received as much justice as it deserves. What perhaps is most impressive in each of the cases we have discussed is this, that the dispossession by a new-comer of a race already in occupation of the soil has marked an upward step in the intellectual progress of mankind. It is not priority of occupation, but the power to utilize, which establishes a claim to the land. Hence it is a duty which every race owes to itself, and to the human family as well, to cultivate by every possible means its own strength: directly it falls behind in the regard it pays to this duty, whether in art or science, in breeding or in organization for self-defence, it incurs a penalty which Natural Selection, the stern but beneficient tyrant of the organic world, will assuredly exact, and that speedily, to the full.[41]

In the same vein, Keith compared the extermination of the Neanderthals with what was happening to the natives of Australia and North America.[42] Over the next few decades he went on the develop a whole theory of human evolution based on tribal conflict.[43]

This appeal to the importance of racial conflict as the mechanism of progress certainly looks like a form of 'social Darwinism.' Note how Sollas openly invokes natural selection as the driving force of race relations. Yet in the same book he ridiculed the Darwinian mechanism of natural selection acting on individual variations.[44] The explanation of this paradox lies in the fact that Sollas and Keith wanted selection to act between races, but looked to some more purposeful mechanism in the actual production of new types. The ideology of race conflict was, in fact, an extension of the non-Darwinian model of evolution that had flourished as an alternative to linear progressionism throughout the Victorian era. The concept of the 'struggle for existence' could be exploited in a variety of ways, some of which had little to do with the original form of Darwinism. In the early twentieth century, the image of conflicting races, each with its own destiny and character, played an important role in the rhetoric of imperialism. It also backed up the call of the eugenics movement for steps to be taken to stave off racial degeneration by preventing the breeding of the

---

[41] See W. J. Sollas, *Ancient Hunters and their Modern Representatives* (London: Macmillan, 1911), p. 383.

[42] Arthur Keith, *The Antiquity of Man* (London: Williams and Norgate, 1915), p. 136.

[43] Keith's views on the positive role of race-conflict were later summed up in his *A New Theory of Human Evolution* (London: Watts, 1948).

[44] Sollas, *Ancient Hunters* (note 41), p. 405.

feebleminded.[45] Eugenics has been linked both to social Darwinism and to the rise of Mendelian genetics in the decades after 1900, but its emphasis on racial character links it also to an earlier, non-Darwinian view of history.

By extending our coverage of the 'Darwinian revolution' into later decades we can see that many of the conventional myths about the impact of the *Origin of Species* must be rejected. Darwin's theory was certainly greeted as an opportunity by those who wanted to push for social reform and an extension of the free-enterprise system. As part of Huxley's campaign to earn science its rightful place in the world, and as a component of Spencer's philosophy of gradual progress, Darwinism was taken up with enthusiasm by certain sections of the Victorian intellectual world. For this to happen, some of Darwin's most important scientific insights had to be pushed aside, to be revived only in the twentieth century.

Those who adopted a more conservative posture were not thereby debarred from accepting the general idea of evolution. Although some opted for creationism at first, there was a steady movement toward the formulation of non-Darwinian theories of development that would preserve and modernize certain aspects of an alternative view of history. For the exponents of orthogenesis and racial conflict, evolutionism also offered an opportunity rather than a threat – although to understand how this was possible we have had to explore the often neglected world of non-Darwinian evolutionism.

---

[45] The eugenics movement was founded by Darwin's cousin, Francis Galton, in the 1880s, but did not gain significant influence until the early decades of the twentieth century; see for instance Daniel Kevles, *In the Name of Eugenics: Genetics and the Uses of Human Heredity* (New York: Knopf, 1985). As Kevles' title indicates, the claim that an individual's character is determined by heredity gained a considerable boost from the emergence of genetics after the 'rediscovery' of Mendel's laws of heredity in 1900. My purpose here is to note that the movement also gained support from those who were more interested in the determination of character by *racial* inheritance – many of whom were not geneticists.

Proceedings of the British Academy, **78**, 149–163

Medical Values in a Commercial Age

W.F. BYNUM

Wellcome Institute for the History of Medicine

EVEN the phrase 'Victorian values' is a reminder that historians write about themselves as well as the past. A volume with this title has different reverberations for us than it would have had for a historian of Lytton Strachey's generation, and even the inclusion of a paper on medicine testifies to recent changes in historical perceptions and practice. Neither science nor medicine rated a chapter in G.M. Young's *Early Victorian Britain*, and only three decades ago, Walter Houghton's *Victorian Frame of Mind* contained but one brief reference to medicine and only cursory material on what is now seen as a much more central Victorian preoccupation: health.[1] The army doctor and sanitary reformer Edmund Parkes (1819–1875) was speaking as a Victorian as much as he was as a doctor when he urged young doctors 'Never [to] think of your life, but always of your health, which alone can make life useful'.[2]

Parkes's coupling of health and usefulness was high praise indeed, for usefulness could easily have served alongside *Duty*, *Thrift* and *Self-Help* as a marketable volume by that quintessential Victorian Samuel Smiles, himself of course originally a trained doctor. In fact, an episode in Smiles's early career points to the theme which I shall discuss here. After a medical

---

Read 13 December 1990. © The British Academy 1992.

[1] G.M. Young (ed.), *Early Victorian England, 1830–1865*, 2 vols (London, 1934); Walter Houghton, *The Victorian Frame of Mind, 1830–1870* (New Haven, 1957).

[2] Quoted by J. Russell Reynolds, 'The Value of Competition', in *Essays and Addresses* (London, 1896), p. 241.

apprenticeship and formal medical study at the University of Edinburgh, and a European jaunt for a quick M.D., Smiles returned to his native Haddington, to pursue a career in medicine. He abandoned Haddington after six years, being, as he recalled, 'among 3000 healthy Scotsmen and in competition with seven other doctors'.[3] Ever the optimist, Smiles settled in Leeds, turning shortly to journalism and then to the writing of those books which so captured the spirit of his age. The doctorate which he proudly displayed on the title pages of his later books was not of the medical variety, but an honorary LL.D. – a higher one in the Victorian scale of values.

Competition in the medical market-place is my theme, then, and while the Victorian medical profession was never so cohesive as to be able to adopt anything like – to use one of our own cant phrases – a 'strategic plan', that profession was, willy-nilly, perhaps, reasonably successful in adapting itself to the changing economic and social circumstances of Victorian Britain. The most striking features of this adaptation were the growth of an occupational diversity and the increasing reliance on the state as an important patron. In that sense, the 1911 National Health Insurance Act was simply a culmination of processes which had been in train at least since the New Poor Law of 1834.

Before examining the variety of medical responses to the spectre of competition, I must mention briefly two matters of relevance: the continuing legacy of individualism, and the size of the medical profession itself.

First, individualism: whatever criteria one chooses as essential defining characteristics of a profession – autonomy, esoteric knowledge, even a rhetoric of altruism – it is clear that Victoria's reign was the crucial period for doctors.[4] Furthermore, it seems to me that recent historical attempts to disparage the 1858 Medical Act as a failure, or worse, because it perpetuated too much of the *status quo*, are all wide of the mark. Irvine Loudon has recently shown that the opportunity for radical transformation of the structure of the medical profession had been missed – in the 1830s and early 40s – and that we should not therefore be surprised that the Act that ultimately came into effect tinkered less than radicals like the doughty Thomas Wakley (1795–1862)

---

[3] T.K. Monro, *The Physician as Man of Letters, Science and Action* (Glasgow, 1933), p. 116; elsewhere, Smiles recalled that there were in Haddington 'more than enough [medical men] to doctor double the population'. (Thomas MacKay [ed.], *The Autobiography of Samuel Smiles, LL.D.* [London, 1905], p. 60).

[4] A standard sociological analysis is Eliot Freidson, *Professional Dominance* (New York, 1970).

might have wished.[5] On the other hand, it seems ironic to see the Act historically in terms of conspiracy and monopoly, as Jeffrey Berlant has done, when the chief source of medical disquiet at the time was that the Act had failed to protect medical men (and the public) adequately from irregulars and quacks.[6] Admittedly, the Act bestowed on regular medical men certain advantages in the medical market place, but it never gave them, nor was it intended to, a monopoly on the individual doctor-patient transaction.

And that was crucial, for the values of the profession at large – both before and after 1858 – placed a premium on the individual encounter between doctor and patient: on the practice, for a fee, of curative medicine. Country surgeon-apothecaries of an earlier generation had been happy enough to call what they did a 'business',[7] and while the professional rhetoric might have been modified in the course of the century, it was still largely through private practice that reputations and fortunes were made, and professional honours secured. The Royal College of Physicians of London had twelve presidents during Victoria's reign, and only with the election of Sir William Jenner in 1881 did it acquire a president who could be described as scientifically distinguished.[8] Even Jenner maintained a large consultancy practice as well as appointments at Victoria's court, the usual pattern for College presidents. It could be argued with some justification that the College of Physicians was a sleepy, conservative place, outside the mainstream of significant professional change.[9] Nevertheless, London continued to act as a medical magnet throughout the century and the leaders of the profession were to be found among the fellowship of the London Colleges.[10] Further, despite

[5] Irvine Loudon, *Medical Care and the General Practitioner*, 1750–1850 (Oxford, 1986); the best description of the long series of acts and successive Parliamentary debates is Charles Newman, *The Evolution of Medical Education in the Nineteenth Century* (London, 1957); a recent attempt to assess the Coleridgean influence on one of the Act's chief architects, John Simon, is T.N. Stokes, 'A Coleridgean against the Medical Corporations; John Simon and the Parliamentary Campaign for the Reform of the Medical Profession 1854–8', *Medical History*, **33** (1989), 343–59.

[6] Jeffrey Berlant, *Profession and Monopoly: A Study of Medicine in the United States and Great Britain* (Berkeley, California, 1975), pp. 153ff, sees the Act as liberal in conception but monopolistic in actual consequence.

[7] A point stressed by Loudon, op. cit. (note 5), pp. 100ff.

[8] The Presidents are listed in vols 3 (p. 343) and 4 (p. 603) of *Munk's Roll*, begun by William Munk and continued by a succession of editors (London, 1878 *et seq.*) where short biographies of them will also be found.

[9] George Clark, *A History of the Royal College of Physicians of London*, 2 vols (Oxford, 1964–6) is a tactful account of the College's history until 1858. A third volume, on the later history of the College, was written by A.M. Cooke (Oxford, 1972).

[10] Jeanne Peterson, *The Medical Profession in Mid-Victorian London* (Berkeley, California, 1978).

the increasing occupational diversity, to be examined more fully below, private solo practice was the model to which most medical students would have aspired and would have hoped, after a few years, to have achieved.

In reality, not all of them could succeed. Was this because there were too many of them? Certainly this was a common complaint from the medical men themselves in the decades before the Medical Act, and one which continued to be voiced throughout the century.[11] An overcrowded profession was bad for the doctors and bad for their public. Doctors suffered a loss of income, patients suffered a loss of quality in their care since, so the argument ran, this professional surplus was always to be found in the dregs of their ill-educated, incompetent colleagues (who rarely managed to get their opinions into print). The real problem, however, especially before 1858 but not solved even then, lay in alternative providers of medical care: quacks, irregulars, practitioners with alternative medical cosmologies, and, perhaps most important, the chemists and druggists who took it upon themselves to sell medicine directly to the public.[12] Despite the economic liberalism of the age, many doctors wanted the state formally to outlaw all unorthodox or alternative practitioners, as a danger to the public's health, and the government's refusal to do this was seen by some as irresponsible. At the very least, they wanted to confine competition to the fraternity itself.

On the other hand, the Medical Register, created by the 1858 Act, did at least and at last officially set the standards by which the fraternity was to be identified. It also required members of it to stand up and be counted if they wanted to benefit from the confidence which the public was supposed to have in the profession. On paper, the Medical Register eased the problem of overcrowding: the census of 1851 enumerated 19,190 medical practitioners, in a population of 17,927,609, or one out of 935 people. The corresponding figures for 1861 are 15,297 in a population of 20,066,224, or one in 1,312.[13] The diminution in the absolute number of individuals calling themselves medical men was a function of the new criteria in effect between 1851 and 1861. Thereafter, for the rest of the century, the ratio of practitioners to population varied but modestly. The

[11] Loudon, op. cit. (note 5), ch. 10; F. Musgrove, 'Middle-Class Education and Employment in the Nineteenth Century', *Economic History Review*, (n.s.) 12 (1959–60), 99–111.

[12] A recent monograph and two collections of essays survey this general area: Roy Porter, *Health for Sale: Quackery in England, 1660–1850* (Manchester, 1989); W.F. Bynum and Roy Porter (eds), *Medical Fringe and Medical Orthodoxy 1750–1850* (London, 1987); Roger Cooter (ed.), *Studies in the History of Alternative Medicine* (Oxford, 1988).

[13] For figures from 1841 to 1971, see Loudon, op. cit. (note 5), p. 309.

drop between 1851 and 1861 was a result of the Medical Act, since after 1858 it was not legal to identify oneself as a 'medical man', even for census purposes, without possessing at least one of a number of the qualifications specified by the Act.

Crude figures like these do not mean too much, since they say nothing about how many of these practitioners were active or how they were distributed throughout the country. Nevertheless, they do suggest that Samuel Smiles was either unlucky in his choice of a place to establish his practice, or exaggerated the extent of his competition, since his figures would give only 375 patients for each doctor in Haddington in the 1830s. There were irregularities of distribution, of course, – London always had more than its share, for example – but as Squire Sprigge remarked in 1905, the very fact that the ratio of population to doctors had been more or less constant for more that forty years, implied that it was 'inherently right'. He at least had no truck with whinging colleagues who complained of too much competition.[14]

Given the structure of the educational institutions and the licensing bodies, there was no chance that numbers would be regulated by the profession itself. Hospital medical schools, university medical faculties and the medical corporations each needed student fees to survive, and more fees to thrive. In the United States, a similar situation produced the pseudo-academic proliferation of proprietary schools offering cut-price degrees.[15] This never happened in Britain. For one thing, the separation of teaching and examination functions between the hospital medical schools and the medical corporations meant that most students were examined by people who had not necessarily taught them. This might have produced an ideal system of checks and balances, though in practice the situation was not nearly so neat. For instance, the universities could both teach and examine, and university medical degrees were registrable in the same way as membership or the licentiate in one of the royal colleges or the Society of Apothecaries. Until about 1850, overwhelmingly the most important university medical school, in terms of degrees, was Edinburgh; the University of London had oppressively and deliberately high standards, with very low pass rates, until the last decades of the century, and the medical schools in Oxford and Cambridge began gradually to attract more students only from

[14] S. Squire Sprigge, *Medicine and the Public* (London, 1905), ch. 2.
[15] Two recent monographs survey medical education in the United States: William G. Rothstein, *American Medical Schools and the Practice of Medicine* (New York, 1987), and Kenneth M. Ludmerer, *Learning to Heal: the Development of Medical Education* (New York, 1985).

the 1860s.[16] Only a minority of the rank and file possessed university medical degrees even by the end of the century, although the present trend was by then well underway. The General Medical Council, created by the 1858 Act, probably did more than its enemies charged, and less than its advocates pleaded, in settling and maintaining educational standards.[17] Its direct powers were limited, but its very existence and functions occupied pride of place in various late Victorian descriptions of the profession, and Sir George Newman was convinced that medical, legal and lay people were unanimous: the General Medical Council had 'achieved order and efficiency in place of chaos and injustice in the profession'.[18]

There existed no single mechanism to regulate professional numbers, and only the barriers of entrance standards and fees could control the size of the cohort setting out in quest of a medical career. The most famous study of what actually happened to medical students was that published in 1869 by (Sir) James Paget (1814–1899), the St. Bartholomew's Hospital surgeon and pathologist. He collected information on the subsequent careers of 1,000 students whom he had taught at Bart's between 1839 and 1859, and concluded, roughly, that about 10% met with either outstanding or considerable success, another 50% with 'reasonable' success, and about 12% with 'limited' success. The remainder – 280 – either failed in their careers, abandoned medicine early, or died during their education or shortly thereafter. In addition, he was unable to trace the whereabouts of another 226, many of whom were probably among the less successful. Consequently, his findings were perhaps more cheerful than the rigours of the profession warranted. The only student which Paget singled out by name was one of his less than successful protégés, the poisoner Dr. Palmer, who had been 'an idle, dissipated student, cursed with more money than he had either the wisdom or the virtue to use well'.[19] A generation later, Squire Sprigge repeated the exercise on a more limited scale, tracing the careers

[16] For London, see Negley Harte, *The University of London 1836–1986* (London, 1986); for Cambridge, cf. Sir Walter Langdon-Brown, *Some Chapters in Cambridge Medical History* (Cambridge, 1946); Sir Humphry Rolleston, *The Cambridge Medical School* (Cambridge, 1932); and Arthur Rook (ed.), *Cambridge and its Contribution to Medicine* (London, 1971). A.J. Engel, *From Clergyman to Don, the Rise of the Academic Profession in Nineteenth-Century Oxford* (Oxford, 1983), barely mentions medical education.

[17] Dr. Russell Smith of the University of Melbourne is presently working on a history of the General Medical Council.

[18] George Newman, *The Building of a Nation's Health* (London, 1939), p. 67; cf. Squire Sprigge, op. cit. (note 14), ch. 1.

[19] James Paget, 'What Becomes of Medical Students', reprinted in Stephen Paget (ed.), *Selected Essays and Addresses by Sir James Paget* (London, 1902), pp. 27–32; cf. Stephen Paget, *Memoirs and Letters of Sir James Paget* (London, 1902), pp. 244–5; and Peterson, op. cit. (note 10), pp. 133–5.

of 250 students who had entered St. George's Hospital Medical School, beginning from 1879. His general conclusions were roughly comparable to Paget's: of 250 students, 63 – about a quarter – failed to qualify for a variety of reasons; from the remaining 187, Sprigge judged that 116 had achieved outstanding, reasonable or fair success, 23 had died within 12 years of qualification and only six had come to grief, including two who ended up in prison. He was unable to say anything about the careers of 20 who were still on the Medical Register, but the fact that they were there implied to him that they were earning some sort of a living through medical practice.[20]

These numbers could be variously interpreted, though both Paget and Squire Sprigge chose to see them in a rosy light, as indicating that medicine offered a good career choice, if only for the energetic and ambitious young man. Following the medical life, Squire Sprigge insisted, was 'worth the candle'. On the other hand, both men were conscious that their own medical schools, Bart's and George's, were prestigious metropolitan institutions and that comparable figures for other medical schools might not be so favourable. In addition, individuals whose careers were untraceable were excluded, and these were unlikely to have been professionally successful. Paget attempted to explain away what could seem to be relatively high death rates for young adults, but neither commented on the fact that the bulk of the professional wastage occurred early on. This was only partially a consequence of the examination system; only a small fraction of those who failed professionally did so because they were unable to pass their exams. Nevertheless, the elaboration of a much more extensive and, so contemporaries believed, searching examination structure was a striking feature of Victorian society, including its medical profession.[21] Even the Royal Colleges, hardly notorious for advocating meritocracies, were forced to change, through the replacement of oral examinations by written ones, the extension of subjects to be examined, and the emergence of mechanisms whereby examiners were appointed as a result of competence rather than seniority.[22] More generally, examining became

---

[20] Squire Sprigge, op. cit. (note 14), ch. 2; Squire Sprigge returned to the theme, with some figures collected by Edward Corner for St. Thomas's Hospital students from 1890–9, in an essay entitled 'Prizes and Performances', in S. Squire Sprigge, *Physic and Fiction* (London, 1921), pp. 148–75.

[21] For a general overview, see Robert J. Montgomery, *Examinations: An Account of Their Evolution as Administrative Devices in England* (London, 1965).

[22] A.L. Mansell, 'Examinations and Medical Education: the Preliminary Sciences in the Examinations of London University and the English Conjoint Board, 1861–1911', in Roy MacLeod (ed.), *Days of Judgement: Science, Examinations and the Organization of Knowledge in Late Victorian England* (London, 1982); Loudon, op. cit. (note 5), pp. 171–88; W.J. Reader, *Professional Men* (London, 1966), ch. 3; Newman, op. cit. (note 5).

itself a kind of mini-industry, providing welcomed income and prestige, and not-so-welcomed drudgery in roughly equal portions.[23] Title pages of medical works often singled out examination appointments alongside hospital and academic posts, an indication of the value the profession began to place on the former.

The competitiveness of the system was explicitly celebrated in prize-giving ceremonies, which, with the opening of session, was one of the two red-letter days in the medical school's annual calendar. Each was occasion for inspirational platitudes, and Prize-Day gave eminent representatives of the profession and of public life more generally oppor-tunity to reflect on such themes as 'The value of competition', the title of Sir John Russell Reynolds' address to the medical students in Bristol in 1885. He reminded his charges that the public rewards of medicine were not so great as those of the church, the bar, or the armed forces, but that the private gratitude of their patients and their patients' families and friends could compensate. It was these latter who would continue the lifelong examination merely begun in medical school: fail your patients and you will fail your profession and in your profession.[24]

Embodied in such injunctions, and in the hierarchies of success by which Paget and Squire Sprigge classified their peers, was the recog-nition that, in the end, private practice was the most pervasive touch-stone. Paget judged 'distinguished success' to have been achieved by obtaining, in this order, 'a leading position in practice in great cities', a place on the honorary staff of a large hospital, an academic chair or some important public office. In reality, attainment of any of the latter three was unlikely except in conjunction with the former. Russell Reynolds singled out three of his contemporaries as worthy of emu-lation: E.A. Parkes, Sir William Jenner and Sir John Simon. They may be more commonly remembered as a sanitarian, hospital consult-ant or civil servant, respectively, but each began as a private practi-tioner and continued to see patients in that capacity for much or all of his career. Of the trio, Parkes (1819–1876) had the least interest in private practice, partly because his health was always delicate and

---

[23] Becoming an examiner in physiology and comparative anatomy for London University in 1856 was one of several posts which helped the young T.H. Huxley cobble together a scientific career. cf. Leonard Huxley, *Life and Letters of T.H. Huxley* (2nd edn, 3 vols London, 1903), I, pp. 213ff.

[24] Reynolds, op. cit. (note 2). A poignant comment on the phenomenon can be found in Shephard T. Taylor, *The Diary of a Medical Student During the Mid-Victorian Period, 1860–1864* (Norwich, 1927), entry for 28 June 1861: 'Distribution of prizes at the College [King's College London], but as there were no prizes for poor me, I purposely kept away.'

partly because his connexions with the army's medical service dictated frequent trips abroad, even during the decade (1849–1860) he was professor of clinical medicine of University College. However, as William Jenner, one of his memorialists, pointed out, he was 'a sound and able practitioner', who simply had not remained long enough in London to rise to the top of the consulting branch of the profession – 'we all know that success in practice is, to some extent, a question of survivorship'.[25] Simon gave up his private consulting rooms in the 1850s, but he retained his surgical consultancy at St. Thomas's until his retirement age.[26]

What the individual patient paying a fee to the individual doctor constituted – whether it was a shilling for an office visit to a poor general practitioner or five guineas or more for half-an-hour of a Harley Street consultant's time – was a vote of confidence. 'The public are our employers, and, in the long run, we shall be what our employers make us,' remarked Robert Brudenell Carter in 1903.[27] Within that context, internal competition was perceived as inevitable, even desirable, and was regulated by a complicated but informal code of intra-professional etiquette, governing such matters as second opinions and poaching patients.[28] Two other major sources of competition, one external and one internal, continued to plague the late Victorian profession. The external one was of course the unresolved one of what doctors still liked to call quackery.

In practice, the most serious economic threat was probably not that posed by unregistered individuals offering their services in the medical market place, whether these were homoeopaths, botanicals, nurses,

---

[25] William Jenner, 'Observations on the Work and Character of the Late Dr. E.A. Parkes, FRS', *Lancet* 1876, ii, 41–3, on p. 41.

[26] Royston Lambert, *Sir John Simon (1816–1904) and English Social Administration* (London, 1963).

[27] R.B. Carter, *Doctors and Their Work* (London, 1903), p. 13.

[28] Ibid., ch. 13 for an Edwardian discussion of medical etiquette; Squire Sprigge, op. cit. (note 14), pp. 243ff also touches on issues of 'second opinions'. An anecdote from Carter (pp. 291–2) illustrates the dilemma from the doctor's point of view: 'An old lady once consulted me, to whom I said that she must undergo an operation without avoidable delay, and who replied that she could not consent to so serious a proposal until she had taken a second opinion. I applauded her decision, and urged that the second opinion should be taken immediately. She assented, but went on to ask me to whom I should advise her to go. I was obliged to say that the answer must depend upon the opinion she desired to receive. If she wished for one which would encourage her to undergo the operation, I could tell her where to get that. If she wished for one which would encourage her in letting things drift, I could equally well tell her where to get that. She was a shrewd old lady, and, after looking at me for a minute with a rather puzzled expression, she said, "Perhaps I had better have it done." I thought so too; and the "second opinion" was not obtained.'

wise-women, or prescribing parsons, but the dispensing chemists and druggists, and patent medicine manufacturers.[29] Relationships between the medical profession and the Pharmaceutical Society were sometimes strained, as doctors complained that would-be patients were going directly to their neighbourhood chemist for advice and medicine, and pharmacists objected that too many doctors still dispensed medicines. As Squire Sprigge remarked:

> The Pharmaceutical Society very properly and strictly forbids its members to prescribe for patients or to take upon themselves the functions of the medical practitioner, but over the counters of scores of dispensing chemists every day and every hour there are given to the public medical advice and medical treatment.[30]

Proprietary medicines like Godfrey's Cordial or Carter's Little Liver Pills were available in a wide variety of shops, and a large mail-order market, often aimed at people suffering from 'shameful' conditions, like venereal disease, female troubles, sexual anxieties or unwanted pregnancies, was cultivated by advertisers. Bartrip has recently examined the *British Medical Journal*'s late Victorian and Edwardian campaign against 'secret remedies'.[31] As a profession, doctors were never entirely happy that the 1858 Act had not protected the public from what they liked to see as its own gullibility, though the more thoughtful of them recognized that they, the doctors, were not, and could not be, disinterested parties in the debate.[32] Late Victorian medical commentators found consolation in the belief that an increased public appreciation of the new scientific medicine would encourage Parliament to outlaw quackery, or at least diminish patients' appetite for quack remedies and self-medication.

A more subtle, internal source of competition also confronted the late Victorian profession: the abuse of the charity system by patients who could afford to pay for the services of a private practitioner. Charity

---

[29] This threat has been emphasized for the early nineteenth century by Loudon, op. cit. (note 5), ch. 6; a detailed local study is Hilary Marland, *Medicine and Society in Wakefield and Huddersfield, 1780–1870* (Cambridge, 1987), pp. 208–51; *idem*, 'The Medical Activities of Mid-Nineteenth-Century Chemists and Druggists with Special Reference to Wakefield and Huddersfield', *Medical History*, **31** (1987), 415–39.

[30] Squire Sprigge, op. cit. (note 14), p. 73. Significantly, he discussed this situation in a chapter entitled 'The Evils of Quackery'.

[31] P.W.J. Bartrip, *Mirror of Medicine, A History of the BMJ* (Oxford, 1990), pp. 189–202; for an example of a late Victorian entrepreneurial quack, cf. William Schupbach, 'Sequah: An English "American Medicine" – Man in 1890', *Medical History*, **29** (1985), 272–317.

[32] E.g. Squire Sprigge, op. cit. (note 14), p. 72: 'The opposition of the medical men to the quack, however legitimate, cannot be called disinterested, and therefore does not weigh with the public'.

was of course big business in Victorian Britain, among which the voluntary hospitals with their out-patient departments, specialist hospitals, lying-in charities, and dispensaries occupied pride of place.[33] These were aimed primarily at the provident poor, that large segment of the population sufficiently independent to fall outside the jurisdiction of the Poor Laws but sufficiently impecunious to be unable to afford the services of a private practitioner and, especially, the nursing and other expenses of a serious illness or operation. Members of the medical profession had a large stake in these establishments, of course, and honorary appointments were keenly sought. Nevertheless, the continued growth of the charity sector was viewed by many practitioners with alarm. Squire Sprigge rated the 'abuse of hospitals' on an equal par with the 'evils of quackery',[34] and radical reformers like the Liverpool doctor Robert Reid Rentoul wanted the whole charity system overhauled.[35]

The problem, as doctors perceived it, was the ease with which waged workers and members of their families could obtain free or cheap treatment through charity. Outpatient attendance in the London hospitals rose by more than 50% between 1887 and 1900, from just over one million to well over one-and-a-half million.[36] Most hospitals employed clerks to investigate the financial circumstances of their patients, and posted the maximum weekly wage which entitled patients to use the charity, or over which payment would be expected. Rentoul cited an enquiry conducted in 1875 by the Charity Organization Society at the Royal Free Hospital in London. Of 641 individuals presenting themselves for treatment at the out-patient department, 12 were deemed able to pay a private practitioner, 231 were eligible to subscribe to a provident society, 169 were suitable, 103 gave false addresses and 69 gave insufficient information.[37] On the other hand, policing patients was not easy, and, in any case, the more patients institutions saw, the easier external fund-raising was among benefactors. The perilous financial state of many charities encouraged them to accept money from whatever quarter, including paying patients and, especially towards the

[33] The standard account of hospitals in England, Brian Abel-Smith, *The Hospitals, 1800–1948* (London, 1964), is still useful if somewhat dated. A recent synthetic study of hospitals in London is Geoffrey Rivett, *The Development of the London Hospital System, 1823–1982* (London, 1986); for the Manchester area, see J.V. Pickstone, *Medicine and Industrial Society: A History of Hospital Development in Manchester and its Region, 1752–1946* (Manchester, 1985).

[34] Squire Sprigge, op. cit. (note 14), chs 5 & 6.

[35] R.R. Rentoul, *The Reform of Our Voluntary Medical Charities* (London, 1891).

[36] The figure is quoted by Squire Sprigge, op. cit. (note 14), p. 58.

[37] Rentoul, op. cit. (note 35), p. 3.

century's end, from working people themselves.[38] In theory, the latter were the objects of the hospitals' charitable exertions. In Birmingham, over half the working population contributed in the 1890s through the Birmingham Hospital Saturday Fund, mostly at a penny a week. This raised close to £20,000 a year for the hospital, but the contributors naturally looked upon their contributions as a form of insurance which entitled them to use the hospital's services.[39] The spectre of municipalization of the voluntary hospitals was raised long before the coming of the N.H.S.

Rentoul wanted a strict separation of the charity and paying sectors and proposed a more systematic prepayment scheme for working men and their families who he thought should be more rigorously excluded from the voluntary hospitals and their outpatient departments. His proposals, made in the late 1880s and early 1890s, were debated by several local branches of the British Medical Association, but sympathy with the problem did not lead to widespread enthusiasm for his solutions.[40]

In the interest of protecting the profession from charity abuse, Rentoul would have had general practitioners offer what was effectively a collective package of basic care, a Public Medical Service, in return for an annual sliding-scale payment based on age and physical condition. Such a scheme would have benefited both doctors and their patients, he thought, and would have left charitable institutions with their original task of providing care for those too poor to pay for it.

Fee-for-service medical practice was still too important ideologically for doctors to make many of them wish to jump on a comprehensive Public Medical Service bandwagon. Nevertheless, in actuality, doctors were earning increasing amounts of money outside the context of fee-for-service practice. The old 'business of medicine' of the late eighteenth century was much more complicated by the end of Victoria's reign. Part of this was the result of the considerable increase, during the last quarter of the century, in contract and club practice.[41] This 'battle of the clubs', as a *Lancet* commissioner put it, divided the medical profession, particularly as doctors believed that many middle class families who could have afforded private fees were joining working class clubs. The General Medical Council

---

[38] In London, hospital charity was co-ordinated, from 1897, by the Prince of Wales' Hospital Fund for London, which became the King Edward's Hospital Fund after Victoria's death. This is discussed in Rivett, op. cit. (note 33), pp. 145ff. Dr. Frank Prochaska has recently completed a history of the King's Fund, as the charity is now called, which will be published by Oxford University Press.

[39] Squire Sprigge, op. cit. (note 14), pp. 60–2.

[40] Jeanne L. Brand, *Doctors and the State* (Baltimore, 1965), pp. 153–5.

[41] David G. Green, *Working-Class Patients and the Medical Establishment* (New York, 1985).

tried to neutralize the most competitive aspects of the situation in 1899 by reminding registered practitioners that advertising fee scales and canvassing for patients constituted unprofessional ('infamous') conduct.[42]

At one level, the ability of organized patient groups to command the salaried services of a general practitioner can be seen as a consequence of an overcrowded or at least a relatively weak profession; on the other hand, the guaranteed salary was a safe bet for a young practitioner and doctors complained that non-collection of fees could be as high as 40% for those practising in working-class areas. Either way, clubs offered an alternative to ordinary solo practice, and many of the structures which the clubs had generated were perpetuated after 1911.[43]

Much of the Victorian occupational diversification, however, occurred in the public sector. The growth after 1834 of the Poor Law Medical Services; after 1845 of the psychiatric network of county lunatic asylums; after 1848 of Medical Officers of Health; the merchant naval service; army, navy and Indian Medical services; a separate colonial medical service; prison, police and factory surgeons; public vaccinators and public analysts; coroners; medical inspectors of passenger ships and of seamen; each of these employed some or many medical men, but more by 1900 than 1850 or 1870.[44] The exact nature of the job, its terms, salary and security, varied widely of course, as did the kind of men likely to be attracted. Recruitment to what was called the Sanitary Service, especially in the larger

[42] Green, (ibid.), has argued that club practice worked well, although the picture of it painted by Squire Sprigge (op. cit., note 14) was much less favourable.
[43] A. Digby and N. Bosanquet have recently examined the economics of medical practice after the 1911 Act: 'Doctors and Patients in an Era of National Health Insurance and Private Practice, 1913–1938', *Economic History Review*, 2nd ser. **41** (1988), 74–94. See, also, N.R. Eder, *National Health Insurance and the Medical Profession in Britain, 1913–39* (London, 1982).
[44] I know of no work which attempts to examine systematically the phenomenon of medical occupational diversification in the nineteenth century, although aspects of it are considered by several of the authors already cited, viz. Loudon, Peterson, Squire Sprigge, Marland and Brand. For material on separate occupational groups, cf. Ruth G. Hodgkinson, *The Origins of the National Health Service* (London, 1967); Andrew T. Scull, *Museums of Madness: The Social Organization of Insanity in 19th Century England* (London, 1979); D.E. Watkins, 'The English Revolution in Social Medicine, 1889–1911', Ph.D. thesis, University of London, 1984; Neil Cantlie, *A History of the Army Medical Department*, 2 vols (Edinburgh, 1974); Chris Hamlin, *What Becomes of Pollution?: Adversary Science and the Controversy on the Self-Purification of Rivers in Britain, 1850–1900* (New York, 1987); Colin Russell, *Lancastrian Chemist: The Early Years of Sir Edward Frankland* (Philadelphia, 1985); Marguerite W. Dupree and M. Anne Crowther, 'A Profile of the Medical Profession in Scotland in the Early Twentieth Century: the *Medical Directory* as a Historical Source', *Bulletin of the History of Medicine*, forthcoming; Marguerite W. Dupree, 'Other than Healing: Medical Practitioners and the Business of Life Assurance During the Nineteenth and Twentieth Centuries', paper delivered at the Autumn Conference of the Economic and Social History Society of Scotland, November 1989.

metropolitan authorities, was vigorous; the Poor Law Medical Officers were less successful as an occupational group and until the 1890s the army was notorious in its dealings with its medical officers.

Nevertheless, the very existence of this diverse group of employment possibilities undoubtedly aided in the task of cobbling together a decent living. Hilary Marland's detailed study of Wakefield and Huddersfield is instructive: in 1835, 35 medical practitioners were practising in these two localities and she was able to identify 23 public posts. In 1851, 47 practitioners were chasing 46 posts. In 1871, after the Medical Act, the practitioners numbered 38, while the posts had risen to 78.[45] Most of the posts were part-time and pluralism was obviously common. A random sample of 100 practitioners from the 1892 *Medical Directory*, 30 London and 70 provincial, revealed that 69 had identified themselves as holding or having held, a paid post or posts in the public or charity sector. I excluded resident physician or surgeon positions in voluntary hospitals, since these were becoming an accepted part of training. No fewer than 13 were or had been public vaccinators and the vaccination service had received £15,638 from central funds, in addition to the more routine contributions made at the local level.[46] Nationally, about 5% of the practitioners in Britain and Ireland were employed in the Sanitary Medical Service, and more than twice that number in the Poor Law Medical Service (also, since 1871, under the Local Government Board). The state even paid doctors for the notification of each case of 13 compulsorily notifiable infectious diseases, including smallpox, diphtheria and scarlet fever.[47]

It would be a mistake to conclude that, even by the century's end, medicine could compete with the Church, the Bar, or the Armed Forces, for the eldest sons of those who ruled Victorian Britain. Nor did the occupational diversity of the profession necessarily lead to greater unity. Even the United States has abandoned *e pluribus unum* as its motto. But diversification and state patronage were, I think, sources and consequences of strength. And no-one can read today Sir John Simon's *English Sanitary Institutions* without realizing that Victorian medicine had had its statesmen, most notably, perhaps, Simon himself. As the chief architect of that

---

[45] Marland, op. cit. (note 29), p. 276.
[46] The *Medical Directory for 1892* (London, 1892), p. 37; for the Victorian Vaccination System, cf. Lambert, op. cit. (note 26), esp. pp. 249–58 and 356–65; and *idem*, 'A Victorian National Health Service: State Vaccination 1855–71', *Historical Journal*, **5** (1962), 1–18. Compulsory vaccination provoked an organized resistance, which has been examined by R.M. MacLeod, 'Law, Medicine and Public Opinion: The Resistance to Compulsory Health Legislation 1870–1907', *Public Law*, Summer and Autumn 1967, 106–28, 188–211; and Dorothy and Roy Porter, 'The politics of Prevention: Anti-Vaccination and Public Health in Nineteenth-Century England', *Medical History*, **32** (1988), 231–52.
[47] W.M. Frazer, *A History of English Public Health, 1834–1939* (London, 1950), pp. 181ff.

alignment of the state and the profession between 1854 and 1876 he had changed the face of medicine. However, he also recognized that medicine was but one of many agencies devoted to combatting what he called the 'politics of poverty' in order to improve 'man's social existence'. For him, the essence of his age and that of his Queen was not simply new wealth and power; but rather 'the constantly increasing care of the community at large for the welfare of its individual parts'.[48]

[48] John Simon, *English Sanitary Institutions* (2nd edn, London, 1897), p. 485.

Proceedings of the British Academy, **78**, 165–182

Victorian Values
and the
Founders of the Welfare State

JOSE HARRIS
University of Oxford

HISTORIANS interested in the roots and rationale of modern social policy
have had to take account of not one but two powerful interpretations of
Victorian values which have been in circulation over the past decade:
two interpretations which are in many respects inconsistent with and even
diametrically opposed to each other. On the one hand we have the model
enunciated in 1983 by the late Prime Minister, in her invocation of the
Victorian values of character, family, effort, thrift and self-help, as values
indispensable to the economic and social recovery of Britain in the 1980s
and 1990s.[1] Mrs. Thatcher did not at any point link her praise of Victorian
values with an explicit attack upon the values of the welfare state. But
many among both her opponents and supporters instantly assumed that
this was in fact what she meant. It was widely believed that Mrs. Thatcher
was favourably comparing the nineteenth century welfare apparatus of
deterrent workhouse, organised charity, and moral discrimination between
deserving and undeserving poor with the system of comprehensive social
services, fiscally-managed full employment and Keynesian consumerism
that had prevailed in Britain since 1945. A distinguished sociologist
portrayed 'Mrs. Thatcher and her circle' as 'entering office in 1979 to
enact a replay of the Poor Law Amendment Act'.[2] And this impression

---

Read 14 December 1990. © The British Academy 1992.
[1] Interview on Nationwide, as reported in the national press, 15 Apr. 1983.
[2] A.H. Halsey, 'A Sociologist's View of Thatcherism', in R. Skidelsky (ed.) *Thatcherism*
(London, 1988), p. 177. See also *New Stateman*, supplement on 'Victorian Values', 27 May 1983.

was reinforced by Mrs. Thatcher's recurrent endorsement of a brand of Christianity that stressed individual identity and private conviction, as opposed to the more organic social Christianity – or alternatively the sheer secularism – of many of her critics.[3]

Mrs. Thatcher's account of Victorian values – or, at least, what was popularly understood as her account – has of course been widely discussed. But in the context of social policy, it was not the only model advanced in the 1980s that juxtaposed Victorian values with the principles and practices of the modern welfare state. An alternative model – and arguably a more polemically powerful one, because more explicit and systematic and detailed than Margaret Thatcher's – was that advanced by the historian Correlli Barnett in his book on *The Audit of War*, published in 1986. Correlli Barnett's account portrayed the contemporary welfare state, not as the antithesis of the Victorian age, but as its major structural and ideological inheritance. In stark contrast to Mrs. Thatcher, Barnett identified the essence of Victorian values as being, not rugged competitive individualism, but sentimental chivalry, disdain for economic materialism, and paternalist concern for the outcast and the poor and the weak. Unlike Mrs. Thatcher, Barnett perceived Victorian Christianity – both the nonconformity of the chapels and the orthodoxy of the established church – as deeply committed to humanitarian collectivism; and he viewed that Christianity as directly responsible for the growth of a socially enervating, economically parasitic, politically corrupt system of state welfare in the mid- and late-twentieth century. In Barnett's view it was precisely this legacy of Victorian values that was directly responsible for Britain's prolonged economic stagnation, widespread disdain for competition and materialism, propping-up of lame ducks and social failures, and long drawn-out national and international decline. The task for reformers, as Barnett saw it, was to throw off this 'Victorian' incubus of Christian humanitarianism, and to replace it by a modern, Germanic-style system of organisation, advanced technology and state investment in competitive national efficiency.[4] Although Correlli Barnett's vision of reform had certain faint resonances of that set out by Mrs. Thatcher,[5] his account of Victorianism was therefore in many ways utterly different from hers: a contrast that appears all the more striking

---

[3] Hugo Young, *One of Us. A Biography of Margaret Thatcher* (London, 1989), pp. 416–26.
[4] Correlli Barnett, *The Audit of War. The Illusion and Reality of Britain as a Great Nation* (1986), pp. 12–19, 36–7, 62, 93, 145–51, 213–33, 279–304 and *passim*.
[5] Mrs. Thatcher's speech to the 1978 Conservative party conference at Blackpool may be seen as foreshadowing Barnett's approach by attacking policies that had their 'roots in the plans for reconstruction in the postwar period when governments assumed all kinds of new obligations'. [N. Wapshoott and D. Brock, *Thatcher* (1983), p. 273]. But no connection was made at this point between the rise of social welfare and the demise of Victorian values.

in view of the fact that several of Barnett's warmest admirers – most notably Sir Keith Joseph and Mr. Nigel Lawson – were also at various times ministers in Mrs. Thatcher's governments and leading campaigners in her crusade for economic regeneration.

Such a contrast nicely demonstrates a fact of which all who are engaged in the study of modern British history must be aware: namely, that Victorian Britain was a large, ramshackle, complex, diverse society which lasted a very long time and embraced a multiplicity of cultural traditions – and is therefore open to a wide variety of often mutually-conflicting stereotyped interpretations. Victorian Christianity subsumed an enormous range of social theologies, stretching from penal substitution and private good works through to a vision of earthly society as the material incarnation of the Kingdom of Christ. Victorian social policy covered a period of more than sixty years: it stretched from the 1830s (a decade haunted as starkly as any late twentieth-century Third World country by the spectre of population outrunning resources and per capita income barely keeping pace with subsistence) through to the 1890s (when the social problem was seen much more in terms of a deviant or inadequate or unfortunate minority who were failing to keep pace with rising overall standards of efficiency and affluence). From this welter of diversity it would not be difficult to select specimen reformers and social administrators whose values and behaviour would either confirm or falsify the models of Victorianism set up by Mrs. Thatcher and Mr. Barnett. In this paper, however, I shall adopt a rather different approach. Instead of starting from an a priori conception of Victorian values about welfare, I shall probe the central concerns of some of the key figures in the social welfare movements of the late nineteenth and early twentieth centuries, and consider what those concerns tell us about the values that they actually held. And I want to suggest that an important clue to those values lies in the habits, practices and aspirations of the organised working-class: habits, practices and aspirations which the founders of the welfare state saw as offering a model that could potentially be adapted and extended to a much larger cross-section of British society, and ultimately to society as a whole. Such an argument may seem perhaps a surprising one, in view of the fact that most social reformers were middle-class, and that social policy is often perceived by historians as a form of imposition upon the working-class of the alien and extraneous values of an officious bourgeoisie. That such an alien imposition did often occur – sometimes deliberately, sometimes unintentionally – cannot be denied. But, whatever may have been the case in the earlier Victorian period, it was not I think the primary or characteristic objective of the founding patriarchs and matriarchs of the welfare state – a group whose heroic epoch I take to be the period from the social crisis of the 1880s down to the setting-up of the national health service and universal social security in the 1940s. As my major matriarchs and patriarchs I shall take Sidney and Beatrice Webb, Helen Bosanquet, Octavia Hill, William Braithwaite, and William Beveridge: a group of people whose political views ranged from state socialism to free market individualism, whose religious views stretched from High Anglican Christianity through Unitarianism to agnosticism and atheism, but whose views of social welfare all revolved around a common set assumptions about both personal morality and collective social norms. That common set of assumptions, I shall argue, was derived par excellence from their interpretation of and admiration for the culture and institutions of the late-Victorian and Edwardian organised working-class. It was in this culture that they found, or thought they found, the escape route out of the Poor Law. And it was there also that they saw embodied the attitudes to work, thrift, community and family life which all of them – albeit by widely differing political and administrative means – sought to promote and replicate as the foundation of social welfare in modern industrial society.

What evidence is there for this interpretation of the underlying principles of the early welfare state? And what precisely were the values that the founding fathers so much admired in working-class social welfare institutions. Evidence that some at least of the roots of the welfare state lay in the self-help institutions of the working-class is writ large in many sources, though much of that evidence has been curiously glossed over or marginalised by social and political historians.[6] Let us take first the idea of the 'National Minimum', a term conceptualised by Sidney and Beatrice Webb in the 1890s. The national minimum is often dutifully cited in studies of social policy as one of the path-breaking principles that heralded a new approach to social welfare; but its precise meaning and context are virtually never fully explored. An important point to be recalled about the 'National Minimum' is that it was first formulated by the Webbs not in one of their works on social policy but in their study of *Industrial Democracy*, first published in 1897. They there made it quite clear that their vision of the national minimum was directly derived from a mixture of the practices of 'old' and 'new' trades unionism. Like the new trades unionists of the 1890s the national minimum was to invoke the use of the legislative power of the state; and it was to use that power to impose upon the whole community the standards of health, safety, income and social security that the older and soundly-established trade unions had obtained for themselves by their own collective voluntary efforts.[7] As is well-known,

[6] Valuable exceptions are Pat Thane, 'The Working Class and State "Welfare" in Britain, 1880–1914', *Hist.J.*, **27**, **4** (1984), pp. 877–900; and Noelle Whiteside, 'Welfare Legislation and the Unions during the First World War', *Hist.J.*, **23**, **4** (1980), pp. 857–74.

[7] S. and B. Webb, *Industrial Democracy* (London, 1897, 1902 edn), pp. 766–784.

the interests of the Webbs shifted in the 1900s away from trades unionism towards more bureaucratic modes of promoting social change. Yet a very similar underlying vision may be found in their arguments for new public social services, which they put forward through the Royal Commission on the Poor Laws in 1905–9. They argued that the 'legislative enforcement' of a 'legally enforced Common Rule' defining basic minimum standards would have exactly the same impact upon the welfare, character and public spirit of the poor and unskilled as three generations of trade unionism had had upon the skilled and organised working-classes. The result, claimed the Webbs, would be the transplantation of trade-union social solidarity, democratic self-discipline, and work and welfare practices into society as a whole; and the end product would be the growth of 'a new principle of social organisation in the progressive recognition and enforcement of the very condition of civilisation itself, the mutual obligation of service from the community to the individual and from the individual to the community'.[8]

Such an idealised vision of the internal culture of the organised working-class is perhaps unsurprising in the writings of Sidney and Beatrice Webb, who had a life-long involvement in the labour movement and were to become prominent figures in the Labour party. But a comparable perspective can also be found in the other social reformers I have mentioned, often in quite unexpected spheres. Octavia Hill, the doyenne of the Charity Organization Society and pioneer of family casework, is often cited as a prime agent for the cultural imposition of bourgeois personal morality and middle-class family life-styles upon the hapless London poor. Yet, as a number of recent studies have made clear, nothing could have been more remote from the prudent, respectable, patriarchal stereotype of the Victorian bourgeois family than Octavia Hill's own life-history – brought up as she was by a mother who was compelled to work, abandoned by a feckless and unstable father, saved from dire poverty only by the patronage of rich relatives, and thoroughly familiar with the personal impact of economic insecurity, uncertain identity, precarious social status and emotional neglect.[9] Octavia Hill's writings on housing management, and her evidence to the Royal Commissions on Housing and on the Aged Poor suggest very forcibly that her vision of prudent, close-knit, independent and authoritarian family life was derived not from the middle-class families of her acquaintance but from what she believed to be the practices and values of artisan families and of those whom

---

[8] Ibid., pp. 790, 807–50.
[9] Gillian Darley, *Octavia Hill* (London, 1990), pp. 17–43; Jane Lewis, *Women and Social Action in Victorian and Edwardian England* (Aldershot, 1991), p. 25

she termed the 'regular casuals' – families whom she had encountered through her contacts with the Co-operative movement and the London Working Men's College and through her work as a housing manager.[10] A similar emphasis upon the life-style of the organised working-class may be detected in the works of Helen Bosanquet. Mrs. Bosanquet is perhaps best-known for her scepticism about Seebohm Rowntree's poverty line[11] and for her resistance to the state social services proposed by the Webbs. On the Royal Commission on the Poor Laws in 1905–9 she was characterised and caricatured by Mrs. Webb as a bastion of old-fashioned individualism. Yet Helen Bosanquet's social philosophy centred not upon atomistic individualism *per se*, but upon what she called 'social collectivism'; by which she meant collectivism mediated not through 'the state' but through 'society'. Collectivism in the form of co-operative societies, trade unions, friendly societies and other mutual self-help agencies she perceived no less than the Webbs as the great progressive, evolutionary force of late-Victorian Britain and as the moral flagship of future industrial society.[12] The disagreement between Mrs. Bosanquet and the Webbs lay not over the substantive issues of collectivism and the need for social services but over the medium of public provision – Mrs. Bosanquet believing that the spread of social collectivism would be not enhanced but hindered and thwarted by the Webbs' vision of an all-embracing, multi-functional administrative state.[13]

The tension between these two visions of collectivism lay at the heart of the most substantial social welfare measure of the Edwardian period: Lloyd George's introduction of compulsory health insurance for nearly all employed persons under the National Insurance Act of 1911. Lloyd George himself had little more than a practical and pragmatic understanding of social welfare administration, little grasp of its relation to wider aspects of

---

[10] *Select Committee on Artizans' and Labourers' Dwellings*, H. of C. 235, 1882, qq. 3305, 3412; *RC on Housing of the Working-Classes*, C. 4402, 1885, qq. 8852, 8862–3; *RC on Aged Poor*, C. 7684. II, 1895, q. 10455. Hill specifically rejected the notion that middle-class standards should be applied to welfare and housing schemes provided for working-men. Unlike other reformers discussed in this paper, however, she had a low opinion of the political and managerial capacities of the skilled working-class, believing that sentiment and the desire for cheap popularity always tended to undermine democratically controlled welfare experiments.

[11] Helen Bosanquet, 'Wages and Housekeeping', in C.S. Loch (ed.) *Methods of Social Advance* (London, 1904), pp. 131–46.

[12] Helen Bosanquet, *The Strength of the People* (2nd edn 1903), pp. 107, 168–70, 237–9.

[13] Ibid., pp. 107–8, 168–70, 234–42; Helen Bosanquet, *The Poor Law Report of 1909*, (London, 1909), pp. 1–12, 144–68; A.M. McBriar, *An Edwardian Mixed Doubles. The Bosanquets versus the Webbs. A Study in British Social Policy 1890–1929 (Oxford 1987)*, especially ch. 8.

social structure and culture. But quite the opposite was true of his chief Treasury assistant, William Braithwaite, the man primarily responsible for negotiating and drafting the health insurance provisions of the 1911 Act. The account of the making of the Act in Braithwaite's diaries revolved around two key administrative and philosophical problems: the problems, first, of how to extend and transplant the social welfare habits of the organised working-class into the lives of the working-class as a whole; and, secondly, of how to do so without thereby violating and extinguishing the hidden mainsprings of that independent working-class culture.[14] Braithwaite was a post-Gladstonian liberal to whom the work-ethic and self-help tradition were not merely valuable in themselves but the lifeblood of national civic virtue. But at the same time he was also a Toynbeeite 'new liberal', very conscious of the fact that by its nature the independent self-help culture of the upper working-class could not automatically penetrate into the lower depths of the casual poor. The core of Braithwaite's work on national health insurance consisted of building into the provisions of the Act a subsidy from the employer and the state (including a 100% subsidy for the lowest-paid workers), whilst at the same time retaining exactly the same kind of administrative rules about self-government, solvency, fraternal aid to the genuinely sick and firm handling of the malingerer, that were inscribed in the rule-books of friendly societies, collecting societies and skilled trade unions. The setting-up of democratic, self-managing, 'approved societies' under the 1911 Act was meant to tie together the twin ethics of state-aid and individualism, and to use those seemingly antagonistic principles not to cancel out but to reinforce each other. As the Explanatory Memorandum of the Insurance Act carefully explained: 'All deficits due to malingering will have to be borne . . . by the members of a defaulting Society . . . and not by the state [so] there is every inducement to economy. Bad management will be promptly and effectively penalised. Good management will be promptly rewarded'.[15]

A very similar perspective underpinned the unemployment provisions of Part Two of the National Insurance Act, and the social philosophy of William Beveridge. Beveridge is often perceived as an anti-labour figure and it is certainly true that he often clashed with leading trade unionists over such issues as decasualisation and labour-discipline. Yet in reality Beveridge's ideas about labour organisation and those of the bulk of trade union leaders were fundamentally similar. They clashed not on substantive

---

[14] H.N. Bunbury (ed.), *Lloyd George's Ambulance Wagon. Being the Memoirs of William J. Braithwaite 1911–12* (London, 1957), pp. 79–81, 93–5, 142.
[15] *National Insurance Bill. Memorandum Explanatory of the Bill as Passed by the House of Commons so far as relates to National Health Insurance*, Cd. 5995, 1911.

policies of organisation and decasualisation but over the fact that trade unionists wanted to confine such policies to their own members and to keep their operation under trade union control; whereas Beveridge wanted to extend such policies to the whole of the workforce, using where necessary the coercive machinery of the state.[16] Such conflicts have tended to obscure a fundamental feature of Beveridge's philosophy of welfare, which is that – no less than the other reformers whom I have mentioned – he admired and idealised the independent self-help culture of the organised working-class. This was very apparent in his evidence to the Royal Commission on the Poor Laws in 1907, where he portrayed the major trade unions as the *only* bodies throughout the whole range of self-help and philanthropic institutions who had taken seriously the problem of maintaining workers during periods of unemployment, without resort to poor relief.[17] And it was apparent, no less than in the case of Braithwaite, in Beveridge's work at the Board of Trade on the construction of unemployment insurance. Prior to the drafting of the National Insurance Act Beveridge drew up a massive compendium of the rules and social security practices of trade unions throughout Britain;[18] and as in the case of health insurance, the provision for unemployment was adapted directly from existing practices pioneered by the trade unions. Rules about the relationship between a worker's contributions and his entitlement to benefit, about registering himself as available for work, about a three-day waiting-period before benefit was payable, about protection of the 'standard rate', about conditions under which a worker might refuse an offer of work, and about the penalisation of malingerers: all were copied, in many cases verbatim, from the rulebooks of such societies as the Boilermakers Union or the Amalgamated Society of Engineers.[19] Moreover, sections 105 and 106 of the National Insurance Act enabled trade unions that preferred to manage their own private

[16] Noelle Whiteside, 'Welfare Insurance and Casual Labour: a Study of Administrative Intervention in Industrial Employment 1906–26', *Econ. Hist. Rev.*, 2nd series, **32**, **4** (1979), pp. 507–22; Gordon Phillips and Noel Whiteside, *Casual Labour. The Unemployment Question in the Port Transport Industry 1880–1970* (Oxford, 1985), pp. 134–6.

[17] Royal Commission on the Poor Laws, minutes of evidence, q. 77832, paras. 72–2 (Cd. 6066, 1910).

[18] *Tables showing the Rules and Expenditure of Trade Unions in Respect of Unemployed Benefits and also showing Earnings in the Insured Trades*, Cd. 5703, 1911.

[19] *National Insurance Act*, 1911, sections 86–8 and schedule 7. These may be compared with the provisions relating to out-of-work donation in the rule-books of, e.g., the United Society of Boilermakers and Iron and Steel Shipbuilders, the Steam Engine Makers' Society, the Shipconstructors and Shipwrights Association, the Friendly Society of Ironfounders, the General Union of Operative Carpenters and Joiners and the Amalgamated Society of Engineers. Most of the rule-books cited in this paper are deposited in the trade union collection at Nuffield College. In addition a few rule-books of lesser-known unions were supplied to me by Mr. C. Hodgskin of Clifton Books.

unemployment insurance schemes to continue to do so, but at the same time to become eligible for the state and employers' subventions under the Act. Contrary to the views of some later historians who have seen the Act as little more than a disguised bureaucratic conspiracy to curtail working-class autonomy, the encouragement to independent labour self-help schemes and the endorsement of the values embodied in those schemes could scarcely have been more obvious.

Similar points may be made about Beveridge's view of welfare a generation later, at the time of the Beveridge Plan of 1942. Beveridge in the early 1940s was called upon to investigate Britain's social security arrangements after what many people believed had been a quarter of a century of failure. The 'approved society' system of 1911 had produced a highly uneven system of national health insurance, under which benefits varied widely in size and scope from one society to another. Some approved societies had successfully maintained the democratic, comradely, *gemein-schaft* ethic of the late nineteenth century self-help institutions. But many had been overtaken by apathy, and many more had been outstripped by the aggressive selling techniques and more 'routinised' bureaucratic practices of the great industrial assurance companies, who had been included in the 1911 Act almost as an afterthought on the same terms as friendly societies and trade unions.[20] And similarly the 1911 unemployment scheme had collapsed in the face of two decades of mass long-term unemployment. A purely abstract and rational-bureaucratic approach to social security in 1942 might have suggested to Beveridge a universal social security system, payable simply out of taxation on proof of need and wholly detached from the constraints of contributory insurance. Beveridge was indeed a very abstract and rational-bureaucratic person; but he was also a repository of certain traditional social principles (what may indeed be termed 'Victorian' values, though not the sentimental, utopian version of Victorian values inexplicably fathered upon him by Correlli Barnett). No less than in the 1900s Beveridge greatly admired the tradition of voluntary saving and self-help, both as a practical medium of welfare, and as a vehicle of thrift, social solidarity, micro-citizenship and personal freedom.[21] And even more than in the Edwardian period he hated the Poor Law and all similar forms of means-tested public relief, as a system of provision

---

[20] Braithwaite, op. cit., p. 95 and following; Bentley B. Gilbert, *The Evolution of National Insurance in Great Britain* (London, 1966), pp. 318–43; Bentley B. Gilbert, *British Social Policy 1914–39* (London, 1970), pp. 270–84.

[21] *Social Insurance and Allied Services. A Report by Sir William Beveridge*, Cmd. 6404, 1942, paras. 375–84. The clearest expression of Beveridge's continuing support for voluntary as well as compulsory thrift came in his post-war study, *Voluntary Action. A Report on Methods of Social Advance* (London, 1948).

wholly alien to modern industrial democracy. Such systems, Beveridge believed, if applied legalistically and economically, treated citizens like serfs; whilst if applied with humanity and generosity, they penalized work, thrift, family life, innovation and labour mobility. In either case they tended to insulate both citizens and government against the need for rational forethought and prevention (trends which he saw as exemplified in the 'uncovenanted benefit' schemes of the 1920s, no less than in the indoor and outdoor relief schemes of earlier generations).[22] As in 1909, therefore, Beveridge in 1942 had little hesitation in opting for a contributory-insurance model of the welfare state. As in 1909, he strove to build into his proposals the principles of financial solvency, maintenance of work-incentives, fraternal help and friendly visiting, disqualification of those whose dependancy was self-induced, compulsory retraining of the long-term unemployed, and 'penal treatment' of malingerers.[23] He now envisaged and recommended, however, that these mutual aid principles could be transplanted into a universal state system and applied not merely to the mass of the working-class but to all levels of British society.

The social welfare values of the late-Victorian and Edwardian skilled working-class were therefore of crucial importance in shaping the principles and structure of the early welfare state. A little more must be said, however, about what those values actually were and about the culture they reflected. The world of trade unions and friendly societies was notoriously a world of almost infinite idiosyncrasy and diversity, and it is impossible to do justice to that diversity in a single brief paper. Several points are of relevance, however, to the reconstruction of Victorian values in the context of social welfare. One is that late-Victorian trade unions and friendly societies were almost never purely instrumental and utilitarian organisations, concerned only with material factors such as wages, hours, working conditions and levels of contribution and benefit. On the contrary, they were miniature republics in the classical sense of that term; self-governing, highly-principled, democratic organisms whose members were required to be active and conscientious practitioners of civic

---

[22] W.H. Beveridge, *Unemployment. A Problem of Industry*, (London, 1930 edn), pp. 150–4, 272–94, 407–10; *Social Insurance and Allied Services*, paras. 21–3.

[23] *Social Insurance and Allied Services*, paras. 66–9, 326, 369, 373, 376. It may be objected that the actuarial provisions of the Beveridge Plan differed from those of voluntary insurance schemes, in that Beveridge envisaged that the State would have no imperative need to 'fund' national insurance because it could meet deficits by using its power to vary levels of taxation (ibid., paras. 24–6). This did indeed differ from the practice of insurance companies and of most friendly societies; but it precisely coincided with the common practice of Trade union welfare schemes, which normally met deficits not by funding but by *ad hoc* levies on members.

virtue and public spirit. It is I think hard to imagine anything more utterly remote from the leaden 'economism' of which British trades unionists were accused by Lenin than the high seriousness of the statements about citizenship and brotherly love with which late-Victorian and Edwardian trade societies such as the engineers, boilermakers, tailors, carpenters and joiners habitually prefaced their rule-books and their articles of association.[24]

A second point is that, like many small republics, the late-Victorian friendly organisations practised an all-embracing system of rigorous self-discipline, compulsory citizenship and behavioural police.[25] An analysis of the terms and conditions by which trade unions managed their social welfare schemes reveals a network of minutely-prescribed horizontal social controls that makes the late nineteenth-century Charity Organization Societies look by comparison like veritable havens of libertarian behavioural permissiveness. In all leading trade unions members were disqualified from sick pay if their illness was brought on by drink, physical violence, or sexual misconduct. Recipients of sick pay were subject to compulsory medical inspection and were regularly visited by brother members, who checked that they were genuinely ill, that they were not secretly employed in work and that they were not engaging in practices harmful to their recovery. Concern on this latter score led nearly all unions to impose on sick members a strict night-time curfew (often 6 p.m. to 8 a.m. in winter, 8 p.m. to 7 a.m. in summer), ostensibly to protect them from 'the rigours of the night air', more probably to protect them from the snare of the public houses and other nocturnal temptations). Similar rules applied to unemployment pay. Members were automatically disqualified from benefit if they were sacked for poor workmanship or gave up their employment for some trivial reason or 'small grievance'. They were required to follow up rumours of job-vacancies and to accept any reasonable opportunity of work offered at the standard rate; and a system of increasingly severe fines and penalties regulated those thought to be 'imposing' or 'not exerting themselves to obtain employment', culminating after a third or fourth offence in expulsion from the union. Such penalties were enforced in all benefit-paying unions by draconian personal surveillance. Members who were not themselves 'imposing' or 'malingering' but who turned a blind eye to the misdeeds of others were themselves subject to loss of benefit

---

[24] See e.g the preface to the Rules of the United Society of Boilermakers and Iron and Steel Shipbuilders (1871, revised 1912), for a highly idealised vision of trade unionism as a cradle of wider citizenship.

[25] The Webbs compared the older-style trade unions to the Landsgemeinden of Uri and Appenzell, a comparison that accurately conjured up not only their day-to-day practical arrangements but the roots of their political philosophy (*Industrial Democracy*, pp. 1–15).

rights, fines and disqualification. 'Special attention', insisted the rules of the United Boilermakers, was to be paid to the behaviour of those who, having exhausted their out-of-work pay, then signed on for sick pay.[26] 'Any president or secretary who fails to impose fines is himself to be fined', declared the rule book of the Amalgamated Society of Tailors and Tailoresses (a body which also threatened to fine any member found guilty of 'upbraiding another for receiving benefits to which he was justly entitled').[27] Moreover, such rules were no mere formalities, designed to satisfy the Registrar of Friendly Societies. In many unions, taking a turn as a 'sick steward' was an absolute obligation upon members, and refusal to do so was punishable by fines and suspension. And personal surveillance was reinforced by the nationwide circulation of information among union branches about malingerers, lapsed subscribers, those not genuinely seeking work and other batteners on the funds.[28] In cases of fraud, however trivial, unions had no hesitation in bringing benefit swindlers before the courts. 'The society had no vindictive feeling', reported the ASE in 1910 on the occasion of the prosecution of a sick member who had altered a benefit cheque for five shillings, 'but they felt that this was a matter which should be brought forward as a warning and deterrent against the committal of similar offences.' When this particular offender was sentenced to five months imprisonment with hard labour he was expelled from the society: 'we are well rid of such characters' was the comment in the union's monthly report.[29]

A third crucial factor was that membership of friendly societies and trade union benefit schemes was at all times necessarily selective and exclusive. Such schemes excluded those unable to pay their subscriptions; they excluded those without the requisite skills; and they systematically screened out those who fell into arrears or who lapsed into anti-social or disorderly behaviour. Moreover, even among those qualified by skill, income and moral propriety, they excluded those likely to prove an abnormal actuarial risk. The rules of the ASE, for example, refused admission to those who were deaf, dumb, ruptured, subject to fits, wore

[26] Rulebook of the United Society of Boilermakers and Iron and Steel Shipbuilers, 1871, revised 1912.
[27] Amalgamated Society of Tailors and Tailoresses, rulebook, 1912.
[28] The monthly reports of the ASE, for example, always included warnings about named members thought to be exploiting their benefit entitlement; and the quarterly reports included detailed lists, usually running into several hundreds, of members disqualified from benefit. The majority of the latter were members who had fallen into arrears with contributions, but they also included members excluded for 'immorality', 'acting contrary to the Society's interest', 'entering under false pretences', 'imposition', 'not refunding benefits improperly received', 'chronic laziness' and 'general bad conduct'.
[29] ASE monthly report, August 1910.

spectacles or had lost the use of more than two fingers (though curiously enough the ASE allowed the membership of those who had lost the sight of one eye, provided they produced a doctor's certificate guaranteeing that sight in the other eye was unaffected). Rule books of the 1900s suggest some slight relaxation of these conditions, and an increasing willingness on the part of the old-established trade unions to admit to their benefit schemes certain groups who had been excluded in earlier years, such as women, apprentices and older workers who could not earn the full standard rate. But throughout the Edwardian period the practical need to maintain actuarial viability clashed with and often eclipsed the growing aspiration of many trade union leaders to represent the wider interests of the whole of the working-class.

Such rules demonstrate both the strength and the limitations of working-class mutual-help schemes as an inspiration and model for more general social welfare. As I have already indicated, the welfare schemes of trade unions and friendly societies provided a powerful normative and practical inspiration to the founders of the welfare state: and many of their procedures were incorporated virtually unchanged into early twentieth-century social welfare legislation. Rules and regulations often ascribed by historians to middle-class hegemony or bureaucratic coercion in fact stemmed time and again from the long-established habits and values of the skilled and organised working-class. Several factors conspired, however, to limit and ultimately to undermine the permanent dominance of such habits and values within the structure of British social welfare. One such limiting influence was the fact that the very same measures which set out to incorporate working-class self-help schemes also brought the state into partnership for the first time with profit-making private insurance. The industrial insurance companies and collecting societies – bodies like the Prudential, the Pearl and the Liverpool Victoria which employed paid agents to sell new policies and collect weekly premiums by house-to-house visitation – had been growing fast in the British economy since the 1880s. With their emphasis on regular saving, they had appeared initially to be closely allied to the Victorian friendly-society ethic. But already by the 1990s their culture of individualised passive consumerism was challenging the tradition of active mutual thrift – and they were beginning to penetrate those lower layers of society that friendly societies and trade unions had never adequately reached, the unskilled casual poor. Even within the skilled and organised working-class, trade unions and friendly societies after 1911 were soon perturbed by a growing tendency among their members to prefer the inertia and anonymity of a door-to-door salesman to the more strenuous demands of democratic self-management: with the result that, far from buttressing the mutual aid tradition, the private insurance companies proved in the long run to be a major source of its destruction.[30]

A second limiting factor was that for several decades after 1900 the voluntary societies themselves and particularly the trade unions looked with ambivalence and suspicion upon the threatened embrace of the advancing welfare state. Traditional liberal mistrust of overweening state power was reinforced during the Edwardian period by the rise of anarcho-syndicalism; and, quite contrary to the expectations of Whitehall reformers, the 1911 National Insurance Act was initially viewed by many skilled workers as a veiled attack upon the rights and privileges of organised labour. They argued with some justification that state-enforced social security would tend to undermine the whole rationale of the voluntarist movement: that it would encourage bureaucratic controls, seduce working people away from active participation in welfare schemes, and – perhaps worst of all – confer social insurance benefits upon those who had neither financially nor morally deserved them.[31] Such views were forcefully expressed by trade unionists who lobbied the Treasury and Board of Trade during the passage of the National Insurance Act; and such lobbying helped to reinforce the protection of trade union and friendly society interests within the state insurance schemes. But acceptance of state subventions necessarily entailed acceptance of new forms of state control, which often provoked bitter disputes within the societies themselves; and uneasy suspicion of government regulation of welfare remained a powerful force in the trade union movement, and to a lesser extent among the friendly societies, throughout the early decades of the welfare state era.[32]

A third important factor was that the compulsory extension of mutual thrift affected not only the substance of social welfare schemes but their methods of management. As I have shown, the framers of the National Insurance Act went to great efforts to preserve and replicate the intimate

[30] Report of a meeting of the executive committee of the Engineering and Shipbuilding trades, 17 Nov. 1911; ASE monthly report, Dec. 1911, p. 15. The share of national insurance business going to trade unions and to democratic friendly societies fell from 35.2% to 24.6% between 1912 and 1938. The rest went to industrial assurance companies or to bureaucratised friendly societies without local branches (*Social Insurance and Allied Services*, para. 54).

[31] PRO, LAB 2/211/LE 500, report of a conference with the Federation of Engineering and Shipbuilding Trades, 18 June 1909; Beveridge Papers, III 37, 'Criticisms of Workmen's Insurance by members of the Executive Council of the Shipbuilders and Engineering Trade Federation', compiled by D.C. Cummings, 29 May 1909; Report of the Ipswich Conference of the TUC, 1909, p. 108.

[32] In the ASE, for example, pressure from the National Insurance Commission for amendment and tightening-up of the Society's rules and statutes led in 1912 to a major split among union members, resulting in the sacking of the executive council by the union's trustees and an expensive and damaging dispute in the High Court.

and self-governing character of established voluntary schemes. The sheer scale of national insurance, however, and the vast range of circumstances and contingencies that had to be catered for, meant that in practice the participating societies were soon overwhelmed by a mass of clerical tasks and routine data-collection that began to undermine and transform their traditional 'friendly' practices and functions.[33] The Act also provided for the popular election of working-class representatives who would sit on advisory panels in a quasi-judicial capacity to hear appeals against refusal of benefit; a provision intended to transmit into the public sector some of the elements of personal participation and moral solidarity believed to characterise the domain of mutual thrift. But when in 1912 the first elections were held for members of unemployment insurance panels only 7% of the insured workforce turned out to vote; and the electoral experiment was eventually abandoned by the Ministry of Labour shortly after the first world war.[34] Such an outcome was perhaps unsurprising. But it demonstrated very clearly the difference between a self-selected elite of the most highly-skilled and educated workers – what the ASE proudly called 'the intelligent and intellectual' working-class[35] – and encircling mass society.

Most important of all, however, was the never-resolved problem that – for all the aspirations of social reformers – rules about personal behaviour and standards of efficiency that had grown out of the experience of small *gemeinschaft*-type organisations rooted in highly-skilled industries and close-knit communities were in the last resort only very imperfectly applicable to the wider context of advanced industrial and democratic society. Braithwaite and Beveridge might borrow the rules of friendly societies and trade unions, but they could only do so selectively. They could and did transplant into the state insurance system the rules about specific instances of malingering and misconduct. But there were limits beyond which they simply could not leave out all the moral and actuarial undesirables – or not, at any rate, without undermining the whole purpose and character of a comprehensive state scheme. And, similarly, personal behavioural controls over contributors that had a certain moral legitimacy within a tight-knit trade-union or friendly-society culture, appeared in the wider impersonal society to be intolerable infringements of personal and civil liberties, and either had to be abandoned or were never introduced

---

[33] ASE monthly report, June 1913, p. 29.
[34] *Courts of Referees. Return setting forth the Statutory Provisions relating to the Constitution of Courts of Referees*, H. of C. 527, 1913. This experience may be compared with that of France, where workers' organisations played a much more active role in the democratic control of state social security schemes (Tony Lynes, *French Pensions*, Occasional Papers in Social Administration, 1967).
[35] ASE monthly report, Jan. 1880, p. 44.

in the first place.[36] National health insurance, for example, could never directly prohibit its beneficiaries from stepping outside their homes at night or from going into pubs; and although some approved societies maintained the old surveillance system down to the second world war, such surveillance was increasingly both unpopular and impracticable.[37] In the 1920s the unemployment insurance system tried to impose but ultimately had to abandon the notorious 'genuinely seeking-work clause' – a clause often seen as an invention of mindless bureaucracy, but which had in fact been initially modelled on the long-standing practice of many benefit-paying trade unions.[38] The onset of mass unemployment inevitably subverted the attempt by the state to harness what had been the universal practice of all benefit-paying unions – that entitlement to benefit both individually and collectively should always be financially adjusted to contributions paid.

In other words, the institutions of self-help culture could leave out the residuum of the unfit and the inefficient, the unfortunate and the long-term unemployed, they could require members to share in democratic self-management, and they could monitor the behaviour of welfare benefi-ciaries – but beyond certain limits the welfare state could not. This problem was very clearly anticipated by the Webbs, who claimed that the healthy conditions produced by the National Minimum would greatly reduce the national quota of 'weaklings, degenerates and other undesirables', but that at the end of the day there would always be a residue of such persons – a group whom the Webbs thought should be permanently incarcerated in humane institutions, where they could no longer infect, drag down and demoralise the rest.[39] Such treatment would be implemented and legitimised not just by state bureaucracy, but by a Rousseau-esque process of continuous popular involvment in social welfare administration ('In a fully-developed democratic state, the Citizen will be always minding other

---

[36] The reports of many unions after 1912, for example, soon began to suggest that the behavioural rules about when a member could or could not vacate or refuse a job of work were much more problematical and irksome when exercised by labour exchange officials than when exercised by fellow-members. (ASE Monthly Journal and Report, Mar. 1913, p. 14; June 1913, p. 18).

[37] Jose Harris, 'Did British Workers want the Welfare State? G.D.H. Cole's Survey of 1942', in J.M. Winter (ed.) *The Working Class in Modern British History. Essays in Honour of Henry Pelling (1983), pp. 204–5.*

[38] ASE monthly report, July 1912, p. 6; Rule-Book of the British Steel Smelters, Mill, Iron, Tin-Plate and Kindred Trades Association, 1917; Rule-Book of the Shipconstructors and Shipwrights Association, 1913. On the gradual perversion of the clause by heavy-handed administrative and legal interpretation, see Beveridge, *Unemployment (1930 edn)*, pp. 279–80, and Alan Deacon, *In Search of the Scrounger*, Occasional Papers in Social Administration, (1976), *passim*.

[39] *Industrial Democracy*, pp. 784–9.

people's business'.[40]) A similar political philosophy of welfare can be detected in the outlook of Beveridge, though usually in a more modest and muted form. Beveridge's earliest writings on social policy had directly linked welfare dependency to loss of citizen rights;[41] and, although he soon rejected this view, he never abandoned the principle that, in order to preserve civic morale, malingerers and fraudulent claimants would have to be dealt with by a mixture of self-policing through the medium 'friendly' volunteers and stern disciplinary procedures enforced by the state. Such self-policing and disciplinary procedures had a crucial though not very conspicuous role in the Beveridge Report of 1942.[42] Their partial collapse and loss of legitimacy in the post-second world war era symbolised perhaps more clearly than any other change the long-term erosion of Victorian values within the structure of the modern welfare state.

How does my account of the genesis of the welfare state relate to the two models of Victorian values that I set out earlier in this paper. Clearly it bears very little relation to that advanced by Correlli Barnett. As I have argued elsewhere, the sentimental libertarianism that Barnett claims to detect in the founders of the welfare state more properly belongs to the secularised poverty lobby that dates from the 1960s than to the practical inheritance of reformist Victorian Christianity.[43] Of the two models, I think that the more genuine historical consciousness belongs to Margaret Thatcher. Her perception of Victorian values does have a direct resonance in the voluntaristic and highly-disciplined social welfare culture of the late nineteenth century friendly societies and benefit-paying trade unions. If, as some of Mrs. Thatcher's aides and advisers have sometimes claimed, her true position on social welfare was really a 'Back to Beveridge' one – then that was a perfectly logical corollary of her perception of Victorian values; a far more logical corollary than the widely-held suspicion that her secret agenda was a return to the Victorian Poor Law.

The flaw in Mrs. Thatcher's reasoning lay not in her account of Victorian values but in her understanding of the kind of society that had made such values possible: namely, an aggregation of small-scale, stable, highly-localised, highly-skilled, face-to-face communities that were only very imperfectly invaded by forces of the free market. Such communities were of course only minority communities even within late nineteenth

[40] Ibid., p. 846.
[41] W.H. Beveridge, 'The Question of Disfranchisement', *Toynbee Record*, Mar. 1905, pp. 100–2; and 'The Problem of the Unemployed', *Sociological Papers*, **3**, (1906), pp. 328–31.
[42] *Social Insurance and Allied Services*, paras. 66–9, 369, 373.
[43] Jose Harris, 'Enterprise and Welfare States', *Trans. R.H.S.*, 5th series, vol. 40, 1990, p. 189.

century society; but for a time in the mid- and late-Victorian years they appeared to many people to offer a model for the universal society of the future.[44] Such a vision was central to the social welfare philosophy of Gladstonian liberalism. The erosion of small-scale, working-class communities and organisations by economic change was already well under way, however, by the early twentieth century: and the very fact that private self-help schemes seemed in the 1900s to have exhausted their capacity for autonomous growth was a major factor in precipitating the advance of state welfare. During the course of the twentieth century the wholesale transition to a market-dominated society was to be to a certain extent arrested by the interruption of two world wars and their economic aftermath; and it was no coincidence that the Beveridge Report received its great acclaim in the midst of the Second World War – a war that temporarily revived much of the sense of corporate fraternity, communal self-discipline, and sharing of scarce material resources that had characterised the old friendly society culture of the late nineteenth century. Such Victorian values were, however, increasingly in tension with the values and practices of post-war Keynesian consumerism; and they perhaps received their death-blow from the accelerated market forces of the past eleven years.

[44] See, e.g. 'Accident Benefit Presentation', ASE monthly report, Feb. 1880, pp. 46–8, the report of a visit to the Society by W.E. Forster. The history and significance of such communities are usefully explored in Patrick Joyce, *Work, Society and Politics. The Culture of the Factory in Later Victorian England* (Brighton, 1980).

Proceedings of the British Academy, **78**, 183–194

The Workhouse

M.A. CROWTHER
University of Glasgow

THE 'Victorian values' associated with the workhouse are not as straight-forward as they might seem. Most obviously, the workhouse was not Victorian at all. Model workhouses could be found in Nottinghamshire and elsewhere well before the passing of the New Poor Law,[1] while the law itself was Georgian, not Victorian. The workhouses also long outlasted the Victorian era, until 1948, though renamed 'Poor Law institutions' in 1913. But the architecture of most workhouses was Victorian; and whether built to house a few hundred rural poor, or over a thousand town dwellers, they dominated the landscape. The Victorians inherited the task of turning the Benthamite utopia of 1834 into a practical system.

The workhouse was intended to restore essential social values previously undermined by indiscriminate outdoor relief. Fear of the workhouse was to be a 'stimulant to exertion and to the observance of thrifty and provident habits.'[2] Moreover, it was to reinforce personal morality and social order.[3] Labourers would support their families, children their aged parents, without relying on a subsidy from the parish. Mothers of bastards would no longer enjoy a parish premium for their errors, nor would the young enter into imprudent marriages expecting a subsidy for each child.

Read 14 December 1990. © The British Academy 1992.
[1] J.D. Marshall, 'The Nottinghamshire reformers and their contribution to the New Poor Law', *Econ.Hist.Rev.*, 2nd ser., **13** (3) (1961), 382–96.
[2] MH 10/1/ circular 2.
[3] S.G. and E.O.A. Checkland (eds), *The Poor Law Report of 1834* (1974), 123, 374.

Employers would be forced to raise wages and workers become more deferential if wages, not subsidies, became the chief economic relationship. All this, with the promise of greatly reduced poor rates, enabled the new system to pass into law with a minimum of Parliamentary opposition. And, in spite of criticism, it remained at the heart of Victorian social administration.

Only in a few recalcitrant unions was the building of the new institutions long delayed. The massive investment, over 13 million pounds for building costs between 1834 and 1883, gained an unstoppable momentum.[4] Yet throughout the Victorian period, the workhouse was a focus not for consensus, but dispute. Very soon after the new law was passed, the enthusiastic certainties of Chadwick's rhetoric were challenged from several quarters, and this debate never died away. Few, apart from the most irreconcilable radicals or paternalists, argued that workhouses be pulled down, but their purpose no longer seemed straightforward.

It is not easy to decide exactly which 'Victorian values' are represented by the workhouses. They proved indestructible, but were enormously disliked, even by the social classes who created them. Today the popular image of the workhouse is entirely negative, its original purposes seeming either misguided or hypocritical. It has become a symbol of the ruthlessness of Victorian capitalism, especially as applied to helpless groups such as children and the elderly. Yet this symbolic status was not created by the twentieth century reinterpreting the nineteenth as the 'Bleak Age.' Rather, the Victorians themselves created it as they continued to support the workhouse with ever larger amounts of finance, while abusing it in political polemic, in public meetings, in the pulpit, in art and in literature.

Studies of the opposition to the Poor Law have, reasonably enough, concentrated on the anti-Poor Law movement of the 1830s and 1840s.[5] This included both the brief period of rural rioting in the southern and eastern counties, and the more durable northern campaigns, led by substantial figures in local politics, like Richard Oastler and John Fielden. Such protests shaded into the Ten Hours Movement, the Rebecca riots in Wales, and ultimately into Chartism. All such activities were at an end by the 1850s; yet amongst the rural working class, especially in the

---

[4] For a detailed geography and costing of workhouse construction, see F. Driver, 'The historical geography of the workhouse system in England and Wales, 1834–1883', *Jnl Hist Geography* **15** (3) (1989), 269–86

[5] The most substantial studies are N.C. Edsall, *The Anti-Poor Law Movement 1834–44* (Manchester, 1971), and J. Knott, *Popular Opposition to the 1834 Poor Law* (1985); cf. also M.E. Rose, 'The anti-poor law agitation', in J.T. Ward (ed), *Popular Movements, c 1830–1850* (1970).

eastern counties, the legacy of bitterness left by the New Poor Law was long, showing itself in occasional rick-burning or cattle maiming.[6] In the towns, the most favoured action was a mass gathering at the workhouse to intimidate the guardians with a demand for outdoor relief in times of unemployment.

Although anti-Poor Law sentiment amongst the working class remained strong, expressed in pamphlet and ballad, melodrama and popular song,[7] members of the ruling classes developed their own forms of criticism. These have been underestimated because most of them were not opposed to the main principles of the new Poor Law. Acceptance of the law, but hostility to many aspects of the workhouse test, characterized upper and middle-class attitudes, and this inconsistency persisted throughout the nineteenth century. This is paradoxical, given the apparent unanimity of Parliament in 1834, although its motives at that time have given rise to considerable historical discussion. Whereas the Webbs and other early historians of the Poor Law described it as triumph for Benthamite utilitarianism, more recent historians have debated the continuing interest of the landed gentry in maintaining control over the new Poor Law unions. It is disputed whether the Act aimed to assert traditional authority over the increasingly violent rural poor, or whether it revealed a new capitalist spirit, or 'Christian individualism', as attractive to Tory squires as to Whig bureaucrats.[8] The events of the decade after 1834 were to show that, however compelling the principle of the law might seem, the workhouse did not command the wholehearted loyalty of its original supporters.

Anti-workhouse attitudes manifested themselves in Parliament soon after the passing of the 1834 Act. According to Gladstone, then a fledgling

[6] See, e.g. A. Digby, *Pauper Palaces* (1978), 224–8; D. Jones, 'Thomas Campbell Foster and the rural labourer: incendiarism in East Anglia in the 1840s', *Social History*, **1** (1976), 9ff.

[7] Some of the popular anti-Poor Law songs are reproduced in Roy Palmer (ed.), *A Touch on the Times: songs of social change 1770–1914* (1974), 260–70.

[8] For the main argument in favour of the continuing landed interest in the Poor Law, see A. Brundage, *The Making of the New Poor Law: the Politics of Inquiry, Enactment and Implementation, 1832–1839* (1978); for the counter argument that the Poor Law reflected the Whigs' concern for both economic liberalism and social order, see P. Dunkley, 'Whigs and paupers: the reform of the English Poor Law, 1830–1834', *Jnl Brit Stud*, **20** (2) (1981), 124–49 and *The Crisis of the Old Poor Law in England 1795–1834: an interpretive essay* (NY, 1982); for the Poor Law as arising from the views of a 'modernized' county gentry, see P. Mandler, 'Tories and paupers: Christian political economy and the making of the New Poor Law', *Hist Jnl*, **33** (1) (1990), 81–103 and 'The making of the New Poor Law *redivivus*', *Past & Present*, **117** (1987), 131–57; for a general debate, see A. Brundage, D. Eastwood, P. Mandler, 'Debate: the making of the New Poor Law *redivivus*', *Past & Present*, **127** (1990), 183–201

member, disenchantment began very early. Although in opposition in 1834, Gladstone himself had strongly supported an Act

> which rescued the English peasantry from the total loss of their independ-
> ence. Of the 658 members of Parliament about 480 must have been [its]
> general supporters. Much gratitude ought to have been felt for this great
> administration. But from a variety of causes, at the close of the session
> 1834 the House of Commons had fallen into a state of cold indifference
> about it.[9]

Early enthusiasm was soon tempered when the effects of the law were considered and as local discontent mounted.[10] The Poor Law Commissioners were originally established for five years, and their powers were then annually extended until 1842, when Robert Peel secured them another five-year term. As each period of renewal approached, although only a small minority supported the abolition of the law, the debate became more heated, and criticism of various features of the Act more intense. The most dangerous moment came in 1841, as Russell's Whig government was collapsing, and the radical chorus against the Poor Law was joined by the voice of Young England. The Webbs attributed this simply to factional strife, political manoeuvres rather than principled debate,[11] but the attitudes expressed in this acrimonious session are worth more attention, for they encapsulate anxieties about the workhouse which were to persist for several generations. Such anxieties were not enough to bring down the Poor Law itself, but they reveal the general confusion on the purpose and management of workhouses, and led to a steady attrition of Chadwick's original idea.

Between 1834 and 1841 the Poor Law, and most particularly the workhouse system, were subjected to violent attack, both in Parliament and the press. Thomas Wakley, redoubtable editor of *The Lancet* and MP for Finsbury, adopted the same approach in the Commons as did *The Times* outside it: they recounted lists of appalling evils in specific workhouses – elderly and infirm people of blameless life torn from their homes and friends when they became destitute, husbands and wives separated in the workhouses, children forced from their mothers, starvation dietaries, brutal and indecent behaviour by workhouse officers, paupers left to die alone in the house without their families in other wards being informed.[12] Added

[9] Quoted in J. Morley, *Life of William Ewart Gladstone* (1908), i, 85

[10] For local Tory objections to the law on paternalist and humanitarian grounds, see G. Himmelfarb, *The Idea of Poverty: England in the Early Industrial Age* (1984), chap. 7.

[11] S. and B. Webb, *English Poor Law History, part II: the Last Hundred Years* (1963 ed.), i, 174 ff.

[12] The stories are fully discussed, and largely discounted by D. Roberts, 'How cruel was the Victorian Poor Law?' *Hist Jnl*, **7** (1) (1963), 97–106; see also U. Henriques, 'How cruel was the Victorian Poor Law?', *Hist Jnl*, **11** (2) (1968), 365–71.

to these were the pamphlets, the broadsides, and, in 1841 the enthusiastic compilation of largely unattributable stories, *The Book of the Bastiles*.[13]

The Poor Law Commissioners and their assistants spent much time investigating such stories, and decided that most of them were untrue. In proven cases, officials were disciplined, since the law gave them no authority for such behaviour. In the Commons, defenders of the Law argued, with considerable justification, that abuses had always existed under the Old Poor Law, and the Commissioners had brought them to light. Historians like David Roberts have argued that the evils of the New Poor Law were much exaggerated; but it is more likely, given the wide range of local studies now available, that widespread abuses of authority did exist. This was not surprising, since the new workhouses were much less open to public scrutiny than the old, and their officers were overworked, untrained, and not always well supervised by the guardians.[14] The early years of the workhouse show a rapid turnover of staff, many of them dismissed for offences against property or paupers. The Commissioners permitted no physical cruelty; but they did sanction a minimal dietary in many parts of the country, monotony, discipline, and separation of families.

Nevertheless, whether the widely publicized stories were true or false, they forced themselves on public attention. Special committees of both Houses investigated them, and MPs became involved in detailed debates about the truth or falsity of certain cases. Wakley, in particular, provoked hours of discussion on such matters in the Commons. The debate of 1841 revealed the Poor Law in an uneasy state after years of public sniping.

The debate began when Lord John Russell tried to extend the Commissioners' powers for a further 10 years, and to amend the Act of 1834 in some minor ways. It revealed a pattern well established in Parliamentary discussion of the Poor Law. Russell's ministry was tottering, but the Conservatives were not inclined to take advantage. As in 1834, few members from either side of the house actually challenged the principles of the New Poor Law, or wished to return to the old. Only Wakley, Fielden and a small group of radicals disliked the New Poor Law enough to aim for its total destruction; in this they were joined by a few paternalist Tories who objected to bureaucracy and interference with local affairs. Among these was Disraeli, just arrived at the bottom of the greasy pole. His attitude later received stern comments from the Webbs, who obviously saw him as a frivolous and irresponsible young man. Disraeli, with the mixture of paternalism and antiquarianism that made up Young England, stressed the need for social cohesion in the parishes: 'the great boast in

[13] G.R. Wythen Baxter, *The Book of the Bastiles* (1841).
[14] M.A. Crowther, *The Workhouse System 1834–1929* (1981), 33–5, 118–25

this country,' he argued, 'had been that society was strong and government weak.'[15]

Around 140 amendments were tabled to Russell's proposals, from a wide spectrum of MPs.[16] Yet the support for most of these amendments was small, rarely able to muster more than 50 votes. The speeches of radical and Tory opponents, spread over several months and often lasting late into the night, taking up interminable pages of *Hansard*, became predictable. Wakley argued that the law was 'unsuited to the charitable and kindly disposition of the people of this country,' Disraeli added that 'to suppose for a moment that . . . the poor population could be controlled and managed by shutting them up in prisons, was to suppose that which was contrary to every principle of humane society.'[17] More interesting were the responses from the large majority supporting the principles of the Poor Law, reminding the objectors that the previous law had become extravagant, cruel, unworkable. But as each speaker defended the new system, he added a clause asserting his right to attack features of it which he found unacceptable.[18] Wakley complained that there was no agreement on whether, or how long, the Poor Law Commission should be extended, or on which parts of the Poor Law were most in need of amendment, and so 'the effect of this difference of opinion was, that there was always a majority in favour of the bill.'[19] Each speaker had his own crotchet, but certain themes began to emerge, some becoming the subject of later legislation.

The chief objection to the workhouse was its rigid separation of families, particularly elderly couples.[20] This had previously been raised in the Lords by a small group of dissident peers, and the Bishop of Exeter, who felt that it was unchristian.[21] Such feelings forced Russell to drop a highly utilitarian clause proposed by the Poor Law Commissioners, that guardians be allowed to make efficient use of their property by renting out empty space in workhouses to one another. The result would be further separation of families and removal of paupers from their own neighbourhood.[22] In fact, rationalization was never permitted except in the case of specialized

---

[15] *Hansard* 56, 8 Feb. 1841, 382. (This and subsequent references are to the third series of *Hansard*). Cf. the comment of one of his successors, 'There is no such thing as society', quoted in H. Young, *One of Us: A Biography of Margaret Thatcher* (1989), 490.

[16] *Hansard* 57, 27 Sept. 1841, 902.

[17] *Hansard* 56, 29 Jan. 1841, 157; 8 Feb. 1841, 378.

[18] E.g. speeches by Knatchbull, *Hansard* 56, Feb. 8 1841, 428; Darby, *idem* 435–8; Somerset, 57, 26 March 1841, 631; Wood, 57, 27 Sept. 1841, 905; Philips, 57, 28 Sept., 957.

[19] *Hansard* 57, 19 March 1841, 401. Cf. also Edsall (1971), 137–8.

[20] E.g. speeches by Darby, *Hansard* 56, 8 Feb. 1841, 437; James, ibid, 445; Somerset, 57, 1 April 1841, 774–5.

[21] *Hansard* 43, 25 June 1838, 986.

[22] *Hansard* 57, 1 April 1941, 774–7.

institutions such as district schools, asylums for the insane, and (later) special institutions for the handicapped. The first rationalization along the lines proposed by Russell came during World War I, when elderly paupers were moved to workhouses with spare capacity to make room for military casualties. Disquiet over elderly married couples continued until 1847, when enough country squires united to amend the law and permit couples over 60 to share a room, if they so requested.[23]

The pervasive tendency in debate, amongst many who supported the workhouses, was to make exceptions of certain groups. The deserving unemployed had their supporters, who wished to operate an outdoor labour test rather than the workhouse test.[24] This power was confirmed by the Poor Law Commissioners in 1844 as a way of solving the intractable problem of sudden slumps in industrial areas, but was widely extended during the nineteenth century.[25] Another amendment, imposing the workhouse test on wives whose husbands were overseas, was dropped because of its possible repercussions on the navy (in 1844 the law was amended to treat these women the same as widows – to prevent their removal from their usual place of residence, and to allow them outdoor relief).[26] Widows, children, the sick and the elderly, all had their champions, who felt that the workhouse test might be bent to favour them. The general unease is exemplified in the unhappy comments of an MP who had supported Poor Law reform and now found himself opposing many of Russell's clauses;

> he hoped that the commissioners would see that a proper allowance was made to the poor, and particularly to the sick poor, that out-door relief should be afforded to as great an extent as possible, and that no such cruelties or inhumanities as had unfortunately more than once taken place in the workhouses should again be permitted.[27]

In May, after months of debate in which amendments were added and dropped, Russell gave up his attempt to amend the Poor Law, and the Commissioners' life was prolonged for only one more year. Peel, coming to power in September, had to take over the task. In 1842, having taken account of some of the most strongly voiced objections to the Law, he was able to prolong the Commissioners' remit until 1847.[28] The opponents of the law were vociferous, but had no alternative to offer. To return to the

[23] 10 & 11 Vict c. 109 s. 23. See also D Roberts, *Paternalism in Early Victorian England* (1979), 257–8.
[24] *Hansard* 56, 8 Feb. 1841, 428, 437.
[25] Webb (1963), II i, 142–50: Driver (1989), 274–5.
[26] *Hansard* 57, 1 April 1841, 788. The 1844 regulations were in 7 & 8 Vict c.101, s.25–6. Widows with illegitimate children were disqualified, however.
[27] *Hansard* 57, 26 March, 638 (Halford).
[28] Russell's Act was 5 Vict c.10, Peel's 5 & 6 Vict c.57.

Old Poor Law seemed impossible, nor did any doubt the need for some kind of institutional provision. Workhouses, once constructed, developed a logic of their own, since they represented a heavy investment, and soon began to fulfil the functions of hospitals and asylums. The government in 1834 had passed, by an overwhelming majority, an act which appeared, by a simple device, to end long-standing grievances. But the act provoked much popular unrest, and aroused great nervousness among many of its original supporters. Unable to go back, the government saw no clear way forward, except perhaps some tinkering with administrative detail.

The workhouse system, therefore, created discord even among supporters of the New Poor Law, and provoked a major clash of Victorian values. It was supposed to invigorate family responsibility, but did so by breaking up families; it was supposed to encourage the industrious worker and discourage idleness and depravity; but in the general mixed workhouse the sick and destitute were mixed together whatever their background: moral classification, apart from a few experiments later in the century, was rarely possible. The ambivalent regard in which workhouses were held by their creators is unintentionally summarized by the Duke of Wellington, in his speech introducing Peel's bill of 1842 to the House of Lords:

> It [the Poor Law bill of 1834] has undoubtedly improved the condition of the working classes, and it certainly does put on a better footing the relations between the working classes and their employers . . . My Lords, I don't mean to say that I approve of every act that has been done in carrying this bill into operation. I think that in many cases those who had charge of the working of the bill have gone too far, and that there was no occasion whatever for constructing buildings such as have acquired throughout the country the denomination of bastiles, and that it would have been perfectly easy to have established very efficient workhouses, without shutting out all view of what was passing exterior to the walls.[29]

If Parliament was prepared to upset workhouse principles by special pleading, the local guardians who administered the law were even more benighted. Poor Law Inspectors regularly complained about the activities of well-meaning but misguided guardians and members of the public, 'these anti-poor-law pseudo-philanthropic agitators' as Edward Carleton Tufnell, the most dedicated of Chadwick's assistants, called them in the early years of the law.[30] For the first decade, Tufnell had to fight against Kent and Sussex guardians anxious to give outdoor relief during hard winters. Their inspector noted testily: 'I am wearied to death with preaching theory to

[29] *Hansard* 65, 26 July 1842, 619–20.
[30] MH 32/71 12 June 45.

these dull-headed people.'[31] Embarrassment was compounded because in some unions the magistrates and clergy were vocal against aspects of the workhouse test.[32]

Nor did these difficulties subside. J.S. Davy, Inspector for most of Yorkshire, reported at length in 1879 on the unsatisfactory habits of guardians in his district. His report came at the end of a decade notable for the Local Government Board's attempts to tighten up the administration of the law, and to reduce outdoor relief. Yorkshire unions, at first resistant to the New Poor Law, were mostly applying either the workhouse test or the labour test by the 1870s, though the workhouses never had enough accommodation to deal with the unemployed during trade depressions. Davy believed that the poor would deliberately apply in large numbers in hard times, knowing that the guardians would be forced to give outdoor relief; he suggested that guardians pack as many beds as possible into the dormitories and corridors of the workhouses, as a deterrent. His report indicated the wide variety of opinions in the district: some guardians were subsidizing men on short-time working to keep families together; others offered test work not as a deterrent but as a form of public works. In Hunslet and Holbeck, 'veritable *"ateliers publiques"*' had been set up, where men on stone-breaking work were paid by the ton; in Saddleworth, where correct principles applied, a man would work a full day for a small fixed sum.[33] One guardian carried economy to excess, another told Davy 'The word pauper as applied to everyone who gets relief from this Board rings most detestably in my ears. Our test men are as honourable as I, & would never trouble us but for the frost.'[34] Philanthropists tried to persuade guardians not to take charitable assistance into account when dispensing relief, while in Bradford, where the same frost had disrupted the building trade, two clergymen 'placed themselves at the head of a mob of several hundred persons, and made a demonstration in front of the Town Hall.'[35] They aimed to persuade the guardians to end the labour test or increase the rate of relief. Although this demand failed, they succeeded, Davy reported, in stirring up much uneasiness in the town.

Historians are now in dispute over the effects of the workhouse test in reducing outdoor relief for able-bodied men after 1834: some have argued that the test succeeded not only in cutting back on relief, but in keeping wages low in areas of labour surplus: others that outdoor relief continued

---

[31] MH 32/69 21 Oct. 1837.
[32] Digby (1978), 211–14. Roberts (1979), 154–6 describes the divisions in attitude which the Poor Law produced among the clergy.
[33] MH 32/98, 13 Feb 1879.
[34] Ibid.
[35] MH 32/98, 30 Jan. 1879.

surreptitiously in many unions, particularly in the north.[36] The debate probably proves no more than that regional practices varied widely. Even if we assume that local guardians followed the requirements of the law in this fundamental matter, there is less doubt that conditions for the indoor poor were not uniform, but depended on the amount of local finance, the state of the building, and the attitudes of both guardians and local pressure groups. Keith Snell, whose admirable work on the southern and eastern counties suggests severe exploitation of the rural poor after 1834, draws much of his evidence from the writings of concerned paternalists, including the clergy.[37] The conflict of values was at its most severe at the local level.

In this discussion of Parliamentary and local debates, little time has been left for the other ways of analysing public response to the workhouse. Here, literary and artistic representations would take a central place. The workhouse was the bogey not only of Chartist pamphleteers, but of middle-class organs like *The Times*, *Punch* and several of the Tory daily papers of London.[38] Dickens was the most famous of many writers who used the workhouse as an essential plot device, and hence helped to shape public perception. Since workhouses were relatively closed to the public gaze, artistic representations possibly had greater significance. Against the views of tract writers such as Harriet Martineau, where the workhouse waited as the inevitable end of the indolent and vicious, was the workhouse of Dickens, or Hardy, or the popular melodrama: where the workhouse existed not to admonish the disreputable, but to terrify the helpless.

In particular, the workhouse system dwelt uneasily alongside another Victorian value: belief in private charity. The Poor Law report of 1834 ended with a veiled attack on private charities for giving indiscriminate relief. Such charities, the report argued, 'are often wasted and often mischievous', and it hinted at the need for government control of their actions.[39] Given that two Bishops had signed the report, perhaps it could go no further;[40] but in 1841 Russell attempted to define the relationship

---

[36] Karel Williams, *From Pauperism to Poverty* (1981) chap. 2; A. Digby, 'The labour market and the continuity of social policy after 1834: the case of the Eastern Counties,' *Econ. Hist. Rev.* **28** (1) (1975), 69–83; William Apfel and Peter Dunkley, 'English rural society and the New Poor Law: Bedfordshire, 1834–47', *Social History*, **10** (1) (1985), 37–68; M.E. Rose, 'The allowance system under the New Poor Law', *Econ. Hist. Rev.* **19** (3) (1966), 607–20.

[37] K.D.M. Snell, *Annals of the Labouring Poor: social change and agrarian England 1660–1900* (Cambridge, 1985), chap. 3.

[38] Roberts (1979), 192–8.

[39] Checkland (1974), 495–6.

[40] Mandler (1990) discusses the relationship between current political economy and religious thought.

between Poor Law and charity. The guardians, he argued, could not distinguish between the deserving and undeserving poor, but had to use the workhouse deterrent in an impartial manner. Only charity could use proper discrimination in identifying deserving recipients of relief.[41] Unfortunately, the Poor Law Commissioners chose that moment to suggest that charity undid the good work of the Poor Law by giving indiscriminate aid, but Sir Robert Peel responded vigorously:

> he should abominate the Poor-law if he thought it relieved the rich from almsgiving . . . it was unwise in the commissioners to issue a public notice announcing that 'a principal object of a compulsory provision for the relief of destitution was the prevention of alms-giving.' One object might be the prevention of mendicancy or vagrancy, certainly not of alms-giving. Good God, it was a complete desecration of the precepts of the Divine law . . .'[42]

For the rest of the century, the relationship between charity and the work-house was uneasy. The law's harshness undoubtedly stimulated charitable activities, at first designed to 'save' deserving cases from the workhouse, and later attempting to permeate the workhouse itself with charitable values.[43] It is virtually impossible to compare the scale of charitable provision with the scale of the poor law; equally, it seems impossible to doubt that the charitable efforts of the kingdom outweighed its public provision. David Owen's deliberately conservative estimate for 1874–5, excluding missionary, Bible, and Tract societies, and unable to estimate casual or personal charity, suggests that nearly £4 million was raised by organized charity in London alone: at the same time, Poor Law expenditure for the whole of England and Wales was around £7.5 million.[44] Charity at all points overlapped with or duplicated Poor Law functions: it provided hospitals, orphanages, almshouses for the elderly, homes for the handicapped, refuges for prostitutes, aid for widows, the unemployed, and the virtuous distressed. Charities such as the Metropolitan Association for Befriending Young Servants, were specifically designed to prevent a vulnerable group from going into the workhouse when out of work. The type of charity constantly denounced by Poor Law authorities – casual giving to beggars – continued unabated, and indeed the Local Government Board frequently argued that it would not be reduced until conditions in workhouse casual wards were improved to the point where people felt no guilt in sending vagrants into them. As an alternative stratagem, the determined efforts of Louisa

[41] *Hansard* 56, 1 Feb. 1841, 172–3.
[42] *Hansard* 57, 19 March 1841, 444.
[43] Crowther (1981), 67–71.
[44] David Owen, *English Philanthropy 1660–1960* (Oxford, 1965), 477; K. Williams (1981), 170.

Twining and other charitable women attempted to bring charitable values into the workhouses by improving conditions in the sick wards and softening the treatment of children and the elderly, while discriminating against the 'undeserving'.[45] Society was not content to let workhouse values take care of all social casualties.

The immense confusion of functions, and the possibility of artful dodgers taking advantage of them, was of course the main impetus behind the famous, if unavailing, efforts of the Charity Organization Society to rationalize Poor Law and charity, by a strict investigation of individual circumstances. Their attitude was enshrined in the Majority Report of the Poor Law Commission in 1909, enjoining charitable aid for the deserving, the Poor Law for the 'residuum'.

The conflict of ruling-class opinions, rather than working-class protest, provides the key for the changing functions of the workhouse during the nineteenth century. Chadwick had never intended it to be purely a deterrent: it was to provide education for the children, and 'indulgences' for the elderly; but in its early years its impact was largely negative. During the course of the nineteenth century it began to shed its punitive image for the helpless poor, with better diets, a wide range of hospital functions, cottage homes for children, and so forth. By 1909 the Webbs were looking forward to a system of specialized and purposeful institutions, whether to heal the sick or set vagrants to compulsory labour.

An examination of the Victorian workhouse system shows that efforts to treat the poor in a mechanistic fashion are likely to be confronted by an equally powerful set of alternative values: in fact, the more strongly the authorities attempt to deter the poor from seeking relief, the more they encourage alternative forms of provision. The workhouse produced a clash of values which might fairly be described as 'Victorian,' since that age was characterized by robust debate, and willingness to take sides. To adopt the terminology of one eminent Victorian, Karl Marx, the thesis of Benthamite efficiency was confronted by its antithesis of paternalism and charity. The workhouse is therefore a symbol, not of certainty, but of conflict.

[45] Her views are outlined in L. Twining, 'Workhouse cruelties', *Nineteenth Century*, **20** (1886), 709–14, and *Workhouses and Pauperism, and Women's work in the administration of the Poor Law* (1898).

Proceedings of the British Academy **78**, 195–215

Victorian Values and Women
in Public and Private

ANNE DIGBY

Oxford Polytechnic

.

THE theme of this paper[1] is the Victorian ideological divide between the public sphere (viewed as a masculine domain concerned with paid work and national politics), and the private sphere (viewed as a female domain concerned with home and family). These contrasts were in some respects ancient ones: the political dimension of public masculine persons and private female persons going back at least to Aristotle.[2] Dichotomies of this kind have had varying force in different historical periods. This paper will suggest that both the ideology and its practical application had particular significance during the Victorian period and the years that immediately followed.

A social construction of gender created gendered dualisms of which private and public was but one. Others included personal and political; nature and culture; biology and intellect; work and leisure; intellect and intuition; rationality and emotionality; and morality and power. Do we need these kinds of female / male oppositions? They involve types of shorthand statements of gendered Victorian values that have been taken over by students of the period. But whilst they impose order they may

Read 14 December 1990. © The British Academy 1992.

[1] I should like to thank Charles Feinstein, Jane Ribbens, the members of the Oxford Women's History Group, and those attending the Conference on Victorian Values in Edinburgh, for their very helpful comments on earlier versions of this paper.

[2] J.B. Elshtain, 'A Consideration of the Public-Private Split and its Political Ramifications', *Politics and Society*, **4** (1974), pp. 453–7.

involve conceptual naïvety or empirical over-simplification. An apparently clear and easy stereotyping conceals the fact that such dichotomies are socially constructed and reconstructed according to specific historical circumstances. Indeed they beg as many questions as they answer. Worse, they tend to exclude the kinds of ambiguities that characterise women's lives. Social historians have recently made attempts to get away from dichotomous models towards those involving greater complexity.[3] Social constructions can define in ambivalent, contradictory, even conflicting ways. I will argue, however, that this confusion created a space which empowered some Victorian and Edwardian women.

It has been said that 'The dichotomy between the private and public is central to almost two centuries of feminist writing and political struggle'.[4] I would like to look at what in historical experience appears to be an intermediate or semi-detached area between public and private. I want to call this the borderland, defined in orthodox terms as 'a land or district on or near a border.'[5] This alerts us to the presence of a boundary, frontier, or brink in gender relations. Whilst there is some ambiguity involved in using a geographical for a social concept, its usage was not unknown to the Victorians themselves. Revealingly, the term borderland made its appearance in writing on insanity, and on social degeneration, during the late nineteenth and early twentieth century.[6] In a chapter entitled 'The Borderland' Henry Maudsley wrote that it was not possible to 'draw a hard and fast line, and to declare that all persons who were on one side of it must be sane and all persons who were the other side must be insane.' Rather there needed to be a recognition of 'the existence of intermediate instances' and of 'a borderland between sanity and insanity.' This was peopled by 'doubtful cases' whose 'peculiarities of thought or feeling or character make them objects of remark among their fellows.'[7] Boundaries of gender behaviour were being challenged at this time not just by feminists but also by men who were termed 'decadent males'[8] because of their subversion of established patterns of masculine behaviour – whether

[3] L. Davidoff, 'Adam Spoke First and Named the Orders of the World': Masculine and Feminine Domains in History and Sociology', in H. Corr and L. Jamieson eds, *Politics of Everyday Life. Continuity and Change in Work and Family* (1990), pp. 231, 239.

[4] C. Pateman, *The Disorder of Women. Democracy, Feminism and Political Theory* (1989), p. 118.

[5] *Shorter Oxford Dictionary* (Oxford, 1980).

[6] See, for example, A. Wynter, *The Borderlands of Insanity* (1875); H. Maudsley, 'The Borderland' in *Responsibility in Mental Disease* (second edn, 1874); T. B. Hyslop, *The Borderland* (1924).

[7] Maudsley, *Mental Disease*, pp. 38–40.

[8] E. Showalter, *The Female Malady. Women, Madness and English Culture*, 1830–1980 (1987), pp. 105–6.

sexual, moral, or economic. A Social Darwinistic framework encouraged psychiatrists of this period to set feminist aspirations – particularly those relating to higher education and entry to the professions – against Britain's imperialistic ambitions.[9]

In 1905 The Senior Physician at Bethlem Royal Hospital, T.B. Hyslop, stated that,

> The removal of woman from her natural sphere of domesticity to that of mental labour not only renders her less fit to maintain the virility of the race, but it renders her prone to degenerate, and initiate a downward tendency which gathers impetus in her progeny . . . The departure of woman from her natural sphere to an artificial one involves a brain struggle which is deleterious to the virility of the race . . . it has very direct bearings upon the increase of nervous instability. In fact, the higher women strive to hold the torch of intellect, the dimmer the rays of light for the vision of their progeny.[10]

Writing much later, in 1924, in a book entitled *The Borderland*, Hyslop showed how Maudsley's ideas of fifty years earlier were still influential in psychiatric thinking. He asserted that 'there is no-hard-and-fast line of demarcation between sanity and insanity. Some authorities make the borderland fairly narrow; others however, make it so wide as to include nearly every departure from the conventional modes of thought and conduct.'[11] Such a view had clear professional advantages in dealing with ambiguous behaviour. And within this borderland, where sanity blended imperceptibly with insanity, the diagnosis of moral insanity was an especially useful one since it had always been particularly fluid. The first English writer to develop the diagnosis of moral insanity, James Cowles Prichard, wrote in 1835 that its characteristics included, 'Eccentricity of conduct, singular and absurd habits, a propensity to perform the common actions of life in a different way from that usually practised.'[12] Here one can see strong continuities of thought in almost a century of writing by men esteemed within the psychiatric profession. And these professional diagnoses were ones that could be socially useful

---

[9] See C. Dyhouse, 'Social Darwinistic ideas and the development of women's education in England, 1880–1920', *History of Education*, 5 (1976), pp. 41–58; S. Delamont and L. Duffin, eds, *The Nineteenth-Century Woman* (1978), chapters 3–4 *passim*; J. Burstyn, *Victorian Education and the Ideal of Womanhood* (1980), chapter 5 *passim*; A. Digby, 'Women's Biological Straitjacket', in S. Mendus and J. Rendall, eds, *Sexuality and Subordination. Interdisciplinary Studies of Gender in the Nineteenth Century* (1989), pp. 208–14.

[10] T.B. Hyslop, 'A Discussion of Occupation and Environment as Causative Factors of Insanity', *British Medical Journal*, 2 (1905), p. 942.

[11] T. B. Hyslop, *The Borderland. Some of the Problems of Insanity* (Popular edition, 1925), p. 1.

[12] J. Cowles Prichard, *A Treatise on Insanity* (1835), pp. 23–4.

in dealing with non-conforming women. Those who were perceived as
rebelling against conservatively drawn gender boundaries might find that
others saw them as inhabiting a psychiatric borderland. The label of moral
insanity was especially useful in this context,[13] and so too, (as we shall see
later in this paper), was that of hysteria.

Whilst contemporary psychiatrists saw the borderland as a highly problematic area, into which women ventured at their peril, I want to
suggest that it could also be a positive place for women to colonise.
In my analysis the application of the term borderland will be extended
from contemporary psychiatric usage to focus on gender boundaries
more generally. There were risks for women in establishing frontier
posts within this social borderland and these varied according to the
behaviour of the colonists. Those who, in demeanour as well as activity, flouted traditional gender conventions might find themselves designated as occupying not only a social borderland, but a psychiatric one
also. What both social and psychiatric borderlands had in common,
however, was their shadowy, shifting, indeterminate, and ambiguous
character.

The extent of this Victorian and Edwardian social borderland was
large since it related to different networks and organisations in political,
social and economic life. It is interesting to speculate on the function
of this social borderland. In a society changing at an unprecedented
pace it allowed flexibility. Given major changes in social structure,
urbanisation and political organisation it was predictable that the period
should witness a challenge to older values. To some extent the borderland
also accommodated class differences within female experience. Significantly, it allowed 'official' Victorian values to be silently transgressed
– by working-class women working outside the home, or by mainly
middle-class women engaging in semi-public activities – but without
formal recognition necessarily having to be taken of such 'frontier vio-
lations'. Two of the interesting topics that will be explored are: what
made crossings over the gender boundary from private to public socially
'visible'; and the related issue of what characterised the social 'invisibility' of so much unofficial female colonisation of the borderland.
Put another way, why did this kind of gender Balkans flare up at
times into open conflict whilst at other times women successfully occupied, and extended, their space? In attempting to answer this question,

---

[13] One who was seen as 'wayward', or evincing an improper (i.e. unfeminine) 'desire for the
male sex', for example, might find themselves labelled as morally insane in an asylum – as
was Lucy F., a patient in the Retreat during the 1840s and 1850s. (A. Digby, *Madness,
Morality and Medicine. A Study of the York Retreat, 1796–1914* [Cambridge, 1985], the
appendix gives her case notes in full.)

within the confines of a brief paper, the analysis focuses first on the political, then the economic, and finally the social aspects of Victorian women's lives.

It was during the transitional period of the late eighteenth and early nineteenth centuries that, according to Catherine Hall, 'gender divisions were reworked' and 'men placed firmly in the newly defined public world of business, commerce, and politics; women were placed in the private world of home and family.'[14] Concentrating our attention first on political movements at this time, there were female middle-class activists in anti-slavery campaigns, but they directed much of their efforts to ensure that other women did not consume sugar grown by slaves in their households. And women were essentially perceived as playing a supportive role in the campaigns on the vote during the 1830s, even within female political unions.[15] Dorothy Thompson places a divide in political forms of activity for working-class women rather later in that they, 'seem to have retreated into the home at some time around, or a little before the middle of the century.'[16] The trend, if not its exact timing, was clear; women's skills and interests came to be utilised increasingly on the margins of mainstream political activity, whereas in an earlier tradition of open politics ordinary women had played a notable part. Then there had been an important tradition of female participation in the food riot (with all its obvious linkages to the household and the female role in managing it), and women were also active in anti-New Poor Law demonstrations, but by the 1840s such endeavours were giving way to other forms of political activism.[17] Within Owenite and Saint-Simonian socialism a radical stance on marriage and divorce, and an associated critique of the nuclear family, gave women more space within integrated communities. Even in this radical culture, however, feminist principles had minimal impact on power structures so that there were few women holding executive positions or acting as lecturers and missionaries.[18] In the Chartist movement of the late 1830s and 1840s there was considerable organisation, speaking and demonstrating done by women. However, relatively few concerned themselves with the particular legal, economic or political disabilities of women as a group, although female Chartists

[14] C. Hall, 'Private Persons versus Public Someones: Class, Gender and Politics in England, 1780–1850', in T. Lovell, ed., *British Feminist Thought. A Reader* (1990), p. 52.
[15] Hall, 'Private Persons', p. 60.
[16] D. Thompson, 'Women and Nineteenth-Century Radical Politics', in J. Mitchell and A. Oakley, eds, *The Rights and Wrongs of Women* (1986), p. 115.
[17] M.I. Thomis and J. Grimmett eds, *Women in Protest 1800–1850 (1982)*, p. 45.
[18] B. Taylor, *Eve and the New Jerusalem* (1983), pp. 219–21.

frequently reiterated their fundamental devotion to their homes and families.[19]

A cultural sharpening of the gender divide during the mid-nineteenth century involved a narrowing of the criteria for female respectability and meant that the ideology of separate spheres became more prominent in politics. This was evident in the campaign against the Contagious Diseases Acts, which enforced medical inspection of female prostitutes in specified garrison and naval towns from the late 1860s to the early 1880s. Whilst the movement was spearheaded by Josephine Butler and had a conspicuous public-speaking and organisational role for women, it was 'couched within the terms of a "separate spheres" ideology' which 'stressed women's purity, moral supremacy, and domestic virtue'.[20] Some localities held separate meetings for men and women because of the perceived delicacy of the subject matter, which was not seen as a suitable topic for mixed company. This had the effect of restricting the public role of women in the campaign.[21] Indeed, it is significant in this context that in 1877 Josephine Butler expressed anxiety to the female executive of the Ladies National Association, that women were being squeezed out of the leadership of this crusade. Partly this was because of the 'ease' with which men were said to combine together, and partly because 'women from long habit have quite naturally stood aside and allowed men to work alone, whilst they themselves try very faithfully to exercise that unseen or domestic influence alone which has hitherto been permitted them.'[22]

The strength of this domestic ideology in mid and late Victorian values meant that concepts of female influence in the political process shared some common ground among later suffragists and anti-suffragists. Whilst they most obviously involved women in clearly opposing views on their role in national politics there was – less obviously – some limited agreement on views of citizenship. The idea of a *female citizenship* as a distinctive participative activity was put forward by the anti-suffragists. This was a gendered view of citizenship; women's objective was the good of the community achieved through operating within a locality and not, as with men, within the national state or empire. 'An Appeal against Female Suffrage' of 1889, signed by Mrs. Humphrey Ward and dozens of other women, argued that women's public and political activity should continue to be that which 'rests on thought, conscience and moral influence' and argued against 'their admission to direct power in that State which *does*

---

[19] D. Thompson, *The Chartists* (1984), pp. 149–50.

[20] J.R. Walkowitz, *Prostitution and Victorian Society. Women, class and the state* (Cambridge, 1980), pp. 256–7.

[21] Walkowitz, *Prostitution*, p. 135.

[22] Quoted in Walkowitz, *Prostitution*, p. 139.

rest on force'. They thus rejoiced in female participation in such local activities as voting for, or becoming members of, School Boards or Boards of Guardians but not in activity relating to Parliament. Significantly, they made a clear distinction between citizenship and the suffrage, since in their view 'Citizenship lies in the participation of each individual in effort for the good of the community.'[23] In the reasoning, (but not of course in the opposing conclusions), this was surprisingly similar to the view of the leading suffragist, Millicent Garrett Fawcett. She advocated the extension of the suffrage to women, because she wanted:

> to see the womanly and domestic side of things weigh more and count for more in all public concerns. Let no one imagine for a moment that we want women to cease to be womanly; we want rather to raise the ideal type of womanhood.[24]

Earlier, philanthropic women had been generally more socially conservative, having a stronger belief in individualistic than collectivist endeavour. Josephine Butler argued in 1869 that parochial charity was 'feminine' in character, whilst large-scale legislative-based welfare systems were 'masculine'.[25] Parochial charity, based on personal ties and moral interaction between donor and recipient, was normatively located in the private sphere, although in practice it involved women in work in the community. Fund-raising for many of these parochial charities was done through a public bazaar. And, as Emily Davies commented,

> It is averred that 'public life' is injurious to women: they are meant for the domestic . . . What is meant by it? . . . Fathers who would shake their heads at the idea of taking their daughters into their own counting-houses, allow them to stand behind a stall at a bazaar . . . [these are] far more public scenes where indeed, publicity is essential to success.[26]

The charitable bazaar thus bridged the public and the private, but in what we might call a socially acceptable borderland. The bazaar allowed women to play a more substantial role in the political process too; in the Anti-Corn Law League female expertise, gained in raising money for charitable purposes, was put to good use in running bazaars and fund-raising fairs.[27]

---

[23] Mrs. Humphrey Ward et al., 'An Appeal against Female Suffrage', text reproduced in J. Lewis, ed., Before the Vote Was Won (1987), pp. 409–11

[24] Millicent Garrett Fawcett, 'Home and Politics', in Lewis, Before the Vote, p. 423.

[25] Quoted in F. Prochaska, The Voluntary Impulse. Philanthropy in Modern Britain (1988), p. 73.

[26] Emily Davies, Letters to a Daily Paper (Newcastle, 1860).

[27] Hall, 'Private Persons', p. 64.

Nineteenth-century philanthropy had became 'womanized'[28] This was such a large area that activity within it could be manipulated in radical or conservative ways by the women it involved. Women had made innovative inroads into what was perceived as male political territory in the earlier anti-slavery movement since this lay in a borderland of philanthropy (private sphere) and politics (public sphere). Conversely female social conservatism informed the later voluntary work of Octavia Hill, a pioneer in housing management and in social work. Her tactics give us some clues on the visibility of women's colonisation endeavours in the borderland.

Hill's '*Letters on Housing*' emphasised 'quiet watchings' where 'improvement depends on personal influence' so that there was a strong linkage between the moral qualities of the private woman and the public good that would result. Here the quality of housing management rather than that of the actual buildings was the vital constituent. To achieve this the employment of *ladies* was crucial. 'Ladies must do it for it is detailed work; ladies must do it, for it is household work; it needs too, persistent patience, gentleness and hope', she wrote. Women had a duty, a Christian obligation to give to others. This should be done unobtrusively and Hill's ideal appeared to be that of things 'silently progressing'. Her stress was on the duty of household management being a mutual one as in Chalmer's concept of charity, where both sides were elevated by the interaction. Each activity involved a moralising, face-to-face relationship of private individuals rather than the bureaucratic numbering of public agencies.[29] Whilst Octavia Hill thought that education, and also property rights for women, were reasonable objectives, significantly she was not in favour of the female suffrage. As a philanthropist, who was dependent on women workers to implement her distinctive ideals of housing manangement, she considered that women in Parliament would be lost to this kind of good works. It would, she considered, be 'fatal . . . for women to be drawn into the political arena'.[30]

Hill's volunteers and workers were usually a generation older than those who became active in local government.[31] How overtly political and public was this activity? In a real sense the civic space became for this later generation an enlargement of the domestic space. Mrs. Fordham, in urging women to become parish councillors (as they were enabled to

---

[28] F. Prochaska, *Women and Philanthropy in Nineteenth-Century England* (Oxford, 1980), p. 223.

[29] E. Southwood Ouvry, *Extracts from Octavia Hill's 'Letters to Fellow-Workers' 1864–1911* (1933), Letter of 1889, p. 28; Letter of 1906, p. 60; Letter of 1883, p. 23; Letter of 1872, p. 11; Letter of 1879, p. 20; Letter of 1906, p. 59.

[30] G. Darley, *Octavia Hill. A Life* (1990), pp. 58, 318–19

[31] Ibid., p. 218.

do in 1894), argued that 'The governmment of the village is but the government of the home, only on a larger scale'.[32] And Mrs. Barker, (a former workhouse visitor, who became one of the very few female chairs of a parish council), urged women to stand as parish councillors:

> Women are so much more earnest about small things than men and parish council work deals with matters of seemingly small import. A polluted well, an overcrowded cottage, a barrier across a footpath, are too trivial for men to make a stir about . . . but . . . these trifles if looked into will reveal further defects to remedy.[33]

Women in local government work, as Patricia Hollis has perceptively analysed them, 'preferred to win consent'; 'substituted domestic values for disciplinary ones' in institutions such as workhouses; and worked for 'a womanly version of the built environment' in health committees. Women used so-called 'female' client-centred skills rather than what were then considered 'male' management skills. 'They worked quietly.' and their challenge 'was softened by ladylike clothes and ladylike language'.[34] In relation to our wider enquiry the *complementarity* of the female contribution is striking and so too was the fact that, like Hill's voluntary work, it was *quiet* work by ladies, or those adopting the demeanour of ladies.

This stress on ladylike behaviour in the bourgeois Victorian feminist movement arguably was, 'an acknowledgement of the power of the dominant ideology rather than a demonstration of belief in it'.[35] But whether Victorian leaders of the education or suffrage movement for women adopted tactics from belief or for strategic reasons is highly problematical. Their private correspondence sometimes threw light on the rationale of their actions. A revealing instance of this was when one experienced campaigner advised a fellow-suffragist on the tactics to be adopted when dealing with male anti-suffragists – whom she revealingly termed 'the enemy':

> I don't think it quite does to call the arguments on the other side 'foolish'. Of course they *are*, but it does not seem quite polite to say so . . . You see the enemy always maintains that the disabilities inflicted upon women are not penal but solely intended for their good, and I find that nothing irritates men so much as to attribute tyranny to them. I believe many of them really

---

[32] Mrs. E.O. Fordham, 'Why Women are Needed as Parish Councillors', *Parish Councils Journal*, 1 March 1896.

[33] *Parish Councillor*, 27 December 1895.

[34] P.Hollis, *Ladies Elect. Women in Local Government, 1865–1914* (1987), pp. 391, 463, 466–8, 472.

[35] R. Billington, 'The Dominant Values of Victorian Feminism', in E. Sigsworth ed., *In Search of Victorian Values. Aspects of Nineteenth-Century Thought and Society* (Manchester, 1988), p. 122.

mean well . . . and it seems fair to admit it and to show that their well intentioned efforts are a *mistake*, and not a crime.[36]

The kind of manipulative stategies adopted by women over the suffrage were also used by female councillors. Local government empowered women through colonising the borderlands effectively, but without subverting the dichotomy of public and private too overtly. Women councillors used 'deviousness and diplomacy . . . [and] carefully avoided any threat or challenge to male hegemony.'[37] Their role was essentially ambiguous in emphasising in different contexts and at different times both equality in competence and difference in experience. Women manipulated the language of separate spheres; it could be used radically to claim public space, or conservatively to confirm gender stereotyping.[38] Significantly, 'they occupied and clearly felt comfortable in, a semi-detached sphere of their own.'[39] It was notable that fifty years elapsed between the municipal and parliamentary franchise for women. In between was what may be called the social housekeeping in the community, that anti-suffrage women saw as the vital component in local government work. Women's contribution in local government also contained an interesting paradox since it apparently contributed virtually nothing to the achievement of women's suffrage in 1918.[40]

Turning to another facet of women's lives, that of the economic, we find that politics and paid work were inextricably linked. The suffrage was based in property, and in the Victorian period the extension of the male suffrage was effectively based on men's property in their labour. The working woman, having a property in work, thus implicitly, yet not overtly, posed a challenge to the separate spheres of public and private, not only in paid employment but also in politics.[41]

The threat posed by paid work was, however, largely obscured from view since it was usually regarded as subsidiary to female work in the home. A description of women's work in the pre-industrial economy was that it was 'An economy of expedients',[42] since it was characterised

[36] Emily Davies, Letter to Barbara Bodichon, 14 November 1865 (B. Stephen, *Emily Davies and Girton College* [1927], p. 108).

[37] Hollis, *Ladies Elect*, p. 390.

[38] Ibid., p. 463; P. Hollis, 'Women in Council: Separate Spheres, Public Space', in J. Rendall, ed., *Equal or Different. Women's Politics 1800–1914* (1987), p. 210.

[39] Hollis, *Ladies Elect*, pp. 471–2.

[40] Hollis, 'Women in Council', pp. 193–4, pp. 462–3.

[41] Davidoff, 'Adam spoke first', pp. 245–6

[42] Hufton used this to describe only the work of spinsters and widows, but Hill extended this to married women as well. (B. Hill, *Women, Work, and Sexual Politics in Eighteenth Century England* (1989), p. 259; O. Hufton, 'Women without men: widows and spinsters in Britain and France in the eighteenth century', *Journal of Family History*, **8** [1984], pp. 355–76).

by low pay and a heavy component of seasonal and part-time work. With industrialisation some features of women's work changed. Women's position in the Victorian labour market has been aptly described as the result of a 'negotiated outcome' between the forces of capititalism and patriarchy.[43] But the outcome was a gendered labour market with working-class women relegated to segregated and low-paid work. Male-dominated trade unions supported the concept of a family wage paid to men, on the assumption that they alone had dependants, including a wife. Henry Broadhurst expressed this view clearly in a speech to the TUC in 1875, where he outlined the main aim of members of a trade union as being to, 'Bring about a condition . . . where their wives and daughters would be in their proper sphere at home, instead of being dragged into competition for a livelihood against the great and strong men of the world.'[44] Unfortunately, an only partial achievement of the family wage then left women in a classic 'Catch 22' position. Since working-class women continued to have to work, in part because many of them had responsibility for dependants, they found themselves as much the victim as the beneficiary of the family wage. The problem of female sweated labour, whether at home or in the workplace was to become notorious. Mary Macarthur, founder of the National Federation of Women Workers (1906–20) commented tartly, 'Don't think of the Empire on which the sun never sets, think of the wage that never rises.'[45]

The family wage, women's work and women's rates were conditioned by values that placed women's responsibilities primarily in the home, in the private sphere. But because, as we have seen, private and public were inter-connected a continuum of sexually segregated work existed in both labour market and household. This might be termed an intermediate zone. Jane Lewis comments incisively that 'women's work is doubly gendered, first being confined to "feminine" tasks, whether paid or unpaid, and second being subordinate to men's work both in the home and in the workplace.'[46] Women's power in the home was influenced, yet not wholly determined by, their command of economic resources. Within the working-class home the stereotypical division of labour was increasingly of the man as provider and the woman as manager, although in practice

---

[43] S. Walby, *Patriarchy at Work: patriarchal and capitalist relations in employment* (1986), p. 155.

[44] H.A. Turner, *Trade Union Growth, Structure and Policy. A Comparative Study of the Cotton Unions* (1962), p. 185.

[45] Quoted in S. Boston, *Women Workers and the Trade Unions* (1987), p. 60.

[46] 'Women's Work in Late Nineteenth Century England', in *The Sexual Division of Labour, 19th and 20th Centuries* (Uppsala Papers in Economic History, **7**, 1989), p. 89.

both women and children regularly supplemented the male wage.[47] In the middle-class home the man was seen as the provider with the woman as manager of resources and, in more affluent households as consumer of luxuries, as well.[48]

This bourgeois economic ideal of economically-dependant Victorian and Edwardian womanhood was an aspiration rather than a universal reality. Ideologically attractive yet economically unattainable for a sizeable minority, survival strategies were needed to bridge the gap. Numbers of middle-class girls needed to be equipped to earn their living and a growth in educational opportunities was partly a response to that need. Yet these institutions reflected the kind of social ambiguities that had engendered them; they were thus a version of the social borderland and displayed its tensions. A particularly clear instance of this was the nonconformist boarding school. In the mid-nineteenth century its concerns were ambivalently poised between schooling and social finishing for those, 'whose breeding was not in doubt but whose future was open to every doubt', as Clyde Binfield has aptly described them.[49] Ambiguity in the objectives of early reformed girls schools during the mid-Victorian period is shown both by the nature of the curriculum (with its balancing of academic subjects by traditional, feminine accomplishments), and by the equivocating statements of their headmistresses, who needed to conciliate traditionally-minded parents. Some institutions were explicit about the need to equip their pupils to earn a living, as was Mill Mount College which opened its doors in 1873 to the daughters of nonconformist ministers. Here, the first principal was told on her appointment that, 'We wish to . . . train pupils not merely to be accomplished, but useful members of society, with good sense and right apprehensions of womanly obligations . . . our desire is to prepare the pupils to be wives, mothers, teachers and missionaries.'[50] But, in responding to a cultural backlash of Social Darwinistic criticism about the advanced nature of their institutions, later headmistresses

[47] E. Ross, 'Labour and Love: Rediscovering London's Working-Class Mothers, 1870–1914', in J. Lewis, ed., *Labour and Love. Women's Experience of Home and Family, 1850–1940* (1986), pp. 84–8, and E. Roberts, '"Women's Strategies", 1890–1940', in *Labour and Love*, pp. 226–8.

[48] P. Branca, *Silent Sisterhood. Middle-Class Women in the Victorian Home* (1975), chapter 2 *passim*; R. Bowlby, *Just Looking. Consumer Culture in Dreiser, Gissing, and Zola* (1985), chapter 2, *passim*.

[49] C. Binfield, *Belmont's Portias: Victorian Nonconformists and Middle-Class Education for Girls* (35th Lecture of Friends of Dr. William's Library, 1981), p. 27. I am grateful to Dr. Binfield for drawing the chapel and the nonconformist school to my attention as instances of the social borderland.

[50] Ibid., p. 28.

seem to have been more conciliatory than their pioneering forbears in stressing the womanliness of their graduands.[51] In the 1890s the Headmistress of Worcester High School recorded that she wanted the character of her school to be that of 'delicate womanly refinement', whilst in 1911 her counterpart at the Manchester High School commented approvingly that 'greater emphasis is now placed on the special duties of women . . . to the community, . . . the family and the home.'[52]

These complexities in bourgeois female lives and aspirations were at least matched by those of working-class women, although the nature of the pressures and dilemmas differed. The central importance of working-class wives and mothers was pointed out by contemporary observers. Lady Bell's influential Edwardian study, *At the Works*, stated:

> The key to the condition of the workman and his family, the clue, the reason for the possibilities and impossibilities of his existence, is the capacity, the temperament, and, above all, the health of the woman who manages his house; into her hands . . . the burden of the family life is thrust.[53]

A recent study by Carl Chinn for the period from 1880 to 1939 has argued that for the lower working-class a 'hidden matriarchy' existed behind 'a facade of male dominance, separation of the sexes and female inferiority'. Here women were 'the driving force', and were not only 'arbiters of their own and their families' lives' but also 'dominant influences within their own communities.'[54] This study of the poor in Birmingham included a telling story of the man who grumbled at his wife's management of the scarce household resources he had provided but found that his sandwiches the next day were filled only with the rent book.[55] The balance of power, as well as division of labour, within a working-class marriage is fittingly illustrated here. In a pioneering use of oral history Elizabeth Roberts focussed on the difference between perceptions and realities in the Lancashire woman's life at this time. She concluded that,

[51] A. Digby and P. Searby eds, *Children, School and Society in Nineteenth-Century England* (1981), pp. 48–52; A. Digby, 'New Schools for the Middle Class Girl', in P. Searby, ed., *Educating the Victorian Middle Class* (History of Education Society, 1982), pp. 13–19
[52] S.A. Burstall and M.A. Douglas, eds, *Public Schools for Girls* (1911), p. 18; M.E. James, *Alice Ottley, First Headmistress of the Worcester High School for Girls, 1883–1912* (1914), pp. 98–9
[53] Lady Bell, *At the Works. A Study of a Manufacturing Town* (Nelson edition, 1913), p. 242.
[54] C. Chinn, *They Worked All Their Lives. Women of the Urban Poor, 1880–1939* (1988), pp. 13, 16–17.
[55] Ibid., p. 163.

'The woman exerted significant power, not so much from legal rights as from moral force . . . [but this] could and did give her considerable economic power'.[56]

Within a rather stark model of Victorian values and gender roles there could thus be greater space for women than an initial view might suggest. Male pride and female deference to a public face of dominant masculinity may have sustained an external public appearance of stereotypical roles even when the internal reality was rather different. This was a situation very similar to that disclosed by anthropological studies of an apparently masculinist Mediterranean culture today. 'There is a marked difference between the public and private behaviour of a man and wife towards each other'; in the seclusion of the home the wife discusses all the affairs of the family, whereas in public she is silent and submissive.[57] Discovering a past dialectic between private experience and the public politics of values in Victorian Britain would be a comparably fascinating exploration.

What were *female* Victorian values as perceived and acted upon? It is necessary here to stress the importance both of the inside and outside, of women's lives.[58] Attempting to understand women's past culture from the inside is obviously as problematic as it is important. Yet when we turn to women's more privatised experience we can see that this included that of being active agents in creating female worlds – both in the private sphere and in what I have termed the social borderland – within a wider patriarchal domain. Women's 'networks' seem to be have been as important then – in giving women support and confidence – as they are now. The role of female institutions and communities was, in this context, highly significant.[59] So too was what we know about well-documented friendships of middle-class women, which could embrace an interesting dialogue between female culture and feminism.[60] These institutions and relationships linked private to public worlds – empowering individuals in each sphere. Feminism was

---

[56] Roberts, *Woman's Place*, p. 110.

[57] J.K. Campbell, *Honour, Family and Patronage. A Study of Institutions and Moral Values in a Greek Mountain Community* (Oxford, 1964), pp. 151–2. See also, J. du Boulay, *Portrait of a Greek Mountain Village* (Oxford, 1974), pp. 101–5 for an interesting discussion of perceptions of the gendered characteristics of men and women.

[58] J.Ribbens, 'Accounting For Our Children. Differing Perspectives On "Family Life" In Middle-income Households' (unpublished PH.D thesis, South Bank Polytechnic and CNAA), p. 54.

[59] M. Vicinus, *Independent Women. Work and Community for Single Women 1850–1920* (1985), p. 289.

[60] J. Rendall, 'Friendship and Politics: Barbara Leigh Smith Bodichon and Bessie Rayner Parkes', in Mendus and Rendall, *Sexuality and Subordination*, p. 163.

also a force for some working women: Ada Nield Chew, Selina Cooper, and the working-women suffragists of north-western England are relatively well-documented illustrations of this.[61] But, arguably, these ideas had a wider resonance in working women's lives, as research into women autobiographers of the period is revealing. Mary Smith, who had had a hard-working life as a teacher, and was later a suffragist, wrote a poem on Women's Claims, that included the lines '"Women's Rights" are not her's only, they are all the world's besides / And the whole world faints and suffers, while these are scorn'd, denied'. In her autobiography she stated feelingly that, 'The inequality of the sexes in privilege and power, was a great cause of the dreadful hardships which women, especially in the lower classes had to suffer.'[62] And Florence Wright, who had been a cook, reflected that 'with some of the feminist ideas I was, and am in full sympathy. I hated the pocket-money wage, and always have believed it would have paid the men's unions to have admitted qualified women on the same terms as men, that is, equal wages for equal work.'[63]

For the more typical working-class woman who left no written testimony, informal social networks in the community apparently offered more immediate sustenance: these tended to link social with material support. Whilst the masculine version of Victorian self-help often emphasised its individualist character, the working-class women's version of this central Victorian value was more usually informed by a strong element of mutuality, organised in an informal rather than formal way. 'The range of help provided by neighbours was immense: children were minded: the sick and dying were fed and nursed; clothes were passed on; funeral teas prepared for the mourners, the dead laid out; shopping done for the elderly; and companionship and friendship provided for all ages.'[64] Not that all was shared among women. It is intriguing, for example, to see how frequently mothers seem to have been reticent with their daughters about such intimate but fundamental areas of female existence as menstruation, sexual intercourse or childbirth.

[61] Ada Nield Chew, *The Life and Writings of a Working Woman* (1982); J. Liddington, *The Life and Times of a Respectable Rebel. Selina Cooper, 1864–1946* (1984); J. Liddington and J. Norris, *One Hand Tied Behind Us. The Rise of the Woman's Suffrage Movement* (1978).

[62] Quoted in J. Swindells, *Victorian Writing and Working Women* (1985), p. 160. Smith published a two volume autobiography in 1892.

[63] F. White, *A Fire in the Kitchen: the Autobiography of a Cook* (1938), quoted in Swindells, *Victorian Writing*, p. 155. White was 75, and in more affluent circumstances, when her autobiography was published.

[64] E. Roberts, *A Woman's Place. An Oral History of Working-Class Women, 1890–1940* (1984), p. 187.

Victorian values as they were publicly depicted were basically masculinist and bourgeois. Their gendered and class view of the separation of functions and spaces was encapsulated in Charlotte Brontë's rueful reflection that men were supposed to do and women to be.[65] Stereotyped Victorian values emphasised a peaceful patriarchy with complementary male and female worlds. One important function of the gender borderlands, I would argue, was to defuse gender tensions, ambiguities and antagonisms. Gender was, and remains, a dynamic category so that changing or competing social constructions of femininities and masculinities could find a space here. Thus an elision could take place where older or outmoded ideas might be transmuted in an evolving society. Middle-class women altered the public world to their own advantage and redefined the public/private boundary in the process of so doing. The semi-detached area of philanthropy, voluntary work, and local government was the main instance of this. For working-class women the intermediate zone of part-time employment was a clear illustration of public/private boundaries being breached. In each case female activity in a borderland was socially largely invisible in the sense of being non-contested, even though each area subverted official Victorian values to a moderate extent.

Here I should like to speculate on the criteria that appear to have operated to define this border at particular points in time. What made certain activities in the borderland zone politically visible in the sense of having to be opposed? It is necessary to distinguish analytically between changes in the activity on the one hand, and changes in the manner in which these activities were performed. I will suggest that women became politically visible in the sense of having to be challenged when both the action, and the conduct which accompanied it, were perceived as an overt challenge to fundamental masculine or patriarchal strongholds.

Some new activities of women in the social borderland appear to have been largely unrecognised as such. Thus, for example, the gradual breakdown of the boundary between private and public achieved by female work in philanthropy, voluntary social work, or even local government, was not perceived as an open challenge to the masculine public domain. Women still appeared to be in an acceptable borderland area because they were using familiar feminine skills in an extended, but not separate, area from their domestic territory. It is significant in my view that women's local government work did not loom large in the final debates on granting the female suffrage; in contemporary perception the two seemed conceptually to be quite distinct. Indeed, it is revealing that the leading female anti-suffragist, Mrs. Humphrey Ward, saw women's local government work

---

[65] E.C. Gaskell, *The Life of Charlotte Bronte* (1857), p. 123.

not as a precursor but as an alternative to the vote. She wanted a wider representation of women 'on municipal and other bodies concerned with the domestic and social affairs of the community.'[66] In contrast to female work in the local community, the campaigns for the female suffrage seemed to many anti-suffragists, both men and women, to threaten ideas of social propriety. Natural gender roles would be over-turned; women would neglect their true concerns – the private ones of home and family, and their moral purity would be contaminated by entry to a public, national politics. Anti-suffragists argued that only men had the physical strength to govern the empire or to wage war; only men had the rational, unemotional approach that affairs of state demanded.[67] In this context Lilias Ashworth's comment about her speaking tour for the suffrage was revealing, 'it was evident that the audiences came expecting to see curious masculine objects walking on to the platform'.[68]

The conflation of the personal and the political in other aspects of Victorian feminism resulted in contemporary controversy over female sexuality. Debates over the 'New Woman', and her representation in late Victorian fiction as the challenger of sexual taboos, led Mrs. Fawcett, the moderate suffragist, to stress in 1895 that in her view feminism did *not* include the concept of free love.[69] It is interesting to note that Harriet Martineau (feminist and best-selling author on political economy), had warned against what she saw as the 'Wollstonecraft order' forty years before this. In her *Autobiography* she wrote:

> I have no vote at elections, although I am a taxpaying housekeeper and responsible citizen; and I regard the disability as an absurdity, seeing that I have for a long course of years influenced public affairs to an extent not professed or attempted by many men. But I do not see that I could do much good by personal complaints, which always have some suspicion or reality of passion in them. I think the better way is for us all to learn and try to the utmost what we can do, and thus to win for ourselves the consideration which alone can secure us rational treatment. The Wollstonecraft order set to work at the other end, and as I think, do infinite mischief . . . I have never regarded her as a safe example, nor as a successful champion of Woman and her Rights.[70]

What Martineau objected to in the 'Wollstonecraft order' was first,

---

[66] Quoted in J. Sutherland, *Mrs. Humphrey Ward. Eminent Victorian and Preminent Edwardian* (Oxford, 1990), p. 300.

[67] B. Harrison, *Separate Spheres. The Opposition to Women's Suffrage in Britain* (1978), chapter 4, *passim*.

[68] Helen Blackburn, *Women's Suffrage* (1902), pp. 110–1.

[69] M. Fawcett's Review of *The Woman Who Did*, in *Contemporary Review*, LXVII (1895), p. 630.

[70] H. Martineau, *Autobiography* (Virago edn, 1983), vol. I, p. 402.

the conflation of individual wrongs with public causes, and secondly, the behaviour that ensued from this, 'violating all good taste by her obtrusiveness in society.'[71]

A more general violation of ladylike norms of behaviour by militant suffragettes resulted after 1905 from feminist frustration at a male-dominated Victorian and Edwardian society's refusal to concede what Martineau had described as a 'rational treatment' of women's political deserts. Emmeline Pankhurst later reflected that, 'We threw away all our conventional notions of what was "ladylike" and "good form"'.[72] A recent study has concluded that 'The suffrage movement had brought women into public visibility in a new and unique way.'[73] The militant campaigns of the suffragettes were indeed an overt and therefore 'visible' challenge to the power distribution of an Edwardian patriarchy. They provoked allegations of unwomanliness, and also of hysteria, a convenient term which bore both a flexible everyday meaning as well as more specialist clinical connotations. *The Times* fulminated in 1908 that 'the more violent partisans of the cause are suffering from hysteria.'[74] The medical profession joined in the public debate. Its most notorious public utterances came from Sir Almroth Wright, who wrote that a doctor contemplating the militant suffragist could not shut his eyes 'to the fact that there is mixed up with the woman's movement much mental disorder; and he cannot conceal from himself the physiological emergencies which lie behind.'[75] Indeed, it was at this time that the government brought psychiatrists to Holloway to see whether hunger-striking suffragette prisoners might be certified as lunatics.[76] The contemporary identification of militant feminism with hysteria was based on perceived similarities: anger, refusal of food, and revolt against the norms of prescribed ladylike behaviour.

Edwardian anti-suffrage cartoons of feminists often contrasted a 'shrieking sisterhood' with an appealing womanliness in its opponents. But the iconography of later anti-suffrage publicity was revealing in its inconsistencies. It portrayed militant women as fitting the categories of a debased and degenerate femininity as it appeared in contemporary psychiatric literature. They were seen both as excessively feminine – and therefore hysterical – and as excessively masculine – and therefore lesbian.[77] These images were in

---

[71] Ibid., p. 400.

[72] E. Pankhurst, *My Own Story* (1914), pp. 61–2.

[73] Vicinus, *Independent Women*, p. 281.

[74] *The Times*, 11 December 1908.

[75] *The Times*, 28 March 1912. Wright, a noted anti-feminist, later expanded his views in *The Unexpurgated Case Against Women's Suffrage* (1913).

[76] M.R. Richardson, *Laugh A Defiance* (1953) pp. 152–4.

[77] L. Tickner, *The Specatacle of Woman. Imagery of the Suffrage Campaign 1907–1914* (1987), pp. 193, 195, 198–9, and illustrations facing p. 211.

part a response to the very 'visibility' of the challenge that militant feminists posed to traditional gender boundaries. In attempting to move women so openly from the private to the public spheres, militant suffragettes aroused deep-seated psychic anxieties and antagonisms in society. It was thus predictable that they should fail to gain the vote.[78]

This discussion of the militant suffragettes has suggested that it was the activity – seeking to move women into a central area of the public sphere – when linked to the extreme tactics that accompanied it, which created a new visibility for feminist aspirations. Women were seen to be moving out of an acceptable social borderland in an attempt to breach what their opponents regarded as an impermeable gender frontier. Suffragettes' campaigns differed from the 'social housework' of earlier political endeavours, where women's gradualism and careful attention to outward social proprieties effectively disguised the extent to which activists had permeated traditional gender boundaries. This interpretation differs from that of Showalter, who has stated that, 'The hunger strikes of militant women prisoners brilliantly put the symptomology of anorexia nervosa to work in the service of the feminist cause.'[79] In contrast, I would argue that this adoption of behaviour, which contemporaries regarded as indicative of mental illness, helped their political opponents; it reinforced their perception that hunger-striking suffragettes were not only inhabiting a social borderland but a psychiatric one as well.

The extremity of opponents' responses in attempting to brand suffragettes as psychologically unstable also attested to radical feminists' fundamental challenge to a male public sphere. Their reponse has certain parallels with hostile reactions to women's earlier attempts to pursue secondary and higher education and thence to enter high-status male professions. In each case central features of female physiology were depicted as pathological, so that woman's reproductive functions were held to disqualify her from sustained political or mental effort. Almroth Wright's coded reference in 1912 – which linked suffragettes' mental illness to 'physiological emergencies' – would have been instantly understood by his readers as referring to this discussion. Contemporary theories of Darwinian evolution and of the conservation of energy apparently provided a 'scientific' rationale for continuing controversy over women's educational, professional and political aspirations. But this recurrent

---

[78] Historians disagree as to whether militancy even raised the position of female suffrage on the political agenda. See, for example, the contrasting assessments of M. Pugh, *Women's Suffrage in Britain, 1867–1928* (Historical Association, 1980), p. 25, and D. Morgan, *Suffragists and Liberals. The Politics of Women Suffrage in England* (Oxford, 1975), p. 159.

[79] Showalter, *Female Malady*, p. 162.

debate can only be fully understood if its timing is related to women's attempts to cross the border into the economic and political strongholds of a masculine public space.[80]

Throughout this paper I have pointed to the importance of boundaries within a borderland. In my conclusion I should like to allude both to the rewards and penalties that women faced when entering this shadowy area. Crossing borders too obviously or prematurely could incur social stigma or social costs. An example of the latter was the social prejudice against educated women as potential wives in certain sectors of society, as can be seen in the endless cartoons directed against 'learned ladies' in late-Victorian issues of *Punch*.[81] Is it therefore surprising that many women maintained a preference for more cautious approaches in the borderland between the private and public spheres? However, it is important to emphasise that women were not merely passive recipients of traditionalist values but creatively shaped their destiny. A gradualist approach to new departures, and the adoption of a socially-conservative rather than radical demeanour, had had notable successes in achieving new frontier posts for women. In defending the militant 'shrieking sisterhood' against allegations of unwomanliness Mrs. Pethick-Lawrence argued that 'you see how much need there is for our "shrieking". It is the duty of every woman here to come and help us shriek.'[82] But many suffragists rejected such tactics as counter-productive, preferring to campaign in a feminine manner for feminist objectives. Moderates appreciated the value of social invisibility within the borderland since, on the one hand this was non-threatening to a public masculinity, and on the other, it allowed women unobtrusively to build up new skills, confidence and identity. This social borderland contained not so much a fixed boundary as a moving frontier – an expanding opportunity for women.

Some of the contradictions and complexities inherent in one aspect of 'Victorian Values' have been highlighted in this paper. The very flexibility of these ideological constraints has meant that they can be resurrected in different contexts; history can be used rather than explicated. Past values are seen in some sense as eternal verities and the nostalgic political appeal of values associated with a 'great' period in our past is only too obvious. But this leaves out of acount the extent to which these values were shared. In this paper I have tried to suggest that there was a lack of consensus over the boundary between public and private spheres; Victorian women

---

[80] Harrison, *Separate Spheres*, chapter 4, *passim*; Digby, 'Women's Biological Straitjacket'; Showalter, *Female Malady*, chapter 6, *passim*.

[81] C. Rover, *The Punch Book of Women's Rights* (1967), pp. 55–72.

[82] Emmeline Pethick-Lawrence, *The New Crusade* (Womens Social and Political Union, 1907).

were faced with a dominant set of values to which they owed only limited allegiance. Many restrictive dichotomies still retain their power within a gendered world today, so that modern feminists continue to see analytical relevance in the concept of public and private spheres.[83]

[83] See, for example, J.B. Elshtain, *Public Man and Private Woman. Women in Social and Political Thought* (Princeton, 1981); J. Siltanen and M. Stanworth, eds, *Women and the Public Sphere. A Critique of Sociology and Politics* (1984); and Pateman, *Disorder of Women* (1989) for recent stimulating discussions on this point.

Proceedings of the British Academy, **78**, 217–224

Victorian Values

ANTHONY KENNY
President of the British Academy

WHEN I was asked to contribute to this symposium, I made clear to the organisers that I was no Victorian scholar. Though I have a passionate interest in some individual Victorians my knowledge of the period as a whole is very patchy, and I would not be competent to write a scholarly publishable contribution.

Instead, I want to do two things. First, very briefly, I want to thank the Royal Society of Edinburgh, on behalf of the British Academy, for hosting and organising this joint symposium. All of us here have experienced the excellence of the organisation and the success of the symposium: I can testify that the great majority of the work has been done by the RSE, while the contribution of the BA has been very slight. We are very honoured to have been associated with the RSE in this venture, and proud that our joint names will appear together on the published proceedings.

Secondly, I want to make some shamelessly personal remarks on the topic of Victorian Values and on the question, put to me by the organisers: do they differ greatly from our own?

I am a philosopher, and as a philosopher I have been brought up to make a distinction between facts and values. So far as I can tell, this conference has so far been much more about Victorian facts than about Victorian values. I will talk, not being a historian, exclusively about values.

In order to judge Victorian values, the question each of us should ask ourselves is not: would I like to be the kind of person the Victorians were;

Read 14 December 1990. © The British Academy 1992.

but: would I like to be the kind of person the Victorians admired. In my own case, the answer to the first question would be a definite no, the answer to the second question would be a qualified yes.

But of course there is something very forced in talking about Victorian Values, as if there were a uniform set of values endorsed by all Victorians. The values of John Henry Newman and John Stuart Mill were as different from each other as the values of Paul Johnson and Paul Foot.

If we are to compare Victorian and contemporary values, it is the wrong approach to ask how far Victorian values survive today. We should start from the other end, and ask how far our own values derive from the Victorian era. Or rather, since 'our values' are at least as heterogenous as Victorian values, I will ask myself how far my own values are Victorian in origin. When I put this question to myself: how many of my values are Victorian? I found, rather to my own surprise, that the answer was: almost every single one of them.

For twenty-five years I worked at Balliol College, Oxford. Though Balliol had eked out an undistinguished existence for some 600 years previously, it was in the Victorian era that it acquired distinction and took on the characteristics for which it is nowadays known. It has remained up to the present day dominated by the ethos and aspirations of its Victorian dons.

For fourteen of the twenty-five years I was a tutorial fellow of Balliol. The role of an Oxbridge tutor is one that was defined in the nineteenth century: tutors as we understand them are a unique and Victorian institution, unknown in other times or places, but surviving there from Victorian times to the present.

The honours school in which I was a tutor was Literae Humaniores or Greats: that mixture of Greek and Latin literature, history and philosophy, which was concocted in the Victorian era to fit the administrators of the British Empire for their allotted task. The school was to teach them skill in abstract thought, in the evaluation of evidence, and in the ability to write concise and elegant minutes. The subject matter of the school was not to be any contemporary or recent European culture: it was to be a culture of the distant past, so as to accustom its students to bridge the chasms between their own culture and cultures of very different kinds, such as they would meet in carrying out their imperial vocation.

For eleven years I was Master of Balliol. As Master, I found my job description simply given: the life of Benjamin Jowett was placed in my hands. It was Jowett who had shown what kind of things a Master of Balliol should do, and what kind of person he should be. It was by the standards he had formulated and incarnated that one was judged and found wanting. On the other hand to be told that, in one or other respect, one resembled him was the greatest compliment that a Master could be given by an old member of the College. At the top of the stairs in the Master's lodgings, just at the entrance to his study, there was a vivid photograph of the old Master. As I would return from chairing some difficult meeting of the Governing Body I was met by Jowett's penetrating gaze, conveying unmistakably 'I would have handled that a lot better than you, young man'.

Even during the late sixties and early seventies, the years of socialist student revolution, the two most popular undergraduate societies at Balliol were the Arnold and Brakenbury Society (a Victorian debating society, now, it must be confessed, more frivolous than in the days of its origins) and a society devoted to community singing of allegedly nineteenth-century songs, which was called the Victorian Society and which held its meetings under a portrait of the Queen Empress.

No doubt it will be argued that Oxbridge, and in particular Balliol, are untypical, anachronistic institutions which are overdue for reform. So too, no doubt, are those other Victorian elitist institutions, the public schools. But even in our egalitarian age almost everyone who has the means and opportunity to do so seems to wish their children to attend one or other of these Victorian educational establishments.

I have now left Balliol and work for two Edwardian institutions: the British Academy and the Rhodes Trust. However, both of these bodies, though founded in the early years of the twentieth century, spend a considerable amount of their effort in the perpetuation of Victorian values.

As President of the Academy, one of my major recent concerns has been to secure public funding for a new edition of the *Dictionary of National Biography*. We are anxious to prolong into the twenty-first century that monument of Victorian scholarship.

As Secretary of the Rhodes Trust, I have to see that scholars elected to Rhodes Scholarships are elected in accordance with the provision of Cecil Rhodes will:

> 'My desire being that the students who shall be elected to the Scholarships shall not be merely bookworms I direct that in the election of a student to a Scholarship regard shall be had to (i) his literary and scholastic attainments (ii) his fondness of and success in manly outdoor sports such as cricket, football and the like (iii) his qualities of manhood truth courage devotion to duty sympathy for and protection of the weak kindliness unselfishness and fellowship and (iv) his exhibition during school days of moral force of character and of instincts to lead and to take an interest in his schoolmates for those latter attributes will be likely in afterlife to guide him to esteem the performance of public duties as his highest aim.'

The approximately one hundred Rhodes selection committees throughout the world are thus dedicated to the task of perpetuating the ideal of a

Victorian gentleman. They are to perpetuate it, of course, in non-British material – and, in recent years, female as well as male material, the words 'manly' and 'manhood' having been struck out of the list of qualifications.

As I travel around the world to visit and observe the operation of these selection committees, from the Liguanea club in Kingston to the Sindh club in Karachi, I am sometimes tempted to feel that the Rhodes Trust is the ghost of the British Empire sitting uncrowned on the grave thereof.

Some of the happiest times of my twenty-five years at Balliol have been the months in summer when I have taken reading parties of my students. Reading parties, as you will know, are quintessentially Victorian institutions, half seminar, half holiday. The chalet to which my wife and I take my students, owned by a Trust of which I am a Trustee, is situated on a spur of Mont Blanc, the Prarion, and was built by a Victorian eccentric, David Urquhart, one-time British Ambassador to the Sublime Porte.

Urquhart held two important theories. First, he believed that the human mind did not work well below an altitude of 6,000 feet: at lower levels the brain was too fuddled by oxygen. Second, he believed that the Turkish bath was the solution to the social problems of the age. In the eighteenth and earlier centuries the poor had been exploited by the rich; but, according to Urquhart, it was only in the nineteenth century that the poor had begun to be despised by the rich. This was because until the nineteenth-century rich and poor had both smelt; but now the rich were sweet and clean, and despised the poor for being dirty. The poor should strike back by taking steam baths, which cleansed the body far more effectively than hours of soaking in tubs of dirty water. Urquhart established a Hammam in Jermyn St, and founded a magazine, the Diplomatic Courier, based at Blarney, Co. Cork, devoted exclusively to propaganda for the Turkish bath. And when the time came for him to retire he built on Mont Blanc a chalet at six thousand feet equipped with a Turkish Bath. It is there that I take my yearly reading parties.

Apart from reading parties, my favourite forms of holiday are Victorian: walking in mountains and viewing Italian works of art. I have no stomach for the unguided technical climbing and elaborate mechanical aids of the twentieth-century mountaineer; if I wish to get to the summit of a high alp I will take an ice axe and secure the services of a local guide like any Victorian. In viewing the beauties of the cities of Italy I find no handbook so instructive and enchanting as the works of Augustus Hare.

When the twentieth century allows me the choice and permits me leisure, I prefer Victorian modes of travel – the train and the steamship – to the twentieth century motor and aeroplane.

For most of my married life I have lived, by choice, in Victorian houses:

first in a Victorian farm labourer's cottage, and later in dwellings designed by Waterhouse and Jackson. Whenever I go into a room I choose a chair which is, or resembles, a Victorian armchair. (Those who collect eighteenth century furniture do so in order to look at it rather than to snuggle into it). When I wash, I prefer to soak in a Victorian tub rather than stand beneath a modern shower. Like the rest of you, I use a Victorian invention to discharge my waste into a Victorian sewer.

From this conference I will go home to spend Christmas according to a ritual laid down in the Victorian period, decorating the house with Victorian symbols, singing carols by Victorian writers and composers, eating a menu derived from Victorian cookbooks, and mimicking Victorian methods of domestic heating.

When I have time for leisure reading, it will almost always be a Victorian novel to which I will turn. I can read, and re-read, for pleasure Trollope, Dickens and Eliot; I can rarely get to the end of a novel short listed for the Booker Prize (though even Booker prizewinners are beginning to realise the attractions of the Victorian age). I can understand the motives of the characters in Victorian novels. I can enter into their griefs, share their hopes, suffer with them in their shame. I can do so in a way which I find very difficult in the case of characters in the novels of Updike, Roth or Murdoch.

When I listen to music, the composers I prefer are those the Victorians loved: Bach, Mozart, Beethoven, Verdi. The works of Gilbert and Sullivan are not my favourite form of musical experience, but I can listen to Savoy Operas with very much greater pleasure than any popular music since the Beatles.

The one really original art form of the twentieth century, the cinema, is one for which I have little taste. Of course I watch the news on television, but in the last six months the only extended television programmes I have watched with pleasure have been the episodes in the rerun of Barchester Towers.

The political institutions under which I live, and am content to live, are essentially Victorian. The British constitutional monarchy today is essentially as it was left by Queen Victoria. The two party system (a system of parties divided by policy issues, rather than patronage networks differentiated by their attitude to the monarch) is essentially the creation of Queen Victoria's Prime Ministers.

Of course, it is not now true, as it was in the days of Iolanthe, that every child is born either a little liberal or a little conservative. But I have come to think that in England it least it would be preferable if the voters were indeed faced with a choice between conservative and liberal parties, rather than between conservative and labour parties.

The criminal and penal system which we attempt to operate is, again, in its essence a product of the Victorian age. The use of imprisonment – rather than death, mutilation, or exile – as the major means of enforcing the criminal law is something which became fully developed only during the reign of Queen Victoria. The very prison buildings which we use in pursuit of this system were almost without exception built during that reign. This fact reflects more credit on the Victorians than it does on us.

There are, of course, differences between Victorian attitudes to penal institutions and those prevalent nowadays. The Victorians emphasized the deterrent purpose of prison; in our age it is more common to talk about reform. The Victorian M'Naghten rules enshrined a view about the relation between crime and insanity which has lost favour in recent times. We, unlike the Victorians, like to have on the statute book laws (such as anti-discrimination laws) which forbid not actions of a specific kind, but actions inspired by a particular motive. In each of these respects – and in others also – I think the Victorians, in comparison with the theorists of our own age, showed a clearer and more realistic grasp of the purpose and scope of the criminal law and the penal system. For all its defects in practice, I believe that Macaulay's Indian Penal Code represents one of the most rationally motivated systems of jurisprudence ever devised.

The most obvious difference between the Victorian era and our own is in relationships between the sexes. I said earlier that in judging Victorian values we have to ask ourselves: would I like to be the kind of person whom the Victorians admired? If asked: would you like to be the kind of husband whom the Victorians admired? I have to give the answer no. This, notwithstanding the fact that the best known of Victorian husbands, Prince Albert, seems to me an admirable figure who did a difficult job well, and made no trouble about adapting his own ambitions to his wife's independent career.

The strongest objection to Victorian morality is that it left a wife very little recourse from marital tyranny. It is perhaps no accident that the most vivid and chilling account of marital tyranny in all literature should be from the pen of a Victorian poet, in Browning's *My Last Duchess*.

But even in the case of marriage and the family, the difference between the Victorian age and our own is much more in respect of practice than in respect of ideals. Even nowadays, most people, when they marry, set themselves an ideal of lifelong monogamy involving the shared raising of children. It is still comparatively rare for a bridegroom, on his wedding day, to think to himself 'Well, I'll stay with Jane for eight years or so, and then I will trade her in for a new and improved model'.

Where we differ from the Victorians is in the degree of sympathy and indulgence which we show to those who are unable to live up to this ideal whether married couples who fall out of love, or women who have children outside marriage. Given the problems which face children from broken homes, or from single-parent families, it is hard to be certain that in this area the Victorians had got it all wrong, and we have got it all right.

Most Victorians believed that morality was objective and absolute: that customs such as slavery and suttee were not just different but wrong. I share their belief, and I think that the Victorians were right to use their power, where they could, to put an end to these institutions. It was this conviction of objective morality that lay behind the paternalism of the Victorian imperial administrators.

Established Christianity is less important in the national life now than it was in Victorian times; many of those who take religion most seriously in the U.K. are not Christians at all, but members of other world religions. Within Christianity, the Roman Catholic Church has grown while the Church of England has lost influence.

But within these two churches the Victorian influence is still strongly felt. The three major parties in the Church of England – high church, liberal, and evangelical – are the heirs of the three parties which fought each other at the time of the Oxford movement. Within Roman Catholicism the Second Vatican Council altered profoundly the aspect which the Church had borne since the First Vatican Council. But the change could be described as the substitution for a model imposed on the Church by one Victorian Cardinal, Manning, of a model inspired by the thought of another Victorian Cardinal, Newman. Indeed, until the present Pope no individual has left such a mark on the Universal Church as these two eminent Victorian converts.

Being myself neither Roman Catholic nor Anglican, I feel at home more with the writings of Victorians such as Clough, Arnold, Stephen and Huxley. Unlike many philosophers of the present day I think both that it matters greatly whether the main doctrines of Christianity are true, and that it is very difficult to be rationally certain either way. I have more sympathy therefore with the agonizing of the Victorians than with those at the present time who think that Christianity can be embraced without struggle or shrugged off with ease.

Of course, I am not myself a Victorian. I have no courage to face the cold bath on rising. I cannot ride a horse. Faced with rioting Pathans I would, I fear, run away rather than stare them down. Like most of us in these post-prohibition days I drink spirits before, rather than wine after, dinner.

But in all these respects I wish I were more, rather than less, like the Victorians. The Victorians were, of course, selfish, greedy, corrupt and hypocritical, as every generation of human beings has been since humanity began. But their ideals – as opposed to their practice – were, I believe, among the noblest recorded in history.

I feel more sympathy with the eminent Victorians than with the sniggers of Lytton Strachey. Our own century has made three great social experiments: communism, fascism, and nazism. Happily all three of these experiments, in Europe at least, appear to be over. Those nations which have fought against these experiments have essentially been fighting to preserve important values of the nineteenth century (parliamentary democracy and a scope for free market individualism) against the depredations of the twentieth. The British people of a century which has twiced waged war on a cruel and gigantic scale have no right to condescend to a reign in which the United Kingdom avoided world and continental war.

Did not the Victorian era suffer from one particularly odious feature, namely hypocrisy? Certainly, the Victorians, to encourage the practice of virtue, exaggerated the degree to which the great figures of their own and previous ages actually lived up to their ideals. This was indeed an error. But we, to palliate our own vices, rejoice in contemplating the failures of past heroes. We like to cut down to our own size our more austere, unselfish, and energetic ancestors.

But surely the Victorians took themselves too seriously? Some of them undoubtedly did. But anyone who believes that the Victorians were incapable of mocking at their own solemnity should read Arthur Hugh Clough's epistolary novel in verse, *Amours de Voyage*.

I have set out the ways in which my own life has been embedded in Victorian institutions and guided by Victorian ideals. I do not know how typical my own experience is. Perhaps I am quite untypical. If so, you Victorianists should take good care of me, as a rare surviving dinosaur not in captivity. But I am inclined to believe that there may be many others who, if they examine themselves, will see that like myself they are fundamentally creatures of the Victorians. If you seek a monument, look within.

Index